A Bibliography of George Crabbe

A Bibliography of George Crabbe

T. Bareham & S. Gatrell

Dawson/Archon Books

First published in 1978

© T. Bareham, S. Gatrell, 1978

Wm Dawson & Sons Ltd, Cannon House
Folkestone, Kent, England

Archon Books, The Shoe String Press, Inc
995 Sherman Avenue, Hamden, Connecticut 06514 USA

British Library Cataloguing in Publication Data

Bareham, Terence
  A bibliography of George Crabbe.
  1. Crabbe, George—Bibliography
  I. Title   II. Gatrell, S.
  016.821'7   Z8197   78-040052
  ISBN 0-7129-0785-8
  ISBN 0-208-01723-2 (Archon)

Printed Letterpress in Great Britain
by W & J Mackay Limited, Chatham

Contents

PREFACE   vii

AI   Works published during Crabbe's Lifetime   1
    Items **AI–A72**

APPENDIX

i   Prospectus for Works 1834   94
ii   Balance Sheet for Crabbe's Works published by John Murray   95

AII   Subsequent Editions of Crabbe's Work   101
    Items **A73–A200**
a)   Editions Published After Crabbe's Death   102
i   British   103
ii   American   110
b)   Letters, Sermons, Etc, Published Posthumously; and Poems Making Their First Appearance in Print Subsequent to the Eight Volume Edition of 1834   114
B   Bibliographical Notes and Articles   119
    Items **B1–B16**
C   Bibliographies of Crabbe   123
    Items **C1–C9**
D   Contemporary Reviews of Crabbe's Work   126
    Items **D1–D74**
E   Full-Length Critical and Biographical Studies   139
    Items **E1–E25**
F   Critical Articles other than Contemporary Reviews of Specific Volumes   145
    Items **F1–F195**

APPENDIX

i   Works of Crabbe in Translation   181
ii   Critical Articles in Languages other than English   181
iii   Other Works with Contributions by Crabbe   182
iv   The Crabbe Apocrypha   183

ADDENDUM
Compiled by Peter New   184

INDEX   187–194

To Tita

Preface

Despite the apparently schizoid nature of this bibliography, the work has actually been written in active collaboration, and we would like to acknowledge the generosity and kindness of the following people without whose help our joint task would have been immeasurably more difficult.

Dr John Pafford, who has allowed us to make extensive use of his fine collection of Crabbe volumes, and offered us much valuable advice.

Lady Norma Dalrymple-Champneys, who has unselfishly given us access to bibliographical material assembled originally by the late Kenneth Povey and added to more recently by herself.

Mr D. H. Merry and Dr J. P. Feather of the Bodleian Library, Oxford, and Mr Brian Jenkins of the Cambridge University Library, who have greatly facilitated the assembly and examination of multiple copies of editions of Crabbe's poetry.

The staff of the Inter-library loans department of the library of The New University of Ulster.

Our correspondents in all of the libraries and institutes to which we have written with enquiries, and who have responded and courteously in almost every case.

The publishers John Murray for making available the ledgers of their firm.

Dr Max Golding of the English Department of The New University of Ulster, Mr Tim Cook, lately of the same department, and Mr Ben Benedikz of the Birmingham University Library, who have traced elusive articles for us.

Messrs Dick Dana and John Price, Edinburgh antiquarian booksellers, who have given technical advice and much encouragement. Ms Jean Gow, who acted as Tony Bareham's research assistant. Ms Rosemary Gilmore, who typed sections of the manuscript.

The Research Committee of The New University of Ulster, who made an award to Simon Gatrell to assist with work on his share of the book.

Professor Thomas C. Faulkner who has been marvellously unselfish in allowing us access to material for his forthcoming edition of Crabbe's letters.

There are separate introductions to the two sections of the Bibliography.

A1

Works Published During
Crabbe's Lifetime

Including the posthumous Collected Edition of 1834

AI

INTRODUCTORY NOTE

This section of the bibliography attempts to describe every impression, issue or state of every edition of Crabbe's poems published during his lifetime; it also includes the major posthumous edition of 1834, and brief notes on prose published while he was alive. It does not deal with manuscript material, nor does it claim to distinguish for certain every edition that was revised by the author; this is partly because we understand that a new edition of Crabbe's poetry has recently been prepared, and while we have not been able to see it, such an edition should contain ample analysis in these areas.

The basis of this section is the two great private collections of Crabbe assembled by John Pafford and my collaborator, Tony Bareham. As the frequency with which their copies appear in the registers attached to each entry attests, without their wholehearted and generous co-operation this task would have been much more difficult, and I would like to offer them my especial thanks.

I have attempted to collate mechanically at least five copies of every volume examined, but in a number of cases this has not been possible, either because libraries would (understandably) not permit valuable or fragile volumes to be sent to centres possessing collating machines, or because insufficient copies have been located. In most other cases visual comparison was made, but occasionally, where readily discernible variants were concerned, I requested reports from librarians concerning copies in their collections. The distinction between first and second hand information is made clear in the registers of copies. Wherever possible the Bareham copy was used as control for collations.

I believe that I have discovered most of the significant variations in the volumes I have examined; I realize, however, that in a majority of cases my available sample has been too small to ensure that others do not survive undetected. Indeed on occasions a hundred copies will not reveal a variant that had a brief life during a print run. It seems to me that there is an acceptable minimum, beyond which the labour of collation does not provide an adequate reward, and I believe I have at least reached such a minimum. There is a real sense in which such an undertaking as this can never achieve completeness, and it is to be hoped that the publication of the bibliography will stimulate further investigations.

Machine collation sometimes provides information of a kind which cannot be seen by the eye unaided, and thus, much of it will not be significant for the scholar or collector using the bibliography, and has not been included. On odd occasions however it provides crucial information, and then it remains part of the main entry. Similarly only the most important variations in the headline typography have been noted.

In the main body of description I have not departed in any radical way from the conventions suggested by Philip Gaskell in his *New Introduction to Bibliography*, though I have an attachment to ^{r} and ^{v} to indicate the sides of a leaf as opposed to ^{a} and ^{b}. The entries are as full as seemed appropriate to the possible uses of the bibliography and the distinguishing of states.

All measurements are in millimetres and are only approximate, in that rules vary in the amount of ink they pick up in each copy, and that type-pages, as may be seen from some entries, vary by as much as three millimetres in either direction, partly because of variable shrinkage in the paper, partly because of loosening of furniture round the formes during the print run.

On occasions the statement in the collation about size of sheet used may be the best guess, in default of any uncut copy.

The combination of full pagination with a list of contents should provide adequate description of the appearance of the leaves; when in the contents statement there appears the statement: Text as No 7 (Gk), this means merely that the same Poems, Letters, Tales or Books appear in the same order.

I have not attempted any kind of analysis of the paper of any volume, and my description of it is based on visual and tangible impression.

Binding is relatively unimportant in a period when most copies were rebound to the purchasers taste; Crabbe's early poems were probably sewn in paper wrappers (see *The Newspaper* p. 12); his books published by Hatchard, and the early volumes by Murray often survive in boards with paper labels, but there is no evidence to show whether these derived from the publisher or the bookseller. Only for the later collected editions did the nineteenth century cloth edition binding appear.

The notes about composition and publication are as full as possible, though the disappearance of Hatchards records leaves a great gap in knowledge from *Poems* to *Tales*, and there appears to be very little material in Crabbe's letters to help the bibliographer. It would be of great interest to know, for instance, to what extent Crabbe was interested in seeing his poems through the press, and with how much care and how often he revised the impressions of his work. The edition of Crabbe's correspondence shortly to be completed may provide more details about such matters. The use of small capitals in quasi- facsimile title-pages creates occasional anomalies, especially in the eighteenth century volumes. For example, in No. A1 the third line of the title-page shows the anomaly clearly: the initial capital of 'In' appears larger than the other upper case letters in the line – but this is not the case in the original which it is intended to represent. The same is true in all similar cases.

S.J.G.

Library Locations

AbU	Aberdeen University Library
AdU	Adelaide University
AL	The Athenaeum, Liverpool
AlU	Alberta University
B	T. Bareham
BL	British Library
BLL	British Library, lending division
BmU	Birmingham University
Bod	Bodleian Oxford
BrU	Bristol University
CaU	Calgary University
CJ	Jesus College Cambridge
CK	Kings College Cambridge
CP	Peterhouse College Cambridge
CSmH	Henry Huntington Library, San Marino
CStJ	St John's College Cambridge
CTr	Trinity College Cambridge
CtY	Yale University
CU–B	University of California Berkeley, Bancroft Library
CUL	Cambridge University Library
DrW	Doctor Williams' Library London
DuU	Durham University
EdU	Edinburgh University
ExU	Exeter University
FlU	Flinders University South Australia
GlU	Glasgow University
HuU	Hull University
IU	University of Illinois, Urbana
KeU	Keele University
KnU	Kent University
LaU	Lancaster University
LcU	Leicester University
LeL	The Leeds Library
LeU	Leeds University
LiU	Liverpool University
LoL	London Library
LoU	University of London

LUC	University College London
McGU	McGill University
McMU	McMaster University
MaU	University of Manchester
MH	Harvard University
MstVU	Mount St Vincent University
MWA	The American Antiquarian Association, Worcester
NeU	Newcastle University
NLS	National Library of Scotland
NLW	National Library of Wales
NN	New York Public Library
NoU	Nottingham University
NUU	New University of Ulster
OEF	English Faculty Library Oxford
OL	Lincoln College Oxford
OO	Oriel College Oxford
OS	Somerville College Oxford
OW	Worcester College Oxford
P	J. Pafford
PPRF	Rosenbach Foundation, Philadelphia
QUB	Queens University, Belfast
QUK	Queens University Kingston Ontario
ReU	Reading University
StAU	St Andrews University
StD	St David's Lampeter
ShU	Sheffield University
SoU	Southampton University
StU	Stirling University
SuU	Sussex University
SyU	Sydney University
ToU	Toronto University
TCD	Trinity College Dublin
TxU	University of Texas Austin
UCNW	University College of North Wales Bangor
UEA	University of East Anglia
UWC	University of Wales Cardiff
UWO	University of Western Ontario
YoU	York University

INEBRIETY

INEBRIETY, | A POEM, | In THREE PARTS. | thick-thin rule 88. | If, when the more you drink, the more you crave, | Is your Complaint; if when the more you have, | The more you want; why not with equal Eaſe | Confeſs as well the Folly, as Diſeaſe? | The Heart reſolves this matter in a trice, | "Men only feel the ſmart but not the Vice." | POPE. – | diamond rule 75 mm. | oval floral ornament | thick-thin rule 42 mm. top, 31 mm. bottom | *IPSWICH:* | Printed and Sold by C. PUNCHARD, Bookſeller, in the Butter-Market, | and by reſt of the Bookſellers, 1775. | [Price ONE SHILLING & SIX-PENCE]

Collation Demy 4⁰ in 2s [π²] a²B–N² = [28] leaves[1]

Pagination [four] pages not reckoned in pagination [i] ii–iii [iv] [3] 4–12 [13] 14–25 [26] 27–49 [50] = [56] pages.

Contents [π1^r and ^{v}] blank or half-title π2^r title-page π2^v blank [i]–iii Preface [iv] blank [3]–49 text [50] blank.

Printer's Imprint N2^r has an ornamental open triangle with the initials GJ inside. These may perhaps be those of the compositor rather than the printer. Otherwise see title-page.

Type Page B2^r p5 123 × 110   K1^r p35 121.5 × 108
          E1^r p15 118 × 109

Signatures on $ 1 in centre of direction line. On occasion (i.e. D, G, H, I, L, M, N) the signature is between the text and the often extensive footnotes.

Catchwords. Every page; when quotations continue over the page, they also have a catchword. Those on E2^v (Invain for In vain) I1^v (no catchwords at all), and K2^v (Who' for Who,) are inaccurate; when the footnote catchwords should have inverted commas, they are only present on M1^r and M1^v.

Headline Page numbers at outer margin; running title in centre.

Paper White laid, no watermark; chainlines horizontal, 26 avge apart, wire lines 1.25 avge apart, pinholes apparently visible at top outer edge of each leaf.

Binding Unknown, but probably in paper wrappers.

Notes on Composition and Publication Written during his years as an apprentice physician at Woodbridge, between 1772 and 1775. It was first collected in Vol.

II of Murray's 1834 edition of the Life and Works of Crabbe (see No 48), where the third part of the poem was suppressed, and did not re-appear until A. W. Ward's edition of the *Poems* in 1907. On a1^r of the Bodleian Library copy is written in Crabbe's own hand, the place-name in cypher "NB – pray let not this be seen at Beccles | there is very little of it that Im not | heartily ashamed off."

The print-run is not known.

Copies Bod; the title-page in this copy is a photograph of that belonging to the copy in the Alexander Turnbull Library in Wellington, New Zealand. PPRF

A2

THE CANDIDATE

1780

THE CANDIDATE; | A | POETICAL EPISTLE | TO THE | AUTHORS OF THE MONTHLY REVIEW. | diamond rule 55.5 mm. | Multa quidem nobis facimus mala ſæpe poetæ, | (Ut vineta egomet cædam mea) cum tibi librum | Sollicito damus, aut feſſo; cum lædimur, unum | Si quis amicorum eſt auſus reprendere verſum, | Cum loca jam recitata revolvimus irrevocati: | Cum lamentamur non apparere labores | Nostros, et tenui deducta poemata filo: | Cum ſperamus eo rem venturam, ut, ſimul atque | Carmina reſcieris nos fingere, commodus ultrò | Arceſſas, et egere vetes, et ſcribere cogas. | HOR. Lib. ii. Ep. I. | diamond rule 56 mm. | LONDON: | Printed for H. PAYNE, opposite Marlborough-Houſe, Pall-Mall. | M DCC LXXX.

Collation Demy 4° A–D⁴ E² = 18 leaves.[2]

Pagination [1–3] 4–34 [35–36] = 36 pages

Contents [1] title-page [2] blank [3]–6 Introductory Address 7–8 To the Reader 9–34 Text [35–36] blank?[12]

Type page p. 14 B3^v 181.5 × 117.
Signatures $ 1 and 2 signed in centre of direction line with the exception of A1.
Catchwords Every page, all are accurate.
Press figures 5 on A3^r and B3^v.
Headline Numerals central, within square brackets.
Paper White laid; chainlines horizontal, 25.75 apart avge, wirelines 1.25 apart avge.

Binding There is no evidence.

Copy BL (apparently the unique copy in public hands.)

Notes on Composition and Publication 250 copies were printed by John Nichols. In a letter to Burke on June 26 1781 Crabbe speaks of these copies 'which I believe are now in the warehouse of Mr Payne the bookseller, as I never heard of any sale they had'.

In later life Crabbe ascribed the failure of his venture to Payne's bankruptcy, though no evidence is produced to support the view. It was first collected as the last piece in Vol. II of the 1834 Life and Works of Crabbe (see No. 48).

A3

THE LIBRARY

1781

THE | LIBRARY. | A | POEM. | publisher's device: JD ornamented | diamond rule 74 | LONDON: | PRINTED FOR J. DODSLEY, IN PALL-MALL. | rule 26.5 | M.DCC.LXXXI. | [Price 2s.]

Collation Demy 4° [A]–D⁴E² = 18 leaves.

Pagination [1–3] 4–34 [35–36].

Contents [1] title-page [2] blank [3]–34 text [35–36] blank.

Direction Line Signed $ 1 and 2 in centre; catchwords on every page, all accurate, though that on D3ʳ (29) does not have the immediately following comma; other catchwords do have attendant punctuation.

Press-figures 2 B4ʳ; 3 A4ʳ, D1ᵛ; 5 A2ᵛ, D4ᵛ; 7 C2ᵛ; 9 B4ᵛ; 10 C1ᵛ.

Headline pages numbered centrally within square brackets.

Type-page variation B1ʳ p 9 174–176 by 128–130
$\qquad$ C3ʳ p21 174.5 – 176.5 by 125.5–127.

Paper white laid, no mark, chainlines 27–28, wirelines 1.25 average.

Binding Stab-holes in gutter; presumably issued in wrappers.

Notes on Collation Variations No textual variants were noted, but in view of the apparently small number of copies of this edition that were printed it is interesting to note that there is substantial evidence of considerable type-shifting during the impression. This is most frequently to be seen in punctuation at the end of lines (particularly semi-colons), in press-figures and in page numbers, but on several pages (notably A2ʳ and D2ᵛ) the text itself shows signs of breaking up.

Notes on Composition and Publication The edition was of c. 250 copies, printed by John Nichols, for subscribers.[3]

A manuscript version of *The Library* exists in the collection of Sir John Murray,[4] and in the Bodleian Library there is a fair holograph copy of the poem in its first edition form. The first of these indicates that work on the poem was certainly under way by 1779. On March 27 1781 Crabbe sent to Burke 'the poem in its former state' as well as a corrected copy[3] and on June 26 he promised to wait on Burke with 'a fresh copy . . . as correct as [I] have power to make it'. At Burke's instigation Dodsley agreed to publish *The Library* for the 200 or so subscribers who had by then been found. It finally appeared on July 24.[5] Burke had singled out *The Library* from among all Crabbe's extant MSS as representative of his growing talent, and it led him directly to champion the destitute poet's cause. So successful was he in this that Dodsley, who had hitherto been reluctant to publish it at all, was eventually moved to turn over to Crabbe all the profits from the sale of the first edition.

Copies B BL(2) Bod CUL CTr DuU LoU; CU-B CSmH CtY IU(2 copies) MH NN TxU.

A4

THE LIBRARY

SECOND EDITION   1783

THE | LIBRARY. | A | POEM.| diamond rule 29 | BY THE REV.D GEORGE CRABBE, | CHAPLAIN TO HIS GRACE THE DUKE OF RUTLAND. | diamond rule 74.5 | THE SECOND EDITION. | thick-thin rule 133 | LONDON: | PRINTED FOR J. DODSLEY, PALL-MALL. | thin rule 29 | M.DCC.LXXXIII. | [Price 2s.]

Collation As first edition.

Pagination As first edition.

Contents As first edition.

Direction Line signed $ 1 and 2 in centre; catchwords on every page, all accurate; press-figures: 1 B4^v, D2^v; 2 C1^v; 3 D4^r; 5 C4^v; 6 B3^v; 7 A4^v; thus the outer forme of [A] has no press-figure.

Headline pages numbered centrally within square brackets.

Paper as first edition; TxU copy has a clearly different, much whiter paper for sigs A–B.

Binding As first edition.

Notes on Collation Variants No textual variants; less obvious type-shifting than in the first edition, though several marks of punctuation at the ends of lines do show displacement.

Notes on Composition and Publication The size of this edition is not known. One line (320) was revised (presumably by Crabbe himself), and there are a number of differences in accidentals, including the addition of the comma to the catchword on D3^r which was noted as missing in the first edition; none of these is likely to have been made at Crabbe's insistence.

Copies B BL Bod CTr LeL LoU; CU-B IU MH TxU.

A5

THE VILLAGE

1783

THE | VILLAGE: | A | POEM. | IN TWO BOOKS. | diamond rule 29 | BY | THE REV^D. GEORGE CRABBE, | CHAPLAIN TO HIS GRACE THE DUKE OF RUTLAND, &c. | thick-thin rule 132 | LONDON: | PRINTED FOR J. DODSLEY, PALL-MALL. | rule 28 | M.DCC.-LXXXIII.

Collation Demy 4° [A]² B–F⁴ = 22 leaves.

Pagination [i–iv] [1] 2–23 [24–25] 26–38 [39–40] = 44pp.

Contents [i] half-title page: diamond rule 74 | THE | VILLAGE: | A | POEM. | diamond rule 70 | [Price 2s. 6d.] [ii] blank [iii] title-page [iv] blank [1]–38 text [39–40] blank.

Direction-line signed $ 1 and 2 in centre of direction line; catchwords on each page; all are correct.

Press-figures: 1 B4^r, C1^v, E4^v, F3^r; 2 D3^v; 3 D2^v, F1^v; 6 E4^r Outer forme of B has no press figure, nor has outer forme of C.

Headline: numerals central, within square brackets.

Type page B3^r 185 by 134.

Paper White laid; chainlines average 27 apart, wirelines average 1.25.

Binding Stab-holes in gutter, presumably sewn in paper wrappers.

Notes on Composition and Publication In an article entitled 'John Nichols, Printer and Publisher' (*The Library*: Vol. XVIII No. 3 Sept 1963) Albert H. Smith prints a letter from Crabbe to Nichols which might seem to suggest a private printing of the Village in 1781. It reads:

My friends wish me to preserve some of the Copies you printed for me, but not to let them be known . . . you will once more be so obliging as to send me in these covers 'the Village' separated from the other Pieces. . . .

This letter is dated 'Beccles Suffolk. Aug. 6, 1781. No copies of such an edition have been recorded. Burke had a completed manuscript of The Village by December 26, 1782. Dr Johnson read and corrected it, returning it on 4 March 1783, and the poem appeared on 23 May of that year. The print run is not known.

Copies B BL(2) BmU Bod CTr CUL(2) LeL LiU LoU P UCNW YoU; CU-B CSmH CtY IU(2 copies) MH(2) TxU(3 copies).

A6

THE NEWS-PAPER

1785

THE | NEWS-PAPER: | A | POEM. | diamond rule 75.5 | BY | The Reverend GEORGE CRABBE, | Chaplain to His Grace the DUKE OF RUTLAND. | diamond rule 74 | E quibus, hi vacuas implent fermonibus aures, | Hi narrata ferunt aliò; menfuraque ficti | Crefcit, et auditis aliquid novus adjicit auctor: | Illic credulitas, illic temerarius error, | Vanaque lætitia eft, confternatique timores, | Seditioque repens, dubioque auctore fufurri. | OVID. Metam. Lib. XII. | diamond rule 74 | LONDON: | PRINTED FOR J. DODSLEY, IN PALL-MALL. | M.DCC.LXXXV. | [Price 2s.]

Collation Demy 4° A–E⁴ = 20 leaves.

Pagination [i–iii] iv [v] vi–vii [viii] [1] 2–29 [30–32] = 40 pp.

Contents [i] title-page [ii] blank [iii]–iv Dedication [v]–vii To the Reader [viii] The Argument [1]–29 text [30] blank [31] advertisement [32] blank.

Direction line signed $ 1 and 2 in centre of direction line (not A1); catchwords on each page, all are accurate.

Press figures: 2 E1ᵛ; 3 D3ʳ, E2ᵛ; 4 A3ʳ; 8 B4ᵛ, C3ʳ; 9 A4ʳ, B1ᵛ, C4ʳ; 10 D1ᵛ.

Headline numerals in brackets in centre.

Type page 187 by 135 ± 1.

Paper laid, chainlines 26.5 average, wirelines 1.25. Pin holes are visible in Bod copy at head of leaves $ 1 and 2 where the binder has not cut the leaf so closely. Presumably those on $ 3 and 4 would have been lost when the fore-edge was trimmed (assuming that the imposition was that of common English quarto). The Hungtington copy has a brownish paper for A1, A4, D1 and D4.

Advertisement Lately published by the same Author. | THE LIBRARY: A POEM. Price 2s. | THE VILLAGE: A POEM. Price 2s. 6d.

Binding An extra bifolium of similar paper wrapped round the outside of the volume, then stabbed and sewn, then a sheet of marbled paper stuck to the bifolium over the stitching. This appears contemporary, though it is possible that the marbled paper was added by the purchaser. This information is from LoU copy, Sterling Library.

Notes on Composition and Publication The poem was written during political pressures which affected both Crabbe's patrons – Rutland and Burke. It appeared on 15 March 1785. The print run is not known.

Note Lines 3–4 on p. 17 of the CtY copy have been altered by a contemporary hand to: sly widow's and the coxcomb's Stint | Dives deep for scandal through an oblique hint. There is no indication of the source or authorship of this alteration.

Copies B Bod BL(2) CTr CUL LeL LoU; CU-B CSmH CtY IU MH NN.

A7

POEMS

1807

POEMS. | BY | THE REV. GEORGE CRABBE, LL.B. | thin-thick rule 24 | Ipse per Ausonias Æneïa carmina gentes | Qui sonat, ingenti qui nomine pulsat Olympum; | Mæöniumque senem Romano provocat ore: | Forsitan illius nemoris latuisset in umbrâ | Quod canit, et sterili tantum cantâsset avenâ | Ignotus populi; si Mæcenate careret. | Paneg. ad Pisones, LUCAN. | thin-thick rule 24 | LONDON: | thin-thick rule 18.5 | PRINTED FOR J. HATCHARD, | BOOKSELLER TO HER MAJESTY, OPPOSITE ALBANY, | PICCADILLY. | thick-thin rule 10 | 1807.

Collation Demy 8° a⁸c⁴π¹ B–R⁸ = 141 leaves.

Pagination [i–v] vi–viii [ix] x–xxv [xxvi] [1–3] 4–17 [18–21] 22–29 [30–33] 34–66

[67–69] 70–92 [93–95] 96–133 [134–137] 138–164 [165–167] 168–187 [188–191] 192–205 [206–209] 210–213 [214–217] 218–236 [237–239] 240–244 [245] 246–252 [253] 254–256 = 282 pages.

Contents [i] half-title: thick-thin rule 27 | POEMS. | thin-thick rule 27.5 [ii] blank [iii] title [iv] printer's imprint: within a thin-rule rectangle 31.5 by 5.5 *Printed by Brettell and Co. | Marshall-Street*. [v] vi–viii Dedication [ix] x–xxiv Preface xxv Contents [xxvi] blank [1]–256 text: The Village Book I, Book II; The Parish Register Part I Baptisms, Part II Marriages, Part III Burials; The Library; The Newspaper; The Birth of Flattery; Reflections upon the Subject – Quid juvat errore, mersa jam puppi, fateri? Quid lacrymæ commissa levant delicta secutæ?; Sir Eustace Grey; The Hall of Justice Part I, Part II; Woman!.

Printer's Imprint p[iv] above, and p256 double rule 50 | PRINTED BY BRETTELL AND CO. | MARSHALL-STREET GOLDEN-SQUARE. | double rule 51.

Direction line: signatures $ 1, 2 in centre of direction line; in prelims only a3^r and c1^r signed. The omission of sig b may indicate revision of the preliminary matter by Crabbe at some time after imposition.

Headline pages numbered centrally.

Ornaments feather, lyre and trumpet: 29, 164
diamond-shaped rose: 187
vase of flowers and grasses: 133, 205, 252
ornamental rule: 213, 236
wavy rule: 234
Finis, within an oval sunburst: 256.

Variation in Printing From a Hinman collation it appears that at some time during the print run the outer forme of $ B was badly shaken; no type was lost as a result of this, but considerable overall distortion of the pages is noticeable. See the register of copies.
Type-page variation D2^v p 36 143.5 – 144.5 by 85–86
H1^v p 98 149.5 – 151 by 83–85
M4^v p168 142.5 – 144 by 83–85

Paper wove; watermark 1806.

Binding Drab blue-grey boards; ivory-coloured spine; label (very worn in CUL copy) thick-thin rule | CRABBE'S | POEMS. | decorative rule | *Price 8s. 6d.*

Notes on Composition and Publication Crabbe's first volume of poetry to appear since *The News-paper* twenty-two years earlier. He had written much in the meantime, including three novels and a volume of poems which he offered Hatchard in 1799 and then withdrew. Serious work on the pieces which comprise *Poems* seems to have commenced about 1802 according to information given to Edward Fitzgerald by Crabbe's son George. *Poems* was published on 29 October 1807.

The print run cannot be ascertained through the loss of the records of the firm of Hatchard.

Copies With outer form of Sig B in state a) B BL CTr YU
in state b) Bod CUL OEF
undetermined Bm U DrW P LoU; IU TxU.

A8

POEMS

SECOND EDITION   1808

POEMS. | BY | THE REV. GEORGE CRABBE, LL.B. | diamond rule 30 | Ipse [etc. as No. 7] LUCAN. | double rule 44.5 | SECOND EDITION. | double rule 45 | LONDON: | double rule 15 | PRINTED FOR J. HATCHARD, | BOOKSELLER TO HER MAJESTY, OPPOSITE ALBANY, | PICCADILLY. | thick-thin rule 7 | 1808.

Collation Demy 8° a^{8}b^6 π^1 (bound indiscriminately after a4^v or b6^v) B–R^{8}S^2 = 145 leaves.

Pagination [i–v] vi–viii [ix] x–xxv [xxvi] xxvii [xxviii] [1 leaf not reckoned in pagination inserted after either viii or [xxviii]] [1–3] 4–17 [18–21] 22–29 [30–33] 34–67 [68–71] 72–94 [95–97] 98–135 [136–139] 140–166 [167–169] 170–189 [190–193] 194–207 [208–211] 212–215 [216–219] 220–238 [239–241] 242–246 [247] 248–254 [255] 256–258 [259–260] = 290 pages.

Contents [i] half-title thick-thin rule 27.5 | POEMS. | thin-thick rule 28 [ii] blank [iii] title-page [iv] printer's imprint thick-thin rule 37 | Printed by Brettell and Co. | Marshall-Street, Golden-Square. | thin-thick rule 36.5 [v]–viii Dedication [ix]–xxv Preface [xxvi] blank xxvii Contents [xxviii] blank [leaf not reckoned in pagination, recto Advertisement to the Reader verso blank] [1]–258 text [as No 7] [259–260] Hatchard's advertisements.

Printer's Imprint p. [iv] above and p. 258 thick-thin rule 32.5 | *Printed by Brettell and Co.* | *Marshall-Street, Golden-Square.*

Direction line $ 1^r and 2^r signed (a3^r only in sig a, and S1^r only in sig S) centrally.

Headline pages numbered centrally.

Ornaments feather, lyre and trumpet: xxv, 29, 135, 189
        Rose 166, 254
        Vase 207
        Ornamental rule 215
        Wavy rule 236
        Finis 258
        Grotesque face 238.

Notes on Printing It is probable that sig S was printed in the same forme as sig b, since evidence of the watermarks shows some copies with no watermark in b, but one in S; otherwise all copies (with one exception) have a watermark in either b1 or b2, and none in S (see table below).

Type-page variation 18^r 138–139.5 by 84–86
        $K1^r$ 151–152.5 by 82.5–86
        $K2^r$ 144–145.5 by 84–86.

Paper white wove; watermarks (see Table below). In addition, the difference between the paper of Sig G and the rest of the book is manifested in the different way that the type takes in this signature in all copies examined; it is evidently of inferior quality.

The following table shows the occurrences of the watermark in the various gatherings of the second edition of Poems, as an example of the complexity found in all watermarked editions.

	B	BL (1)	BL (2)	BmU	Bod	CUL	LoL	OEF	P (1)	P (2)	StD	LoU
a	4	4	2	3	2	3	1	3	2	2	1	3
b	1	1	—	—	1	1	1	2	1	—	1	2
B	2	4	1	4	1	3	3	4	3	4	3	2
C	3	2	3	4	2	3	1	2	1	4	2	1
D	1	2	1	4	1	2	3	1	1	1	2	2
E	3	4	3	4	2	3	1	3	3	1	2	3
F	3	3	1	4	1	2	4	2	1	1	1	2
G	3/6	3/6	1/8	1/8	4/5	2/7	3/6	4/5	3/6	1/8	3/6	2/7
H	4	4	4	2	3	4	3	1	4	4	1	4
I	2	1	1	2	1	3	1	4	3	2	4	3
K	3	2	1	4	1	2	3	2	2	2	3	2
L	3	4	2	4	3	2	2	4	2	2	4	4
M	4	2	2	4	2	4	2	1	4	4	4	4
N	4	4	4	2	2	2	2	2	3	2	4	2
O	3	2	1	2	1	2	3	1	3	2	4	2
P	4	3	1	2	1	3	2	3	4	2	2	3
Q	2	4	2	2	3	1	1	4	2	1	2	4
R	2	1	1	4	3	1	4	3	4	2	4	4
S	—	—	—	1	—	—	—	—	—	1	—	—

Notes to the Table There is no observable pattern here, and none should be expected. The wove paper is made with the countermark, in this instance a date, 1808 near the bottom left-hand side of the mould, and its position in the printed sheet depends on whether the sheet was taken inverted, or reversed, or both, or neither. Thus there are four potential positions of the mark, on the first, second, third, or fourth leaf of a gathering. Sig G was printed on paper with a different mark: Ms & [Co?] 1807, placed near the bottom right-hand side of the mould. This may indicate a different time of printing, even a stop-press correction; on the other hand it may simply indicate that it was worked by a different press. Also, in copy B there is the mark 1807 on the Advertisement to the Reader, presenting similar possibilities.

Binding Drab grey boards.

Notes on Composition and Publication Published in August 1808 at the increased price of 10/6, according to the English Catalogue of Books. This second edition was quite extensively revised by Crabbe, and the compositors altered the framework of punctuation, particularly with regard to commas and initial capitals.

Copies With Advertisement after a2^v: TxU.
    With Advertisement after a4^v: B BL(2) BmU Bod CUL P(1); CtY.
    With Advertisement after b6^v: LoL LoU OEF P(2) StD; IU.
    BL(1) has no Advertisement, and also has Longman's advertisement dated June 1 1808 bound in after Hatchard's advertisements.

A9

POEMS

THIRD EDITION

POEMS. | BY | THE REV. GEORGE CRABBE, LL.B. | diamond rule 29 | Ipse [etc. as No. 8] LUCAN. | double rule 44 | THIRD EDITION. | double rule 44.5 | 𝕷𝖔𝖓𝖉𝖔𝖓: | thin-thick rule 14.5 | PRINTED FOR J. HATCHARD, | BOOKSELLER TO HER MAJESTY, OPPOSITE ALBANY, | PICCADILLY. | thick-thin rule 7 | 1808.

Collation Demy 8° a^{8}b^{6}B–R^{8}S^2 = 144 leaves.

Pagination [i–v] vi–viii [ix] x–xxv [xxvi] [xxvii] [xxviii erroneously printed as xxvii] [1–3] etc as No. 8 = 288 pages.

Contents [i] half-title double rule 82 | POEMS. | double rule 82.5 [ii] blank [iii] title-page [iv] printer's imprint rule 33 | *Brettell & Co. Printers,* | *Marshall-Street,* *Golden-Square.* | rule 33 [v]–viii Dedication [ix]–xxv Preface [xxvi] blank [xxvii] Advertisement to the Reader xxvii (in fact xxviii) Contents [1]–258 text (as No. 7) [259–260] Advertisements.

Printer's Imprint [iv] above and 258 rule 31 | *Printed by Brettell and Co.* | *Marshall-Street, Golden-Square.* | rule 32.

Direction line signatures as No. 8.

Headline as No. 8.

Ornaments feather, lyre and trumpet: xxv, 135, 189
        Rose 207
        Ornamental rule (1) 215, 238
        Finis 258
        Cherub with trumpet 166, 254
        Ornamental rule (2) 29.

Notes on Printing It seems clear that the prelims of this edition were at least partly printed from standing type of the second edition: this is the explanation for the error in the numeration of the Contents page, and on page xxi line 22, the second a in the word 'appropriate' is in a different font in both second and third editions. Many smaller idiosyncracies are repeated. However, there are also differences, both to lineation (cf xi) and type itself (cf author/Author in p. xix line 13). There is no doubt, however, that the text was reset, though with no authorial revision.

Type-page variation 127 I8^r 144 by 85.5
             129 K1^r 148–150.5 by 84–84.5
             131 K2^r 143.5–145 by 84.5–86.

Paper inferior quality white wove, gives very bad quality to imprint, opacity very poor, some signatures, particularly P are very prone to foxing, though EdU copy has P unfoxed, the only copy examined in which this was the case. Watermarks are sig. a: M^s & [Co.] 1807, (as was sig. G in the second edition); sig. F 1807; all other sigs. 1808.

Binding Blue boards, ivory spine. Label reads:
thick-thin rule | CRABBE'S | POEMS. | rule | Third Edition | thick-thin rule | Price 10s. 6d. | thin-thick rule.

Copies B(1) B(2) BL Bod CUL EdU LaU P(1) P(2) UCNW; IU TxU.

A10

POEMS

FOURTH EDITION TWO VOLUMES 1809

POEMS | BY | THE REV. GEORGE CRABBE, LL.B. | diamond rule 22 | Ipse [etc. as No. 7] LUCAN. | rule 67 | IN TWO VOLUMES. | VOL. I. (II.) | rule 67 | FOURTH EDITION. | diamond rule 17 | 𝕷𝖔𝖓𝖉𝖔𝖓 | PRINTED FOR J. HATCHARD, | BOOKSELLER TO HER MAJESTY, OPPOSITE ALBANY, PICCADILLY. | thin-thick rule 7 | 1809.

Collation Foolscap 8° Vol. I. [a]–b⁸B–I⁸ = 80 leaves Vol. II. [A]² B–P⁸ = 114 leaves.

Pagination Vol. I. [i–v] vi–viii [ix–xi] xii [xiii] xiv–xxxi [xxxii] [1–3] 4–23 [24–27] 28–39 [40–43] 44–91 [92–95] 96–127 [128] = 160 pages
Vol. II. [i–iv] [1–3] 4–57 [58–61] 62–99 [100–103] 104–131 [132–135] 136–155 [156–159] 160–166 [167–169] 170–197 [198–201] 202–208 [209] 210–218 [219] 220–223 [224] = 228 pages.

Contents Vol. I [i] half-title double rule 69 | POEMS. | double rule 69 [ii] blank [iii] title-page [iv] printer's imprint within a rectangle of rules 39 by 7 Brettell & Co. Printers, | Marshall-Street, Golden-Square. [v]–viii Dedication [ix] Advertisement to the second edition [x] blank [xi] xii Advertisement to the reader (Muston 1809) [xiii]–xxxi Preface [xxxii] Contents [1]–127 text (to The Parish Register Part II as No. 7) [128] blank
Vol. II [i] half-title as Vol. I [ii] blank [iii] title-page [iv] printer's imprint thick-thin rule 30 | Brettell, & Co. Printers, | Marshall-Street, Golden-Square. [1]–223 text (from Parish Register Part III, as No. 7) [224] Printer's imprint thick-thin rule 31 | Brettell & Co. Printers, | Marshall-Street, Golden-Square.

Printer's Imprint Vol. I p. [iv] above and p. 127 double rule 70.5 | Printed by Brettell and Co. Marshall-Street, Golden-Square. | double rule 71.5
Vol. II p. [iv] and p. [224] above.

Direction line signed $ 1 and $ 2 in centre of direction line. $ 1ʳ also has VOL. I.(II.) at gutter margin.

Headline running titles over double rule, pages numbered at outer margin.

Notes on Printing There are frequent differences in the punctuation of this edition when compared with the third, particularly in the matter of capitalizing substantives, which seems to be in a totally fluid situation at this period in the development of punctuation in printing. There appear to be no revisions made by Crabbe.

Type-page variations Vol. I F3^v p 70 112–112.5   by 72–73
13^v p118 111.5–112.5 by 71–72
Vol. II F2^v p 68 111.5–112.5 by 71.5–75
I1^v p114 105–106   by 70.5–71.5

The register must have slipped alarmingly in the BL copy at page 68 of Vol. II.

Paper Off-white wove. Countermark OM
1807

Binding Advertisements suggest that this edition was published in boards at a price of 10s. 6d.; otherwise no evidence.

Copies B BL Bod BrU HuU LoU P(1) P(2).

A11

POEMS

FIFTH EDITION TWO VOLUMES   1810

POEMS: | BY | THE REV. GEORGE CRABBE, LL.B. | decorative rule 21.5 | Ipse (etc. as No. 7, until) *Lucan.* | rule 71 | IN TWO VOLUMES. | VOL. I. (II.) | rule 71 | FIFTH EDITION. | decorative rule 18 | **London:** | PRINTED FOR J. HATCHARD, | BOOKSELLER TO HER MAJESTY, 190, OPPOSITE ALBANY, | PICCADILLY. | thin-thick rule 7 | 1810.

Collation Vol. I Foolscap 8° [a]–b^{8}c^{4}B–I^8 = 84 leaves
Vol. II as No. 10.

Pagination Vol. I [i–v] vi–ix [x–xiii] xiv–xv [xvi–xvii] xviii–xxxix [xl] [1–3] 4–23 [24–27] 28–39 [40–45] 46–92 [93–95] 96–127 [128] = 168 pages
Vol. II as No. 10

Contents Vol. I [i] half-title double rule 68 | POEMS. | double rule 67.5 [ii] blank [iii] title [iv] printer's imprint rule 39 | Brettell and Co. Printers, | Marshall-Street, Golden-Square, London. [v]–ix Dedication [x] blank [xi] Advertisement to Second Edition [xii] blank [xiii]–xv Advertisement to the Reader [xvi] blank [xvii]–xxxix Preface [xl] Contents [1]–127 text (as No. 10) [128] blank
Vol. II [i] half-title double rule 67.5 | POEMS. | double rule 67 [ii] blank [iii] title-page [iv] Printer's imprint as Vol. I [1]–223 text (as No. 10) [224] double rule 39.5 | Brettell and Co. Printers, | Marshall-Street, Golden Square, London.

Printer's Imprint Vol. I p. [iv] above and p. 127 double rule 71 | Printed by Brettell and Co. Marshall-street, Golden-square | double rule 71
Vol. II p. [iv] and p. [224] above

Direction line only $ 1 signed, otherwise as No. 10.

Headline as No. 10.

Note on printing The BL copy appears to have point holes at the top centre of $ 1 and 2. If the imposition is common octavo as it appears to be, then either points must have been placed on the longer sides of the tympan or else the paper placed with the longer edges running across the width of the tympan. The fact that the paper was foolscap, a relatively small size, might have influenced this arrangement, if it was indeed the case.[6] In the matter of Capitalization referred to in the notes to No. 10 this edition is much clearer, in that the practice of capitalizing significant substantives has almost completely been abandoned here; apparently a decisive change by Brettell's compositors.

Type-page variation Vol. I F3^v p 70 112–113   by 70–71
              13^v p118 110.5–112 by 71–74
      Vol. II F2^v p 68 111–111.5 by 70.5–71.5
            I1^v p114 105–106   by 71–72.5

Paper off-white wove; countermark $\frac{\text{OM}}{1808}$

Binding Drab grey boards. Spine label reads thick-thin rule | CRABBE'S POEMS. | rule | VOL. I. (II.) | thick-thin rule | Price 10s. 6d[.] | thin-thick rule.

Notes on Composition and Publication In this edition some poems were extensively revised by Crabbe – *The Parish Register* in particular – while other longer established poems, like *The Library* have no revisions.

Copies B BL BLL Bod BrU CK P.

A12

POEMS

SIXTH EDITION TWO VOLUMES   1812

As No. 11, except thick-thin rules 25 and 19 replace the decorative rules, SIXTH EDITION. for FIFTH EDITION. and 1812. for 1810.

Collation Foolscap 8° *Vol. I* [a]–c^8 B–I^8 = 88 leaves
                Vol. II as No. 10.

Pagination Vol. I [i–v] vi–ix [x–xiii] xiv–xv [xvi–xvii] xviii–xlv [xlvi–xlviii] [1 etc.] as No. 11 = 176 pages
Vol. II as No. 10.

Contents Vol. I [i] half-title thick-thin rule 25 | POEMS. | thin-thick rule 25 [ii] blank [iii] title-page [iv] blank [v]–ix Dedication [x] blank [xi] Advertisement to Second Edition [xii] blank [xiii]–xv Advertisement to the Reader [xvi] blank [xvii]–xlv Preface [xlvi] blank [xlvii] Contents [xlviii] blank [1]–127 text (as No. 10) [128] Printer's imprint thick-thin rule 67 | Printed by J. Berttell, Marshall-Street, Golden-Square, London.

Vol. II [i] half-title as *Vol. I* [ii] blank [iii] title-page [iv] Printer's imprint rule 61 | Printed by J. Brettell, Marshall-Street, Golden-Square, London. [1]–223 text (as No. 10) [224] Printer's imprint thick-thin rule 67 | Printed by J. Brettell, Marshall-Street, Golden-Square, London.

Direction line as No. 11.

Headline running titles over thick-thin rule; pages numbered at outer margin.

Notes on Printing From variations only to be discerned under a collating machine it appears there were two settings of *Vol. II* π. This is only to be expected, since the prelims of *Vol. I* were expanded to fill three full gatherings in eights. The available sample was not large enough to suggest whether there were more than two varieties.

Type-page variation Vol. I F3^v p 70 110–111 by 70–72
13^v p118 110.5–111 by 72–75
Vol. II F2^v p68 110–111 by 71–71.5
I1^v p114 105–106 by 71.5–74

Paper white wove; countermark $\frac{\text{OM}}{\text{1811}}$

Notes on Composition and Publication This edition is a resetting of No. 11 with no authorial revision. Occasional errors in No. 11 (e.g. Vol. II p. 211 line 16 *And left amind,*) are corrected, but others creep in (e.g. Vol. II p. 51 line 7. *It's worn to the th' thread*).

Copies B(1) B(2) BLL BmU Bod P QUB.

A13

POEMS

SEVENTH EDITION 1812

POEMS. | BY | THE REV. GEORGE CRABBE, LL.B. | rule 22 | Ipse (etc. as No. 7 with omission of diaerisis in *Maeoniumque*) *Lucan*. | rule 22 | SEVENTH EDITION. | thick-thin rule 18 | LONDON: | PRINTED FOR J. HATCHARD, | BOOKSELLER TO HER MAJESTY, OPPOSITE ALBANY, | PICCADILLY. | thick-thin rule 7 | 1812.

Collation Demy 8° [a]–b^8 B–R^{8}S^4 = 148 leaves

Pagination [i–v] vi–viii [ix–xi] xii [xiii] xiv–xxix [xxx–xxxii] [1–3] 4–17 [18–21] 22–29 [30–35] 36–68 [69–71] 72–94 [95–97] 98–135 [136–139] 140–166 [167–169] 170–189 [190–193] 194–207 [208–211] 212–215 [216–219] 220–238 [239–241] 242–246 [247–249] 250–256 [257–259] 260–262 [263–264] = 296 pages.

Contents [i] half-title thick-thin rule 25 | POEMS. | thin-thick rule 25 [ii] blank [iii] title-page [iv] Printer's imprint rule 41 | J. Brettell, Printer, Rupert-Street, | Hay-Market, London. [v]–viii Dedication [ix] Advertisement to the Second Edition [x] blank [xi]–xii Advertisement to the Reader [xiii]–xxix Preface [xxx] blank [xxxi] Contents [xxxii] blank [1]–262 text as No. 7 [263–264] Advertisements.

Printer's Imprint p. [iv] above and p. 262 rule 40 | J. Brettell, Printer, Rupert-Street, | Hay-Market, London.

Direction line $ 1 signed in centre of direction line (except [a]) Press figure: 5 on [a] 8^v p. xvi; b2^v p. xx; H2^v p. 100; H4^r p. 103; K2^r p. 131; K7^r p. 141; M2^r p. 163; M3^r p. 165; O1^v p. 194; P3^r p. 213; P8^r p. 223; Q3^r p. 229; Q7^v p. 238.

Headline running titles central, numerals at outer margin; Book or Part number is at gutter margin where appropriate, roman numerals within square bracket. Errors in this system: p. 74 point missing; p. 80 Part I. for Part II.

Notes on Printing It was not possible to compare any of the copies on a collating machine, but it seems probable that there were two settings of sig. S.

Type-page variation B7^v p 14 143–143.5 by 81.5–82
H4^v p104 143–144 by 82.5–85
O2^v p196 148–148.5 by 82.5–85

Paper off-white wove. Has three countermarks apparently randomly distributed through the volume, though since only three copies have been examined, no firm conclusion can be drawn. They are $\frac{1811}{W}$, W and TM. The last appears only on sig. R in the copies examined. Sig. E in P copy has no countermark at all. Of the three copies seen, Bod had a countermark in sig. S, B and P had not.

Binding According to Hatchard's advertisements this edition was issued in boards price 10s. 6d. No copy so bound has been seen.

Copies B Bod P

A14

POEMS

SEVENTH EDITION, SECOND ISSUE ('EIGHTH EDITION')   1813

This is in every respect identical with No. 13, with the exception of EIGHTH EDITION. for SEVENTH EDITION., and 1813 for 1812 on the title page.

[a]2^r, the title-page has the countermark $\frac{1811}{W}$ and there is no other mark in the gathering; while not conclusive evidence, it suggests that the title-page is integral – such a conclusion is reinforced by the upper serifs on the M of POEMS which are missing in both 13 and 14. The two copies of this issue I have seen are rebound too tightly to check physically whether the title-page is integral. If the title-page *is* integral, it seems possible that Sig. [a] was printed with both seventh and eighth edition title-pages in the same print run, Hatchard attempting to anticipate the likely demand, and preserving the novelty of a 'new' edition, while saving on composing costs. However, in default of further copies of this issue such a conclusion must remain debatable.

Copies P; CtY
    Also issued were Poems: 1816 'Eighth Edition' in two variant states and Poems: 1817 'Ninth Edition'. The entries for these issues are on p. 53

A15

THE BOROUGH

FIRST EDITION   1810

THE BOROUGH: | A | POEM, IN | 𝕿wenty-four 𝕷etters. | BY | THE REV. G. CRABBE, LL.B. | rule 84 | PAULO MAJORE CANAMUS. – VIRGIL. | rule 84 | 𝕷onbon: | PRINTED FOR J. HATCHARD, | BOOKSELLER TO HER MAJESTY, 190, OPPOSITE ALBANY, | PICCADILLY. | thick-thin rule 7 | 1810.

Collation Demy 8° [a]–b⁸c⁴d²B–Y⁸Z⁶ = 196 leaves

Pagination [i–v] vi–ix [x–xi] xii–xli [xlii–xliv] [1–3] 4–14 [15–17] 18–27 [28–31] 32–42 [43–45] 46–64 [65–67] 68–74 [75–77] 78–89 [90–93] 94–103 [104–107] 108–115 [116–119] 120–130 [131–133] 134–146 [147–149] 150–160 [161–163] 164–176 [177–179] 180–190 [191–193] 194–200 [201–203] 204–210]211–213] 214–221 [222–225] 226–234 [235–237] 238–251 [252–255] 256–265 [266–269]

270–281 [282–285] 286–296 [297–299] 300–312 [313–315] 316–326 [327–329] 330–344 [345–348] = 392 pages.

Contents [i] half-title thick-thin rule 83.5 | THE BOROUGH: | 𝔄 𝔓oem. | thin-thick rule 83 [ii] blank [iii] title-page [iv] printer's imprint double rule 43 | *Brettell and Co. Printers,* | *Marshall-street, Golden-square, London.* | double rule 42 [v]–ix Dedication [x] blank [xi]–xl Preface xli Contents [xlii] blank]xliii] thick-thin rule 83 | THE BOROUGH. | thin-thick rule 82 [xliv] blank [1]–344 text: Letter 1 General Description; Letter 2 The Church; Letter 3 The Vicar – The Curate, &c.; Letter 4 Sects and Professions in Religion; Letter 5 Elections; Letter 6 Professions – Law; Letter 7 Professions – Physic; Letter 8 Trades; Letter 9 Amusements; Letter 10 Clubs and Social Meetings; Letter 11 Inns; Letter 12 Players; Letter 13 The Alms-House and Trustees; Letter 14 Inhabitants of the Alms-House – Blaney; Letter 15 Inhabitants of the Alms-House – Clelia; Letter 16 Inhabitants of the Alms-House – Benbow; Letter 17 The Hospital Governors; Letter 18 The Poor and their Dwellings; Letter 19 The Poor of the Borough – The Parish Clerk; Letter 20 The Poor of the Borough – Ellen Orford; Letter 21 The Poor of the Borough – Abel Keene; Letter 22 The Poor of the Borough – Peter Grimes; Letter 23 Prisons; Letter 24 Schools. [345–348] Advertisements

Printer's Imprint above p. [iv] and p. 344 rule 39 | Brettell and Co. Printers, | Marshall-Street, Golden-Square, London.

Direction line signatures $ 1 signed (except [a]); also B2, C2, D2, F2, G2 and H2; in centre of direction line.

Headline pages numbered at outer margin; running title in centre; letter number at gutter margin thus: on recto *Letter* 1.] etc, on verso [*Letter* 1. etc. (on half-title pages introducing each Letter the numeral is roman rather than arabic.) Variation from norm in headline: p. 38 the Letter number is missing.

Notes on Printing p. 5, B3ʳ, exists in two states; the variations occur in lines 13 and 20, which in one version read 'wide stream descry,' and 'His tingling fingers', while in the second state they read 'wide stream descry' and 'His tingling Fingers'. Of the 33 copies so far examined or reported on, 19 have the former version, 14 the latter.

A Hinman collation reveals that several other formes, especially the outer formes of C and D and the inner formes of Q and R, have experienced severe type-shifting or distortion. It is not possible to establish which version of p. 5 is the earlier, though from the context it seems probable that the compositor setting the surrounding lines (assuming without warrant other than probability that there was no change in compositor at that place) would have used a capital letter for 'Fingers'. The second edition follows 'fingers' version, but again this may only indicate that they used as copy a randomly chosen volume which happened to read thus.

It is also perhaps worth noting that the fascimile title-page in the Aldeburgh Exhibition catalogue (p. 30) does not have the double hyphen between 𝕿𝖜𝖊𝖓𝖙𝖞 and 𝖋𝖔𝖚𝖗; there is no note of the provenance of the facsimile.

Type-page variation F8ᵛ p 80 151–152   by 85–86.5
N4ᵛ p184 150.5–151.5 by 83.5–85.5
S8ᵛ p272 145.5–146   by 85–86
Z2ᵛ p340 150.5–152.5 by 83.5–85

Paper off-white wove, countermark 1809.

Binding Boards, grey or blue; label reads THE | BOROUGH | A 𝔓𝔬𝔢𝔪, | BY | G. CRABBE | *Price* 10s 6d.

Notes on Composition and Publication Begun at Rendham in 1804 and finished at Muston in December 1809, the volume was published in 1810, probably in April, though Crabbe's son says February. *The English Catalogue of Books* supports the April date and quotes the price of the volume as 10/6. The print run cannot be ascertained. It should be noted that the Scholar Press facsimile of this edition was taken from the CUL copy, which is defective, in that it lacks [a]1 and d2.

Copies (examined) (Fingers) B(1) BL Bod CUL P; CU-B MH TxU (fingers) B(2) CTr LoU; CSmH CtY(2 copies) IU.

Copies (reported) (Fingers) DuU EdU LoL LcU MaU (2 copies) ReU TCD YoU; ALU CaU McGU ToU (fingers) MaU(1 copy) NeU NoU NLS(2 copies) NLW ShU UCNW; AdU McMU.

A16

THE BOROUGH

SECOND EDITION   1810

As 15, escept inserted between the second rule and 𝕷𝖔𝖓𝖉𝖔𝖓: is *SECOND EDITION, REVISED* | ornamental rule

Collation Demy 8° a–c⁸B–Z⁸ = 200 leaves

Pagination [i–v] vi–ix [x–xi] xii–xl [xli] xlii–xlv [xlvi–xlviii] [1–3] 4–14 [15–17] 18–27 [28–31] 32–41 [42–45] 46–64 [65–67] 68–74 [75–77] 78–89 [90–93] 94–103 [104–107] 108–115 [116–119] 120–130 [131–133] 134–146 [147–149] 150–160 [161–163] 164–175 [176–179] 180–190 [191–193] 194–200 [201–203] 204–210 [211–213] 214–221 [222–225] 226–234 [235–237] 238–251 [252–255] 256–265 [266–269] 270–281 [282–285] 286–297 [298–301] 302–314 [315–317] 318–328 [329–331] 332–347 [348–352] = 400 pages

Contents [i] half-title thick-thin rule 83 | THE BOROUGH: | A Poem. | thin-thick rule 84 [ii] printer's imprint rule 32 | J. Brettell, Printer, | Marshall-street, Golden-square. [iii] title-page [iv] blank [v]–xl as No. 15 [xli]–xliv Advertisement xlv Contents [xlvi] blank [xlvii] thick-thin rule 83 | THE BOROUGH. | thin-thick rule 83 [xlviii] blank [1]–347 text as No. 15 [348] blank [349–352] Hatchard's advertisements.

Printer's Imprint above p. [ii] and p. 347 rule 39 | John Brettell, Printer, | Marshall-Street, Golden-Square, London.

Direction line signatures $ 1 and 2 signed except a1 and a2, (a3 is signed) E2, I2, O2, P2, Q2, and R2. Signature in centre of direction line, (note that all these leaves were also not signed in first edition).

Headline as No. 15 though with different variants in typography.

Notes on Printing The variations in typographical details in the headline such as points omitted or raised, or type battered shows expected variation from copy to copy, indicating the deterioration due to type-batter. However, there is one copy, P(1) which has a remarkably long list of unique variations in this respect, including numbers omitted, points present where others have none, and points omitted where others have them. A machine collation of this copy makes it clear that while it uses the same types as the other copies, there is significant movement which might suggest a re-impression. There are very few differences observable without mechanical aid, apart from the headline differences already mentioned. Two examples: p. 114, last line P(1) has two inverted commas, as would be expected, the others only one; p. 280 the fragmentary last word begins below the 'e' in 'pleasant' in P(1), but under the 'l' in others.

It is, as both title-page and Advertisement announce, a revised edition. The revision in this instance was undertaken because both Hatchard and Crabbe were criticized by periodical writers for the poor presentation of the first edition.

Type-page variation F8ᵛ p 80 151.5–153 by 83.5–85.5
N4ᵛ p184 150.5–151 by 82–84.5

S8ᵛ p272 146–147   by 83–87
Z2ᵛ p340 145.5–148 by 84–86.5

Paper off white wove, countermark 1810, or 1809 apparently random. A better quality paper than most.

Binding Drab grey boards: label reads: THE | BOROUGH | [A] | 𝕻𝔬𝔢𝔪. | BY | G. CRABBE | rule | 𝔖𝔢𝔠𝔬𝔫𝔡 𝔢𝔡𝔦𝔱𝔦𝔬𝔫. | rule | *Price* 12*s*[.]

Copies B Bod CK LaU OEF P(1) P(2) QUB SoU YoU.

A17

THE BOROUGH

THIRD EDITION   1810

THE BOROUGH: | A | 𝕻𝔬𝔢𝔪, | IN | TWENTY-FOUR LETTERS. | BY | THE REVᴰ GEORGE CRABBE, LL.D. | thick-thin rule 7 | PAULO MAJORA CANAMUS. – VIRGIL. | thin-thick rule 7 | rule 70 (70.5) | THIRD EDITION. | *IN TWO VOLUMES.* | rule 70 (70.5) | VOL. I. (II.) | ornamental rule 18 | 𝕷𝔬𝔫𝔡𝔬𝔫: | PRINTED FOR J. HATCHARD, | BOOKSELLER TO HER MAJESTY, 190, OPPOSITE ALBANY, | PICCADILLY. | thick-thin rule 7 | 1810.

Collation Foolscap 8° *Vol. I* [a]–c⁸B–M⁸N² = 114 leaves
Vol. II [A]²B–O⁸P⁴ = 110 leaves

Pagination Vol. I [i–v] vi–ix [x–xi] xii–xlii [xliii] xliv–xlvi [xlvii–xlviii] [1–3] 4–15 [16–19] 20–31 [32–37] 38–48 [49–51] 52–72 [73–75] 76–83 [84–87] 88–101 [102–105] 106–116 [117–119] 120–128 [129–131] 132–143 [144–147] 148–163 [164–167] 168–179 [180] = 228 pages
Vol. II [i–iv] [1–3] 4–18 [19–21] 22–34 [35–37] 38–46 [47–49] 50–58 [59–61] 62–70 [71–73] 74–84 [85–87] 88–103 [104–107] 108–119 [120–123] 124–137 [138–141] 142–155 [156–159] 160–174 [175–177] 178–190 [191–193] 194–211 [212–216] (misprinting 209 as 109) = 220 pages.

Contents Vol. I [i] half-title double rule 66 | THE BOROUGH: | 𝔄 𝕻𝔬𝔢𝔪. | double rule 66 [ii] printer's imprint rule 34 | J. Brettell, Printer, Marshall-Street, | Golden-Square, London. [iii] title-page [iv] blank [v]–ix Dedication [x] blank [xi]–xlii Preface [xliii]–xlvi Advertisement [xlvii–xlviii] Contents [1]–179 text; (Letters 1–11, as No. 15) [180] blank.
Vol. II [i] half-title double rule 67 | THE BOROUGH: | 𝔄 𝕻𝔬𝔢𝔪. | double rule 66 [ii] printer's imprint rule 35 | J. Brettell, Printer, Marshall-Street, | Golden-

Square, London. [iii] title-page [iv] blank [1]–211 text; (Letters 12–24, as No. 15) [212] blank [213–216] Hatchard's advertisements.

Printer's Imprint Vol. I p. [ii] above and p. 179 rule 62.5 | J. Brettell, Printer, Marshall-Street, Golden-Square, London.
Vol. II p. [ii] above and p. 211 rule 40.5 | Printed by J. BRETTELL, | Marshall-Street, Golden-Square, London.

Direction line signatures \$ 1 signed (except [a]) in centre of direction line; in *Vol. I* E2 and F2 are also signed. *Vol. I.* (*II.*) appears at the gutter margin of the direction line on \$ 1.

Headline above a double rule approx. 70, running title in centre, page number at outer margin, letter number within square brackets at gutter margin, arabic, as first edition. Various typographical differences; for one of significance see notes.

Notes on Printing p. 53 (E3^r) of *Vol. I* has two states, revealed by three variants: in the headline, Letter / Leteer; in the last line of text, darkness / darkuess; and in the footnote, For an account / Far an acconnt . . . year / yerr. In this case, unlike the first edition of *The Borough*, it is clear enough that the second element in each pair is the earlier, and that this page must have been very ill proof-read by the printers; the presses must have been stopped when the bad state of the page was noticed, and corrections made. A Hinman collation of variant copies indicated that there was no noticeable disturbance of other pages in the forme, though it is interesting that E2 and F2 are the only leaves of the inner formes signed. The misprinted page number in *Vol. II* was apparently not noticed. That Brettell allowed the faulty sheets to go onto the market indicates perhaps his slovenliness as a printer, which remains a general impression throughout his work with Crabbe.

More particularly, when (as a sample) Letter 22 in the second and third edition is compared the following significant compositorial errors appear:
2 p303 Still have they being?   3 p161 Still have they being!
2 p303 Such Peter sought   3 p162 Such Peter bought
where in both cases the sense is radically altered. Note also the incorrect degree assigned to Crabbe in the title-pages.

Type-page variation Vol. I D3^v p38   110–111   by 71–72.5
                   E3^r p53   114.5–115.5 by 70.5–73.5
                   H5^v p106 113.5–115   by 71.5–73.5
         Vol. II D6^v p44   106.5–108   by 70–73
                   L8^v p160 114–115   by 72.5–74

Paper off-white, countermark $\frac{\text{OM}}{1808}$, randomly in each gathering.

Binding Presumably in boards (none so seen).

Note on Composition This edition was not revised by Crabbe

Copies (examined) (Letter) B(2) BL BrU CUL P(1) P(2)
                (Leteer) B(1) Bod BmU CK SyU; CSmH CtY MH TxU
                (2 copies)

Copies (reported on) (Letter) KeU.
                   (Leteer) UEA; CaU.

A18

THE BOROUGH

FOURTH EDITION   1812

THE BOROUGH: | A Poem, | IN | TWENTY-FOUR LETTERS. | BY | THE REV. GEORGE CRABBE, LL.D. | thick-thin rule 7 | PAULO MAJORA CANAMUS. – VIRGIL. | thin-thick rule 7 | rule 70 | FOURTH EDITION. | *IN TWO VOLUMES.* | rule 70 | VOL. I. | ornamental rule 21.5 | London: | PRINTED FOR J. HATCHARD, | BOOKSELLER TO HER MAJESTY, 190, OPPOSITE ALBANY, | PICCADILLY. | thick-thin rule 7 | 1812.

Vol. II as *Vol. I* except Poem,; VOL. II.; rules of 67; different ornamental rule; last thick-thin rule 8.

Collation As No. 17.

Pagination As No. 17.

Contents As No. 17.

Printer's Imprint Vol. I p[ii] rule 36 | J. Brettell, Printer, Marshall-street, | Golden-square, London. and p. 179 rule 37.5 | Printed by J. Brettell, | Rupert-street, Haymarket, London.
Vol. II p. [ii] rule 35 | J. Brettell, Printer, | Rupert-street, Haymarket, London. and p. 211 rule 36 | Printed by J. Brettell, | Rupert-street, Haymarket, London.
Direction line signature $ 1 signed in centre of direction line; VOL. I. (II.) at gutter margin of $ 1. The following leaves have press figure 5: G4^r, G7^r, H5^r, 16^r and ^{v}, K4^v, K5^v, L7^v, M6^v, M8^r, in *Vol. I*; H8^r and ^{v}, I1^v, I6^v, L4^v, L5^v, P4^v in *Vol. II*.

Headline as No. 17 with different typographical variations.

Notes on Printing Reset edition, correcting some of the errors in the third edition, e.g. *Vol. II* p. 168 *sternnest* becomes *sternest*. It appears that Brettell moved shop during the printing of this edition.

Type-page variations Vol. I D3ᵛ p38   109.5–111 by 70.5–71.5
                               H5ᵛ p106 114–115   by 71
                Vol. II D6ᵛ p44   104.5–105 by 69.5–72.5
                          L8ᵛ p160 104–104.5 by 71.5

Paper off-white; no watermark. In BmU copy, which seems to be not cut down in binding, there are pin holes at the top centre of each of the first four leaves. This may indicate that the points are on the shorter rather than the longer edges of the tympan. (Cf. No. 11).

Binding Boards, price 12s.

Copies B BL (Vol. II only) BmU OL P.

A19

THE BOROUGH

FIFTH EDITION   1813

THE BOROUGH: | A | POEM, | IN | 𝕿𝖜𝖊𝖓𝖙𝖞-𝖋𝖔𝖚𝖗 𝕷𝖊𝖙𝖙𝖊𝖗𝖘 | BY | THE REV. GEORGE CRABBE, LL.D. | rule 33 | PAULO MAJORA CANAMUS. – VIRGIL. | rule 33 | *FIFTH EDITION.* | thick-thin rule 18 | LONDON: | PRINTED FOR J. HATCHARD, | BOOKSELLER TO HER MAJESTY, OPPOSITE ALBANY, | PICCADILLY. | rule 7| 1813.

Collation Demy 8° [a]–c⁸B–Y⁸Z⁴AA² = 198 leaves

Pagination [i–v] vi–ix [x–xi] xii–xl [xli] xlii–xliv [xlv–xlviii] otherwise as No. 16, to 347, which is misprinted as 243 [348] = 396 pages

Contents [i] half-title thick-thin rule 25 | THE BOROUGH: | 𝔄 𝔓𝔬𝔢𝔪. | thin-thick rule 25 [ii] blank [iii] title-page [iv] printer's imprint rule 37 | J. BRETTELL, Printer, Rupert | Street, Haymarket, London. otherwise as No. 16, except there are no trade advertisements at the end.

Printer's Imprint above p. [iv] and p. 243[347] rule 37 | J. BRETTELL, Printer, Rupert | Street, Haymarket, London.

Direction line signature $ 1 signed in centre of direction line (except [a]).
Press figure 5 on B5ᵛ, B7ʳ, E1ᵛ, G3ʳ, H7ʳ, I5ʳ and K5ʳ.

Headline numeral at outer margin, running title in centre, LETTER I.] etc. at gutter margin; thus letter numerals change from arabic to roman. There are the usual typographical variations, including] missing on p. 13, and LETTER IV for LETTER VI on p. 87.

Notes on Printing The misprint of 347 as 243 is unusual, in that two figures are incorrect. It may be a coincidence that 243 is R2^r while [347] is AA2^r. It may also be that an error was made, and incorrectly amended; it is barely plausible that a 2 could be mistaken for a 7, and that the number was reversed.

Type page variations C8^v p32 147.5–148 by 85–85.5
                   K8^v p114 154   by 88.5
                   Q2^v p228 150–151 by 82–84
                   Y2^v p324 151–152 by 82.5–84.5

Paper off-white wove, counter mark either W or $\frac{1811}{W}$.

Binding No evidence, probably boards.

Copies B Bod P; CtY.

A20

THE BOROUGH

FIFTH EDITION, SECOND ISSUE (A NEW EDITION)   1820

THE BOROUGH: | *A POEM,* | IN | TWENTY-FOUR LETTERS, | BY | THE REV. GEORGE CRABBE, LL.B. | rule 22 | PAULO MAJORA CANAMUS. – VIRGIL. | rule 21.5 | *A NEW EDITION.* | thick-thin rule 24.5 | LONDON: | JOHN MURRAY, ALBEMARLE-STREET. | 1820.

Collation Demy 8° [a]^8(±[a]1 and 2) b–c^{8}B–Y^{8}Z^{4}AA^2.

Pagination As No. 19.

Contents [i] half-title THE BOROUGH. [ii] printer's imprint LONDON: PRINTED BY THOMAS DAVISON, WHITEFRIARS. [iii] title-page [iv] blank otherwise as No. 19.

Notes This is a second issue of the fifth edition with Murray's cancel title-page; it seems clear that there must have been something of a downturn in Crabbe sales if copies of an 1813 edition were still available in 1820. In Murray's ledgers there is an entry for the printing of titles; presumably this issue is one of those to which the entry refers.

Copy P

A21

CtY copy of this is identical with No. 20 except the rules measure 17, 17 and 22 respectively.

Also issued was the Borough 1816 'Sixth edition' in two variant states. The entry for this is on p. 54.

A22

TALES

1812

TALES. | BY | THE REV. GEORGE CRABBE, LL.B. | diamond rule 34 | LONDON: | PRINTED FOR J. HATCHARD, | BOOKSELLER TO HER MAJESTY, OPPOSITE ALBANY, | PICCADILLY. | thick-thin rule 7 | 1812.

Collation Demy 8° [a]⁴b⁸B–CC⁸ = 212 leaves.

Pagination [i–ix] x–xxii [xxiii–xxiv] [1–5] 6–21 [22–25] 26–40 [41–43] 44–60 [61–63] 64–75 [76–79] 80–103 [104–107] 108–124 [125–127] 128–141 [142–145] 146–157 [158–161] 162–172 [173–175] 176–187 [188–191] 192–207 [208–211] 212–223 [224–227] 228–244 [245–247] 248–263 [264–267] 268–281 [283–285] 286–305 [306–309] 310–325 [326–329] 330–339 [340–343] 344–358 [359–361] 362–375 [376–379] 380–398 [399–400] = 424 pages.

Contents [i] half-title thick-thin rule 25 | TALES. | thin-thick rule 25 [ii] blank [iii] title-page [iv] Printer's imprint rule 36 | Printed by J. Brettell, | Rupert-street, Haymarket, London. [v–vii] Dedication [viii] blank [ix]–xxii Preface [xxiii] Contents [xxiv] blank [1] second half-title thick-thin rule 80 | TALES. | thin-thick rule 80 [2] blank [3]–398 text Tale 1 The Dumb Orators; or, the Benefit of Society; Tale 2 The Parting Hour; Tale 3 The Gentleman Farmer; Tale 4 Procrastination; Tale 5 The Patron; Tale 6 The Frank Courtship; Tale 7 The Widow's Tale; Tale 8 The Mother; Tale 9 Arabella; Tale 10 The Lover's Journey; Tale 11 Edward Shore; Tale 12 'Squire Thomas; or, The Precipitate Choice; Tale 13 Jesse and Colin; Tale 14 The Struggles of Conscience; Tale 15 Advice; or, The 'Squire and the Priest; Tale 16 The Confidant; Tale 17 Resentment; Tale 18 The Wager; Tale 19 The Convert; Tale 20 The Brothers; Tale 21 The Learned Boy. [399–400] Hatchard's advertisements.

Printer's Imprint p. [iv] above and p. 398 rule 41 | J. Brettell, Printer, Rupert-Street, | Hay-market, London.

Direction line signature $ 1 signed in centre of direction line (except [a]). The following leaves have the press-mark 5 in the direction line b3ʳ; G1ʳ or G8ᵛ, G2ʳ, P2ʳ, Q7ᵛ, S6ʳ and ᵛ, U4ᵛ, X4ᵛ and CC4ᵛ; one of these (P2ʳ) is in fact in the last line of text, while those copies with the figure on G1ʳ and G8ᵛ are distinguished in the register below.

Headline running title in centre, page number at outer margin, Tale number at gutter margin thus: TALE I.] etc.

Notes on Printing There are four separate areas of variation in this edition, indicating three separate states:

1 Of the 39 copies examined or reported on 9 have K3 as integral, 30 have it as a cancel leaf; see register of copies for locations.

2 Of the 39 copies 17 have the press figure on G1ʳ, 22 on G8ᵛ; see register of copies for locations.

3 BL and G1U are the only copies so far examined or reported on to have (correctly) an inverted comma at the end of line ten on p. 131 (K2ʳ); (this variation combined with 4).

4 The most straightforward variation is one which probably applies to other editions as well, though this is the only one where positive identification has been made; BL and GIU copies are printed on large paper, presumably relating to the Hatchard advertisements for the second edition of Tales which says that there are 'a few copies on splendid Royal Octavo'.

Hinman collation showed no variants between any of the states apart from that noted above on K2ʳ; however there was often some distortion and occasionally independent movement of single lines which might indicate a possible new impression. (This is particularly the case with the BL large-paper copy).

The relative infrequency of the integral state of K3 makes it probable that the alteration necessitating the cancel-leaf was made late in the print-run. I presume that a fair proportion of copies had already been sewn, and the new leaf cut from the revised sheets of K to replace the defective K3, while the revised sheets were incorporated into the unsewn copies.

There is nothing here, nor in the first edition of Crabbe's next volume of poems, *TALES OF THE HALL* to indicate whether the cause of the presses being stopped was authorial intervention.

The lack of significant variation in sig. G is perhaps surprising; indeed the only explanation for the difference in placing of the press figure may be that the press figure had to be moved for some reason during the print run; normally this variation would be taken to imply two impressions, but machine collation does not support such a conclusion.

The presence of the inverted comma in only two copies may suggest that these were printed early in the run, and that the inverted comma soon dropped out of the forme. Other evidence suggests that this was a fairly inaccurately printed edition; for example, p. 172 an asterisk is missing from the last line; p. 274 line 19: 'now' should be 'own'; p. [329], 3 lines from the foot, a question mark has been omitted.

Type-page variations F3^v p70 148–149 by 84–86

K3^v p134 148–149 by 82–87

O6^v p204 152–152.5 by 82–84.5

U5^v p298 146.5–148 by 84–85

BB8^v p348 151.5–152 by 84.5–86

Paper off-white wove, countermarks variously W, MT, and $\frac{1811}{W}$; no apparent pattern.

Binding Boards, blue or grey sometimes blue spine, grey boards and vice versa. Label on spine reads: decorative border | TALES, | IN | 𝔙erse. | BY | G. CRABBE. | rule 3 | Price 12*s*. | decorative border.

Notes on Composition and Publication According to an advertisement in *The Times* of September 14 1812, *Tales* was published on that day, though earlier dates have been suggested on dubious evidence. Since the dedication is dated Muston, 31 July 1812 the publication date 'in the early part of the year' indicated by Crabbe's son seems a manifest error. Though advertisements used as end-papers have no primary value in assessing date of issue it is interesting to note that MH copy has advertisements for Ballantyne dated December 10th 1811, NN copy is a presentation copy to Mr R Crabbe from the Author.

Copies (examined) K3 integral BL Bod CTr; CtY K3 cancel B CUL LoU P (3 copies); CSmH IU (3 copies); MH (2 copies) NN. Press figure on G1^r Bod LoU; CSmH IU (2nd copy) on G8^v B BL CTr CUL P (3 copies); CtY IU (1st, 3rd copies) MH (2 copies) NN. Inverted comma at the end of line 10 on K2^r p. 131 BL. Large paper copy BL.

Copies (reported on) K3 integral OS UEA YU; AdU McMU. K3 cancel AL EdU CJ CStJ GlU MaU NeU NLS(2 copies) ReU SoU StU SuU UCNW; CaU MStVU QUK. Press figure on G1^r AL CJ EdU MaU NeU SoU SuU UCNW UEA; CaU McMU MStVU QUK. Press-figure on G8^v CStJ GlU NLS(2 copies) OS ReU StU YU; AdU G1U is the only additional copy to have the inverted comma at the end of line 10 on K2^r, p. 131. It is also the only additional large-paper copy; this seems to be clear confirming evidence of a separate issue; the surprising, even irreconcilable element is that BL has K3 integral, and G1U is reported to have it as a cancel leaf.

A23

TALES

SECOND EDITION 1812

TALES. | BY | THE REV. GEORGE CRABBE, LL.D. | rule 42 | *IN TWO VOLUMES.* | rule 42 | SECOND EDITION. | thick-thin rule 7 | VOL. I. (VOL II.) | ornamental rule 17.5 | 𝔏onbon; | PRINTED FOR J. HATCHARD, | BOOKSELLER TO HER MAJESTY, 190, OPPOSITE ALBANY, | PICCADILLY. | thick-thin rule 8 | 1812.

Collation Vol. I Foolscap 8° [a]⁴b⁸B–O⁸ = 116 leaves
Vol. II Foolscap 8° [A]² B–P⁸Q⁶ = 120 leaves

Pagination Vol. I [i–ix] x–xxiii [xxiv] [1–5] 6–24 [25–27] 28–44 [45–47] 48–66 [67–69] 70–82 [83–85] 86–113 [114–117] 118–136 [137–139] 140–155 [156–159] 160–172 [173–175] 176–188 [189–191] 192–205 [206–208] = 232 pages.
Vol. II [i–iv] [1–3] 4–21 [22–25] 26–39 [40–43] 44–63 [64–67] 68–86 [87–89] 90–105 [106–109] 110–132 [133–135] 136–153 [154–157] 158–169 [170–173] 174–190 [191–193] 194–209 [210–213] 214–235 [236] = 240 pages.

Contents Vol. I [i] half-title thick-thin rule 69 | TALES. | thick-thin rule 70 [ii] blank [iii] title-page [iv] printer's imprint rule 30 | Printed by J. Brettell, | Rupert-Street, Haymarket, London. [v–viii] Dedication [ix]–xxiii Preface [xxiv] Contents [1] double rule 70 | TALES. | double rule 70 [2] blank [3]–205 text (Tales I–X as No. 22) [206–208] blank.
Vol. II [i] half-title double rule 69.5 | TALES. | double rule 70.5 [ii] blank [iii] title-page [iv] printer's imprint rule 37.5 | Printed by J. Brettell, | Rupert-street, Haymarket, London. [1]–235 text (Tales XI–XXI as No. 22) [236] Errata.

Printer's Imprint Vol. I p. [iv] above and p. 205 rule 37 | J. BRETTELL, Printer, Rupert- | Street, Haymarket, London.

Vol. II p. [iv] above and p. 235 rule 37 | J. BRETTELL, Printer, Rupert | Street, Haymarket, London.

Direction line signature $ 1 signed in centre of direction line; VOL. I.(II.) at gutter margin on $ 1 with the exception of Vol. I b1ʳ. The following leaves have press mark 5 in direction line: Vol. I G5ᵛ and M8ᵛ; Vol. II B2ᵛ, G2ᵛ, H3ʳ and I2ᵛ.

Headline Above a double rule, there is a running title in the centre, page number at outer margin, [TALE I. etc. at gutter margin. There is a variant state of the inner forme of Vol. I sig. B; some copies examined have [*Tale* 1. There appears to be no type variation in the rest of the page when variant states are compared, so stop-press correction seems the most likely kind of change. There are also a number of other errors, including Vol. I D3ʳ TALF; M1ʳ omits bracket; N4ᵛ TALE XI. instead of IX. Vol. II E7ʳ TALE XIII.) instead of].

Notes on Printing The list of Errata indicates revisions rather than compositorial errors; the references are all correct, though it is interesting to note that Vol. I p. 182 line 11 was already changed from the first edition, 'knew' becoming 'know'. In a sample collation no revisions were revealed, so it may be that this change was compositorial. There are a number of compositorial errors not corrected, such as Vol. I p. 166, four lines from the end, the last word reads 'mour', not 'mourn', and Vol. II p. 159, in the last line there is 'voiee' instead of 'voice'.

A Hinman collation reveals that the title-pages of Vol. I and Vol. II were printed from the same types, with the necessary substitution of II for I; it may be that in making this substitution the full point was dropped.

Type-page variations Vol. I D5ᵛ p42 114.5–115 by 72
I8ᵛ p128 113–114 by 71–71.5
O3ᵛ p198 114–114.5 by 69.5–71
Vol. II D8ᵛ p48 113.5–114 by 71
K4ᵛ p136 113–114 by 69–72
P3ᵛ p214 110   by 70.5–71.5

Paper slightly coarser texture than usual, and apparently no watermark; wove.

Binding No information, presumably boards.

Copies (examined) TALE I. BrU *Tale 1*. B BmU Bod CUL P.

Copy (reported on) TALE I. NLW.

A24

TALES

SECOND EDITION, SECOND ISSUE or SECOND IMPRESSION (THIRD EDITION)   1813

Title page as No. 23 with the following exceptions:

THIRD EDITION. for SECOND EDITION., the restoration of the point between VOL. and II., and 1813 for 1812.

Collation As No. 23.

Pagination As No. 23.

Contents As No. 23.

Notes This is probably the sheets of the second edition issued with new first preliminary gatherings (i.e. Vol. I [a] and Vol. II π). QUB copy has integral title-pages (all other copies were too tightly bound to distinguish) but machine collation shows no noticeable distortion of types such as would be expected from a reimpression of the same types, except on the title-pages themselves clearly, and the remainder of Vol. I [a] less clearly. In every copy so far seen on the Errata page at the end of Vol. II the 'd' has dropped from 'blind' in the note referring to Vol. I p. 177, whereas no copy of the second edition so far examined has this omission; this would be explained if it were assumed that π and O were imposed in the same forme, and that they were reimpressed for this 'issue'. Further evidence to support this hypothesis is the presence of the press-figure 5 on the same pages as in the second edition.

Every copy seen has the correct version of the headline in the inner forme of Vol. I sig. B, and this might lead to suspicions of a reimpression; the statistical sample is perhaps not great enough for any conclusion to be drawn.

The paper is similar to that of the second edition, with no watermark. Other typographical evidence is conflicting; the headline variants remain the same, and Vol. II p. 159, the last line still contains 'voiee'; on the other hand Vol. I p. 166, four lines from the end, 'mourn' is printed correctly.

Copies B BL Bod CK KeU KnU P QUB.

A25

TALES

THIRD EDITION ('FOURTH EDITION')   1813

TALES. | BY | THE REV. GEORGE CRABBE, LL.B. | thick-thin rule 15 | *FOURTH EDITION.* | double rule 81.5 | LONDON: | PRINTED FOR J. HATCHARD, | BOOKSELLER TO HER MAJESTY, OPPOSITE ALBANY, | PICCADILLY. | thick-thin rule 7 | 1813.

Collation Demy 8° [a]⁴b⁸[B]⁸C–CC⁸ = 212 pages.

Pagination As No. 22 = 424 pages.

Contents [i] half-title thick-thin rule 25 | TALES. | thin-thick rule 25 [ii] blank [iii] title-page [iv] printer's imprint rule 43 | J. Brettell, Printer, | Rupert Street, Haymarket, London. Otherwise as No. 22.

Printer's Imprint above p. [iv] and p. 398 rule 38 | Printed by J. Brettell, | Rupert Street, Haymarket, London.

Direction line: signature $ 1 signed in centre with the exception of [a] and B; C2 is also signed.

Headline as No. 22 though with different errors, e.g. H8ᵛ (p. 112) has IV for VI, M3ᵛ (p. 166) has XI for IX, and U8ʳ (p. 303) has no bracket.

Type-page variations F3ᵛ   p70   149–149.5 by 84–85
                K3ᵛ   p134 148   by 83.5–85
                O6ᵛ   p204 152–152.5 by 81–84
                U5ᵛ   p298 147   by 83.5–85
              BB8ᵛ p348 153–153.5 by 84–85

Paper poor quality, off-white wove, countermark 11.

Notes This edition is a reset version of the first edition, with rather less than one difference per page in a sample collation; it would require a full collation to establish the extent to which Crabbe himself was responsible for the changes – some are clearly his, as at line 3 of p. 100; others seem to be simple corrections or punctuation changes which might be attributed to a careful reader. It is at least clear that Crabbe took an interest in this edition.

Copies B Bod P; TxU.

A26

TALES

THIRD EDITION, SECOND ISSUE ('FIFTH' EDITION)   1814

Title-page identical to No. 25 except *FIFTH EDITION.* for *FOURTH EDITION.* and 1814. for 1813.
    Hinman collation suggests that this is sheets of the 'fourth' edition published with a cancel title-page, though all copies examined have been rebound too tightly to allow establishment of the existence of such a title-page; all headline errors are repeated.

Copies Bod LeU P.

A27

TALES

FOURTH EDITION ('SIXTH' EDITION)   1814

TALES. | BY | THE REV. GEORGE CRABBE, LL.D. | rule 41 | *IN TWO VOLUMES.* | rule
41 | SIXTH EDITION. | thick-thin rule 7 | VOL. I. (II.) | decorative rule | 𝕷𝖔𝖓𝖉𝖔𝖓: |
PRINTED FOR J. HATCHARD, | BOOKSELLER TO THE QUEEN, 190, OPPOSITE ALBANY, |
PICCADILLY. | thick-thin rule 7 | 1814.

Collation As No. 23.

Pagination As No. 23, printing Vol. I p. 22 as 32.

Contents Vol. I [i] half-title double rule 71 | TALES. | double rule 71 [ii] blank
[iii] title-page [iv] printer's imprint rule 35 | J. Brettell, Printer, | Rupert Street,
Haymarket, London. [v–viii] Dedication [ix–xxiii] Preface [xxiv] Contents [1]
𝕿𝕬𝕷𝕰𝕾. [2] blank otherwise as No. 23 to 205 [206] blank [207–208] Hatchard's
Advertisements.

Vol. II [i] half-title double rule 71 | TALES. | double rule 71 [ii] blank [iii] title-
page [iv] printer's imprint rule 35 | J. Brettell, Printer, | Rupert Street,
Haymarket, London. [1] 𝕿𝕬𝕷𝕰𝕾. otherwise as No. 23 to 235 [236] blank.

Printer's Imprint Vol. I on p. [iv] above and p. 205 rule 36 | J. Brettell, Printer, |
Rupert Street, Haymarket, London.
Vol. II on p. [iv] above and p. 235 rule 34 | J. Brettell, Printer, Rupert Street, |
Haymarket, London.

Direction line signature $ 1 signed in centre, gutter margin of $ 1^r has VOL. I. (II.)
There appears to be a different pattern of press-marking in this edition, for in
the fold of the gutter there are the following figures:

Vol. I pp. 18, C1^v; 63, E8^r; 70, F3^v; 87, G4^r; 110, H7^v; 116, M3^v and 182, N3^v
have figure 1. 118 I3^v and 130, K1^v have 3.

Vol. II pp. 14, B7^v; 18, C1^v; 38, D3^v; 94, F7^v; 112, H8^v; 122, I5^v; 131, K2^r;
142, K7^v; 162, M1^v; 186, N5^v and [210], P1^v have figure 3, while 146, L1^v has
figure 1. These figures are often impossible to see because of the tightness of the
binding; all noticed in all volumes have been included. The pattern of their
presence varies from copy to copy, and there may be further figures that I have
not observed.

Headline as No. 23 without the variant of the inner forme of Vol. I sig. B. and with different accidental errors, e.g. above under pagination, and Vol. II p. 34 where XI is printed for XII.

Type-page variations Vol. I D5ᵛ p42 115.5   by 72–72.5
I8ᵛ p128 115–116 by 69–71
O3ᵛ p198 113.5   by 70.5–71
Vol. II D8ᵛ p48 114.5   by 69–71
K4ᵛ p136 114.5–115 by 72–73
P3ᵛ p214 111.5   by 73

Paper at least three kinds used, not consistently in different copies, having respectively the countermarks 1810, 1812 and IVY MILL. The last of these appears to be a slightly superior quality; all cream wove.

Binding presumably boards.

Notes There are variations of punctuation in the text, all of which in a sample collation with Nos. 23 and 25 appear to be compositorial normalizing. There is no evidence of authorial revision. The Errata in the second edition are incorporated in the text here.

Copies B BmU Bod CTr P.

A28

TALES

FOURTH EDITION, SECOND ISSUE ('SEVENTH' EDITION)   1815

TALES. | BY | THE REV. GEORGE CRABBE, LL.D. | rule 41.5 | *IN TWO VOLUMES.* | rule 41.5 | SEVENTH EDITION. | thick-thin rule 7 | VOL. I. (II.) | decorative rule | 𝕷onbon: | PRINTED FOR J. HATCHARD, | BOOKSELLER TO THE QUEEN, 190, OPPOSITE ALBANY, | PICCADILLY. | thick-thin rule 7 | 1815.

Binding TxU copy blue boards, grey spine; label missing.

All other details as No. 27.

Notes This is probably the sheets of the 'sixth edition' with a new title-page. It has a selection of the marginal figures noted under the sixth edition, though on many pages the volume was bound too closely to check. It has similar misprints to the 'sixth edition'; e.g. Dutchess in the title to the Dedication and Vol. I p. 22 is printed as 32.

Copies P; TxU.

Note For the third issue of these sheets see Vols. III and IV of WORKS 1816; No. 35 p. 52 below.

A29

TALES

FOURTH EDITION, FOURTH ISSUE (A NEW EDITION) 1820

TALES: | BY THE | REV. GEORGE CRABBE, LL.B. | rule | *IN TWO VOLUMES.* | rule | A NEW EDITION. | VOL. I. (II.) | thick-thin rule | LONDON: | JOHN MURRAY, ALBEMARLE-STREET. | 1820.

A bifolium cancellans π1ʳ half-title TALES. | π1ᵛ Printer's imprint LONDON: | PRINTED BY T. DAVISON, WHITEFRIARS. π2ʳ title-page π2ᵛ blank. Vol. I has Hatchard advertisements. Both have Brettell imprint also.

This is a further issue of the 'sixth' edition of Tales.

Copy BL.

A30

TALES

FIFTH EDITION (A NEW EDITION) 1820

TALES: | BY THE | REV. GEORGE CRABBE, LL.B | rule 18.5 | *IN TWO VOLUMES.* | rule 18.5 | A NEW EDITION. | VOL. I (II.) | thin-thick rule 23 | LONDON: | JOHN MURRAY, ALBEMARLE-STREET. | rule 7 | 1820.

Collation Vol. I foolscap a⁴b⁸B–P⁸.
     Vol. II Foolscap [A]² B–R⁸.

Pagination Vol I [i–v] vi–vii [viii–ix] x–xxii [xxiii–xxiv] [1–3] 4–23 [24–27] 28–46 [47–49] 50–71 [72–75] 76–90 [90–93] 94–124 [125–127] 128–148 [149–151] 152–169 [170–173] 174–188 [189–191] 192–205 [206–209] 210–224.

     Vol II [i–iv] [1–3] 4–23 [24–27] 28–42 [43–45] 46–67 [68–71] 72–92 [93–95] 96–113 [114–117] 118–143 [144–147] 148–168 [169–171] 172–184 [185–187] 188–200 [207–209] 210–227 [228–231] 232–235 [256].

Contents Vol I [i] half-title TALES. [ii] Printer's imprint LONDON: | PRINTED B

THOMAS DAVISON, WHITEFRIARS[.] [iii] title-page [iv] blank [v] vi–vii Dedication [viii] blank [ix]–xxii Preface [xxiii] Contents [xxiv] blank [1] TALES. [2]–224 text.

Vol II [1] TALES. [ii] Printer's imprint LONDON: | PRINTED BY THOMAS DAVISON, WHITEFRIARS. [iii] title-page [iv] blank [1] TALES. [2]–225 text [256] Printer's imprint LONDON: | PRINTED BY THOMAS DAVISON, WHITEFRIARS.

Printer's Imprint Vol. I p. 224 Printed by Thomas Davison, Whitefriars, London.
Vol. II p. 256 LONDON: | PRINTED BY THOMAS DAVISON, WHITEFRIARS.

Direction line $ 1 and 2 signed on right of signature line, with the exception of Vol. I [a]; on left of signature line is VOL. I. (II.).

Headline arabic page numbers on outer margin, roman Tale number at gutter margin, Tale title in centre.

Paper White wove, no mark.

Binding Not known.

Note This was printed in a run of 750 copies, some of which were sold separately; others were included in the seven volume version of Works when Hatchard's 'sixth' edition was exhausted. By June 1822 only 232 copies had been sold at the wholesale price of 5/-, and the remainder were sold off at 2/-, leaving Murray with a loss of £42 16s on the impression. By this time all of Hatchard's stock had been sold, and so Murray presumably decided to cut his losses on this edition and print the 1823 Foolscap Works version of *Tales* rather than attempt to incorporate it into the 1823 Works. In fact it would pretty nearly have covered Murray's sales of the 1823 works up to the time he remaindered it to Tegg in 1829. Apparently Murray had alternative first gatherings printed with different title-pages for separate issue and Works issue. Priority is not ascertainable.

Copy MH.

A31

TALES OF THE HALL

FIRST EDITION   1819

TALES OF THE HALL. | rule 27.5 | BY | THE REV. GEORGE CRABBE, LL.B. | rule 27 | *IN*

TWO VOLUMES. | VOL. I. (II.) | thick-thin rule 24.5 | LONDON: | JOHN MURRAY, ALBEMARLE-STREET. | rule 7 | 1819.

Collation Vol. I Demy 8° [a]⁸b⁴B–X⁸Y⁴ = 176 leaves.

Vol. II Demy 8° π⁴B–Z⁸AA². = 182 leaves.

Pagination Vol. I [i–v] vi [vii] viii–xx [xxi] xxii–xxiv [1–3] 4–19 [20–23] 24–33 [34–37] 38–57 [58–61] 62–83 [84–87] 88–107 [108–111] 112–128 [129–131] 132–169 [170–173] 174–215 [216–219] 220–236 [237–239] 240–273 [274–277] 278–326 [327–328] = 352 pages.

Vol. II [i–v] vi–viii [1–3] 4–47 [48–51] 52–88 [89–91] 92–111 [112–115] 116–136 [137–139] 140–185 [186–189] 190–214 [215–217] 218–234 [235–237] 238–271 [272–275] 276–294 [295–297] 298–326 [327–329] 330–353 [354–356] = 364 pages.

Contents [i] half-title TALES OF THE HALL. [ii] printer's imprint LONDON: | PRINTED BY THOMAS DAVISON, WHITEFRIARS. [iii] title-page [iv] blank [v]–vi Dedication [vii]–xx Preface [xxi]–xxiv Contents [1]–326 text as follows: BOOK I THE HALL, BOOK II THE BROTHERS, BOOK III BOYS AT SCHOOL, BOOK IV ADVENTURES OF RICHARD, BOOK V RUTH, BOOK VI ADVENTURES OF RICHARD CONCLUDED, BOOK VII THE ELDER BROTHER, BOOK VIII THE SISTERS, BOOK IX THE PRECEPTOR HUSBAND, BOOK X THE OLD BACHELOR, BOOK XI THE MAID'S STORY either [327–8] blank, or [327] blank [328] printer's imprint as p. [ii] above.

[i] half-title TALES OF THE HALL. [ii] printer's imprint as Vol. I [iii] title-page [iv] blank [v]–viii Contents [1]–353 text as follows: BOOK XII SIR OWEN DALE, BOOK XIII DELAY HAS DANGER, BOOK XIV THE NATURAL DEATH OF LOVE, BOOK XV GRETNA GREEN, BOOK XVI LADY BARBARA; OR, THE GHOST, BOOK XVII THE WIDOW, BOOK XVIII ELLEN, BOOK XIX WILLIAM BAILEY, BOOK XX THE CATHEDRAL-WALK, BOOK XXI SMUGGLERS AND POACHERS, BOOK XXII THE VISIT CONCLUDED [354] printer's imprint as Vol. 1 [355–6] advertisements.

Direction line signatures $ 1 and 2 signed on right of direction line except Vol. I b2 and Y2 and Vol. II AA2. On the left of the direction line is VOL. I. (II.).

Headline Books I–VII have TALES OF THE HALL. in the centre of each page, the number at outer margin, and the book number at the gutter margin; books VIII to XXII have the title of the book on recto pages and TALES OF THE HALL. on verso pages, otherwise the same.

Notes on Printing There appear to be three easily perceptible variant states of the sheets of the first volume. (1) In many copies P6 is a cancel-leaf; this is always associated with (2) the appearance in the headline on P8ʳ of THE OLD BACHELOR. when it should read THE PRECEPTOR HUSBAND. and (3) the printer's imprint on

$Y3^v$, where other copies have it on $Y4^v$. Three of the four possible variations of the copies with P6 integral have so far appeared, see register of copies for details. It seems very likely, since the cancel leaf is always found with THE OLD BACHELOR and the imprint on $Y3$, that these sets of sheets were already sewn, and they represent the earlier states of their respective leaves.[8] THE OLD BACHELOR and the imprint on $Y3$ exist in very nearly identical numbers and it may be that they were altered to THE PRECEPTOR HUSBAND and $Y4$ at the same time.

Nine copies of this edition were machine collated in order to discover whether there were other differences not readily observable by visual comparison. The results are tabulated below. Copies A = Bod; B = LoU; C = B(1); D = B(2); E = OEF(1); F = OEF(2); G = CUL; H = CK; I = BL. Unfortunately these comparisons had to be carried out in three different libraries, so it was not possible to obtain comparisons between every volume.

The most surprising result is the appearance of three versions of P6, rather than the two that might be expected: these are C and H, the only two integral copies examined; A and F which have a cancel leaf, and B, D, E, G and I, which differ in several respects from A and F. If A, B and C are taken as representative of the three groups, the following basic differences were noted:

$P6^r$

A cf. B: the gap between second and third sections is a different width.

A cf. C: Lines 1, 3 and 11 show horizontal motion, but the gap between the second and third section remains constant.

B cf. C: Lines 1 and 3 (possibly also 2) move horizontally; the gap mentioned above is radically different.

$P6^v$

A cf. B: Lines 10, 18, 19 and 20 show horizontal motion.

A cf. C: Lines 1, 10, 19 and 20 show horizontal motion but in a different configuration from A cf. B.

B cf. C: Lines 2, 10, 18, 19 and 20 show horizontal motion in a similar fashion to A cf. B.

With small differences attributable to the state of the paper in the various volumes the other copies behave similarly.

As far as the rest of sig. P is concerned, the situation was

A cf. B: movement noted on $P1^r$ and $P4^r$.

A cf. C: no movement, though the headline on $P8^r$ is different as noted above.

B cf. C: movement noted on $P4^r$ (and in the case of G $P1^r$ also).

Two other signatures displayed a significant amount of movement: the outer forme of sig. R and both formes of sig. H.

The implications of this pattern of variation are not apparent; particularly obscure is the explanation for two apparent variations in the cancel-leaf. The types appear to be identical in all three varieties of configuration, so the most acceptable conclusion seems to be progressive type-batter leading to distortion.

The entry for *Tales of the Hall* in Murray's ledgers combines the first and second editions; there are discrepancies in the figures which probably made this necessary for accounting purposes. The average cost of printing a copy over the two editions was $2s. 4\frac{1}{2}d.$; calculated at this rate the figures would suggest that 2855 copies of the first edition and 1645 of the second were printed. The average number of copies per ream over the two editions was 11.1; calculated at this rate the figures suggest that 2785 copies of the first edition and 1715 copies of the second edition were printed. These figures are not exact, of course, because it must be presumed that more than 4500 copies overall were printed; but there is scarcely room here for a concealed impression which the three varieties of P6 noted above might indicate. It may well be that, since the second edition was set partially from standing type, the work at Davison's shop on the two volume *Tales of the Hall* was more or less continuous, the decision to print a second edition being taken before the first edition was completed. In support of this it will be remembered that the original order of 250 reams of demy paper seems to imply an original intention to print a smaller number of copies than 3000, though it is possible that the number of sheets the volumes required was underestimated originally by the printer; either way it seems clear that the deficiency was only made up when paper for the second edition was ordered. The new impression of Vol. I sig. P would require at most 6 reams, and so is not a crucial factor here.

Type-page variations Vol. I D8^v p48 139.5–141 by 82.5–84
P1^v p210 128–130 by 83–84
Vol. II H4^v p104 140–141 by 83.5–85
P7^v p222 127–128 by 83–84.5

Paper white wove, no watermark or countermark.

Binding B(1) is bound in the familiar blue boards with grey spine; the label reads TALES | OF | THE HALL. | BY THE | REV. G. CRABBE. | rule 5 | TWO VOLUMES. | 24s. | rule 4.5 | VOL. I. (II.).
B(2), which is a copy presented by Crabbe to Wm. Crowfoot Esqr, is bound in rather thicker brownish-grey boards throughout. The label reads the same as B(1). MH(2) is bound in rose-pink boards; TxU(3) has brown covers, pink spine.

Murray, unlike Hatchard, was not a retail bookseller, and so it is possible that there was no specific binding for these volumes, or for any other subsequent to this date: it is not known in what state the volumes were sold to the trade.

Notes on Composition and Publication Crabbe was working on a new volume as early as 1814, for just prior to publication he spoke of 'four years labour, and of late almost incessant' (Huchon p. 405) and in December 1818 he had his corrections and additions ready for 'Our first sheet' as he wrote to Murray (idem). Indeed some kind of arrangement with a publisher may have existed as early as 1815 for he wrote that year to Miss Charter

> 'By the way can you give me any short stories especially of
> Ghosts and Apparitions .... for here I have pledged myself
> Idiot as I am) to compose another Book.'
> (Broadley and Jerrold p. 131)

The development of the work can be traced through Crabbe's correspondence, particularly that with Mary Leadbeater.

By October 1817 he reported that the setting for his new work – to be called 'Remembrances', was to be a village but . . . 'my people are of a superior class. . . . I have a considerable number of Tales. . . . I hope to copy my now scattered papers within about three months. . . . I do not know . . . whether my tragic or lighter tales . . . are most in number....' (Leadbeater Papers p. 350). A full year later he reported to the same correspondent:

> 'My verses are not yet entirely ready, but do not want
> much that I can give them. Sometime in the passing
> year I believe some publisher will advertise them.'
> (ibid pp. 347–348)

He had clearly made up his mind at this stage to try publishers other than Hatchard who had hitherto handled all his work since 1807.

Early in December 1818 Murray offered £3,000 for the copyright of the new volume together with all Crabbe's previous works. Samuel Rogers nearly upset this arrangement by trying to get Longmans to offer more, but £1,000 was the most they would go to, and there were anxious moments lest Murray had heard of this. He stuck to his bargain, however, and £3,000 was paid to Crabbe as agreed.

The book was published on July 3rd 1819 possibly in an edition of 3,000. In his diary Tom Moore, the poet and friend of Crabbe and Murray, wrote 'Even if the whole of the edition were sold, Murray would still be £1,900 minus.' The Table in appendix II indicates the book loss on this edition (if the figures are accurate), when sales are set against the £3,035 paid for the copyright and stamp, was £1,825.

Copies (examined) Integral | Preceptor Husband | Y3: QUB(2) Integral | Preceptor Husband | Y4: B(2) BmU CK P(1) QUB(1); IU(2) TxU (1, 2)

Cancel | Old Bachelor | Y3: B(1) BL Bod CP CUL OEF(1) OEF(2) P(2); IU(1) TxU(3)

Copies (reported on) Integral | Preceptor Husband | Y4 KeU(1); UWO
Integral | Old Bachelor | Y3: LoL UEA(1); McGU McMU ToU
Cancel | Old Bachelor | Y3: BrU LcU LoU KeU(2) KeU(3) NLW OO ReU
ShU StU SuU UCL UEA(2) YoU; AdU(2 copies).

There are 26 copies with P6 cancel, 16 with P6 integral
32 copies with imprint on Y3^r, 10 with imprint on Y4^r
31 copies with THE OLD BACHELOR on P8^r
11 with THE PRECEPTOR HUSBAND.

A32

TALES OF THE HALL

SECOND EDITION (PARTLY RESET) 1819

TALES OF THE HALL. | BY | THE REV. GEORGE CRABBE, LL.B. | rule 27.5 | *IN TWO VOLUMES.* | VOL. I. (II.) | diamond rule 10 | A NEW EDITION. | thick-thin rule 25 | LONDON: | JOHN MURRAY, ALBEMARLE-STREET. | rule 7 | 1819.

Collation As No. 31.

Pagination As No. 31.

Contents As No. 31 with printer's imprint on Y4^v p. 328 of Vol. I.

Direction line signatures as No. 31.

Headline as No. 31 except that books I–VII have the title of the Book on the recto of each leaf, as in the other Books.

Type-page variations Vol. I D8^r p48 141–142 by 84–85.5
P1^v p210 129–129.5 by 82–84.5
Vol. II H4^r p104 139.5–140 by 82–83.5
P7^r p222 127.5–129 by 82.5–84

Paper As No. 31.

Binding Probably similar to No. 31.

Notes Machine collation shows that most of the text was reset for this edition. The same types were used for Vol. I sig. [a] b and Y. Vol. II is more difficult; the type used for the first edition was very little battered, so distinguishing characteristics are not often apparent. The only signatures that seem clearly the same are C, P, R, S, T, X and Y; the inner formes of B, O and Q also seem identical. F, L and M are clearly reset. The other signatures present more or less evidence of batter and distortion, but their relation to the first edition is not clear. Only three copies of this edition were available for machine collation, and it may be, in the light of the Murray Ledgers, (see p. 46 and pp. 95–98) that some volumes which have first-edition title-pages may have second-edition types, or else that this second edition in fact consists of rather more than 1,500 copies.

Notes on Composition and Publication Apparently 1,500 copies of this New Edition were printed, but the entry in Murray's Copies Ledger B includes both first and second editions, as well as the copies bought from Hatchard. Both editions were sold by Murray at 14/- and by June 1822 only 330 were left on hand; in July 1822 these were sold for 2/- each. Excluding the Hatchard books (on which Murray made a modest profit of £38 13s. 6d.) the profit for these two editions was £1,579 1s. 5d.; but of course this had to be set against the £3,000 Murray paid for the copyright of Crabbe's work. For further details see Appendix II. The retail price of both editions was £1 4s.

Copies B Bod CK CUL P StAU.

A33

TALES OF THE HALL

THIRD EDITION   1820

TALES OF THE HALL. | BY THE | REV. GEORGE CRABBE, LL.B. | rule 17.5 | *IN THREE VOLUMES* | VOL. I. (II.) (III.) | rule 17.5 | A NEW EDITION. | thick-thin rule 22 | LONDON: | JOHN MURRAY, ALBEMARLE-STREET. | 1820.

Collation foolscap 8º:
> *Vol. I* [a]⁸b⁴B–N⁸O⁶ = 114 leaves
> *Vol. II* [A]⁴B–O⁸P⁴Q² = 114 leaves
> *Vol. III* [A]⁴B–P⁸Q⁴R² = 122 leaves.

Pagination Vol. I [i–v] vi [vii] viii–xix [xx–xxi] xxii–xxiii [xxiv] [1–3] 4–18 [19–21] 22–30 [31–33] 34–52 [53–55] 56–76 [77–79] 80–99 [100–103] 104–120 [121–123] 124–159 [160–163] 164–203 [204] = 228 pages

Vol. II [i–v] vi–vii [viii] [1–3] 4–20 [21–23] 24–57 [58–61] 62–109 [110–113] 114–155 [156–159] 160–195 [196–199] 200–218 [219–220] = 228 pages.

Vol. III [i–v] vi–vii [viii] [1–3] 4–23 [24–27] 28–70 [71–73] 74–97

[98–101] 102–117 [118–121] 122–154 [155–157] 158–176 [177–179] 180–207 [208–211] 212–234 [235–236] = 244 pages.

Contents Vol. I [i] half-title TALES OF THE HALL. [ii] printer's imprint LONDON: | PRINTED BY T. DAVISON, WHITEFRIARS. [iii] title-page [iv] blank [v]–vi Dedication [vii]–xix Preface [xx] blank [xxi]–xxiii Contents [xxiv] blank [1]–203 text, Books I–VIII as No. 31 [204] printer's imprint LONDON: | PRINTED BY THOMAS DAVISON, WHITEFRIARS.

Vol. II [i] half title as Vol. I [ii] printer's imprint as Vol. I p[204] [iii] title-page [iv] blank [v]–vii Contents [viii] blank [1]–218 text, Books IX–XIV as No. 31 [219] blank [220] printer's imprint as Vol. I p[204].

Vol. III [i] half title as Vol. I [ii] printer's imprint as Vol. I p[ii] [iii] title-page [iv] blank [v]–vii Contents [viii] blank [1]–234 text, Books XV–XXII as No. 31 [235] blank [236] printer's imprint as Vol. I p[204].

Direction line signatures $ 1 and 2 signed on outer margin of direction line except Vol. I b2 Vol. II P2, Q2 and Vol. III Q2 and R2. At gutter margin of $ 1 there is VOL. I. (II.) (III.).

Headline as No. 31.

Note on Printing The sheets of this edition were also used in the seven volume collected poems of 1820 and the eight volume collected poems of 1823. From one copy of the latter, it is clear that Vol. III sig. Q was printed as Q^8, and Q2, 3, 6 and 7 used to carry the prelims for the volume; (DuU, where the whole of Q is bound in.) Probably Vol. II sig. P was printed in the same way. From a Hinman collation it also appears that there were at least two settings of Vol. II sig. Q and Vol. III sig. R; in the copies of these sheets examined only two varieties of each have been found. There is not enough information to suggest how they might have been printed, however, though it is possible that the two settings of each signature were all set together on one 8° gathering.

Paper white wove.

Binding Blue-grey boards; label reads rule | TALES | OF | THE HALL. | BY THE | REV. G. CRABBE. | rule | *Three Vols.* | VOL. I. (II.) (III.) | rule | 18s. | rule.

Notes on Composition and Publication 3,000 copies of this edition were printed, and by June 1822 1,394 had been sold, on the common basis of 25 as 24, at the price of 10/- the three volumes; the entry in Murray's ledgers then shows that between 1822 and 1829 of the remaining 1,606, 502 were sold as Coffee-House sales at the same rate, presumably to form part of the 8 volume works of 1823.

Finally, in 1829 or 1830 the last 1104 were sold to Thomas Tegg the publisher and bookseller at 25 as 24 for 3/–. The proportion of this edition that was bound as part of the seven volume Works can not be established from the Ledgers. The retail price of these volumes was 18/–. For further details see Appendix II.

Copies B Bod.

A34

LINES

1822

Only two copies of this have been seen and they may be defective. They have no title-page.

Collation Possibly pot 2° π².

Contents [1]–3 text [4] blank.

Printer's Imprint p3 PRINTED BY JAMES BALLANTYNE AND COMPANY, | FOR WILLIAM BLACKWOOD.

Type page p2 141 by 92.

Paper white, marked C WILMOT | 1822, leaf size 227 by 187 cut down.

Copies CUL NLS.

A35

WORKS

IN FOUR VOLUMES

1816

VOL. I POEMS

THE | WORKS | OF THE REVEREND | GEORGE CRABBE, LL.B. | rule 13.5 | *IN FOUR VOLUMES*. | thin-thick rule 13.5 | VOL I. | POEMS. | rule 22 | *LONDON*: | PRINTED FOR J. HATCHARD, | BOOKSELLER TO THE QUEEN, OPPOSITE ALBANY, PICCADILLY. | rule 10 | 1816.

Collation Royal 18° in sixes a–c⁶B–Y⁶ = 144 leaves.

Pagination [i–iii] iv–vi [vii–xi] xii–xiii [xiv–xv] xvi–xxxiv [xxxv–xxxvi] [1–2]

3–16 [17–18] 19–26 [27–30] 31–63 [64–66] 67–89 [90–92] 93–121 [132–134] 135–161 [162–164] 165–184 [185–186] 187 [188] 189–200 [201–202] 203–206 [207–208] 209–227 [228–230] 231–235 [236–237] 238–244 [245–246] 247–249 [250–252] = 288 pages.

Contents [i] title-page [ii] printer's imprint rule 36.5 | Printed by J. Brettell, | Rupert Street, Haymarket, London. [iii]–[vii] Dedication [viii] blank [ix] Advertisement to the second edition [x] blank [xi]–xiii Advertisement to the reader [xiv] blank [xv]–xxxiv Preface xxxv Contents [xxxvi] blank [1]–249 text as No. 7 [250] blank [251–252] advertisements.

Printer's Imprint p.[ii] above and p. 249 rule 37 | Printed by J. Brettell, | Rupert Street, Haymarket, London.

Direction line signatures $ 1 and $ 3 signed in centre of direction line, with the exception of the title-page.

Headline numerals at outer margin, running title of poem and (where appropriate) Book or Part number in centre.

Paper off-white, poor quality; no mark.

Binding Drab brownish grey boards as usual. Labels read thick-thin rule | CRABBE'S | WORKS. | rule | IN FOUR VOLUMES | rule | VOL. I. (II.) etc | 𝔓𝔬𝔢𝔪𝔰. | [Price, erased in the only copy I have seen, as it was a presentation set from the author] | thin-thick rule.

Notes The Bodleian copy of this edition has double title-pages in all volumes; the integral title-page as above, and the cancel title-page for the eighth edition of *Poems*, and the sixth edition of *The Borough*. It also has H W Pickersgill's portrait of Crabbe as π1ᵛ, engraved by Robert Newton, which has beneath it the letterpress THE REV. GEO. CRABBE L.L.B. | LONDON: | PUBLISHED 1ˢᵗ MAY 1816 BY JOHN HATCHARD, | PICCADILLY.

VOL. II THE BOROUGH

THE | WORKS | OF THE REVEREND | GEORGE CRABBE, LL.B. | rule 14 | *IN FOUR VOLUMES.* | thin-thick rule 14 | VOL. II. | BOROUGH | rule 22 | *LONDON:* | PRINTED FOR J. HATCHARD, | BOOKSELLER TO THE QUEEN, OPPOSITE ALBANY, PICCADILLY. | rule 10 | 1816.

Collation Royal 18° in sixes A⁶b⁶c⁴B–BB⁶CC² = 162 leaves.

Pagination [i–iii] iv–vi [vii] viii–xxviii [xxix] xxx–xxxi [xxxii] [1–2] 3–12 [13–14] 15–23 [24–26] 27–36 [37–38] 39–54 [55–56] 57–62 [63–64] 65–75 [76–78]

79–87 [88–90] 91–97 [98–100] 101–110 [111–112] 113–124 [125–126] 127–135 [136–138] 139–149 [150–152] 153–162 [163–164] 165–170 [171–172] 173–178 [179–180] 181–187 [188–190] 191–198 [199–200] 201–212 [213–214] 215–223 [224–226] 227–237 [238–240] 241–250 [251–252] 253–263 [264–266] 267–276 [277–278] 279–292 = 324 pages.

Contents [i] title-page [ii] printer's imprint rule 37 | Printed by J. Bretell, Rupert Street, | Haymarket, London. [iii]–vi Dedication [vii]–xxviii Preface [xxix]–xxxi Advertisement [xxxii] Contents [1]–292 text as No. 15.

Printer's Imprint p.[ii] above and p. 292 rule 36 | Printed by J. Bretell, | Rupert Street, Haymarket, London.

Direction line signatures $ 1 and $ 3 signed in centre of direction line except A1 and c3.

Headline page numbers at outer margin, running title of each letter title in centre, arabic letter numbers at gutter margin.

Paper As Vol. I.

Binding As Vol. I.

VOLS. III and IV TALES

THE | WORKS | OF THE REVEREND | GEORGE CRABBE, LL.B. | rule 14 | *IN FOUR VOLUMES.* | thin-thick rule 14 | VOL. III. (IV.) | TALES. | rule 22.5 (22) | LONDON: | PRINTED FOR J. HATCHARD, | BOOKSELLER TO THE QUEEN, OPPOSITE ALBANY, PICCADILLY. | rule 10 | 1816.

Collation Vol. III foolscap $8°$ π^1[a]^4(— [a]1 and 2) b^{8}B–O^8 = 115
Vol. IV foolscap $8°$ π^1B–P^{8}Q^6 = 119.

Pagination Vol. III [leaf not reckoned in pagination] [v–ix] otherwise as No. 23
Vol. II [i–ii] [1–3] otherwise as No. 23.

Contents Vol. III $\pi 1^r$ title-page $\pi 1^v$ printer's imprint rule 37 | Printed by J. Brettell, | Rupert Street, Haymarket, London. [v–viii] Dedication rest as No. 27
Vol. IV [i] title-page [ii] printer's imprint rule 37 | Printed by J. Brettell, | Rupert Street, Haymarket, London. [1] 𝕿𝕬𝕷𝕰𝕾. rest as No. 27.

Notes These are the sheets of the 'sixth' edition issued for a third time with a cancel title-page as Vols. III and IV of the 1816 Works. They have the characteristic error in the dedication: DUTCHESS.

Copies B Bod St AU.

A36

Poems

EIGHTH EDITION   1816

POEMS: | BY | The Rev. GEORGE CRABBE, LL.B. | rule 14 | Ipse (etc. as No. 7)
Lucan. | rule 14 | *EIGHTH EDITION.* | rule 14 | 𝕷𝖔𝖓𝖉𝖔𝖓: | PRINTED FOR
J. HATCHARD, | BOOKSELLER TO THE QUEEN, 190, OPPOSITE ALBANY, | PICCADILLY.
| thick-thin rule 7 | 1816.

This is a separate issue of No. 35 Vol. I, with a cancel-title page, the verso of
which has no printer's imprint.

Copies LeU P(2) YoU.

A37

One copy seen of 36 has the following variations on the cancel title-page: for
LL.B. it has LL.D.; for all the 14 rules it has wavy 12.5 rules. It also has printer's
imprint rule 35.5 | Printed by J. Brettell, | Rupert Street, Haymarket, London.

Copy BL.

A38

Poems

NINTH EDITION   1817

This is apparently a sub-issue of No. 36, perhaps bearing the same relationship
to it as 14 does to 13. The only differences from No. 36 noticeable without
mechanical comparison are the alteration of EIGHTH EDITION. to NINTH EDITION.
and 1816. to 1817. on the title-page. The volume was bound too tightly to
suggest whether the title-page or the first gatherings are cancels.

Copy MH.

39

POEMS

('A NEW EDITION')   1820

POEMS: | BY THE | REV. GEORGE CRABBE, LL.B. | rule 10.5 | Ipse etc. (as No. 7)

Lucan. | rule 17.5 | *A NEW EDITION.* | rule 17 | LONDON: JOHN MURRAY, ALBEMARLE-STREET. | 1820.

This again is an issue (the fourth) of No. 35 Vol. I, with a cancel-bifolium. [i] half-title POEMS. [ii] Printer's imprint LONDON: PRINTED BY T. DAVISON, WHITEFRIARS. [iii] title-page [iv] blank. Murray also issued this printing as part of the seven volume works of 1820 (No. 43).

Copy B.

A40

THE BOROUGH

SIXTH EDITION 1816

THE BOROUGH: | A | 𝔓oem, | IN TWENTY-FOUR LETTERS. | BY | The Rev. GEORGE CRABBE, LL.B. | rule 14 | PAULO MAJORA CANAMUS. – VIRGIL. | rule 14 | *SIXTH EDITION.* | rule 14 | 𝔏ondon: | PRINTED FOR J. HATCHARD, | BOOKSELLER TO THE QUEEN, 190, OPPOSITE ALBANY, | PICCADILLY. | thick-thin rule 7 | 1816.

No printer's imprint on [ii], otherwise it is a second issue of the sheets of No. 35 Vol. II.

Copy Bod.

A41

One copy seen has the following variations in the title-page: LL.D. for LL.B.; 12.5 wavy rules for first two 14 rules, omitting the third altogether. On [ii] there is the following printer's imprint: rule 33 | Printed by J. Brettell, | Rupert Street, Haymarket, London.

Copy BL.

A42

THE BOROUGH: | *A POEM,* | IN | TWENTY-FOUR LETTERS. | BY THE | REV. GEORGE CRABBE, LL.B. | rule 17.5 | PAULO MAJORA CANAMUS. – VIRGIL | rule 17.5 | *A NEW EDITION.* | thick-thin rule 22 | LONDON: | JOHN MURRAY, ALBEMARLE-STREET. | 1820.

A further issue (**the third**) of the sheets of 35 Vol. II with a cancel-bifolium

[i] half-title THE BOROUGH. [ii] Printer's imprint LONDON: | PRINTED BY T. DAVISON, WHITEFRIARS. [iii] title-page [iv] blank. Murray also issued this impression as part of the seven volume works of 1820 (No. 43).

Copy B.

TABULATION OF THE COLLECTED EDITIONS 1816-1823

1816	1820(a)		1820(b)	1823
POEMS	←		←	
BOROUGH	←		←	
[TALES I '6th edn'	←			
TALES II ,,]	←			
	[TALES OF THE HALL I 3rd edn	←	←	
	TALES OF THE HALL II ,,	←	←	
	TALES OF THE HALL III ,,]	←	←	
			TALES I	
			TALES II	
				POEMS
				BOROUGH I
				BOROUGH II
				TALES I
				TALES II

A43

WORKS

IN SEVEN VOLUMES 1820

THE | WORKS | OF THE | REV. GEORGE CRABBE, LL.B. | rule 17.5 | *IN SEVEN VOLUMES.* | rule 17.5 | VOL. I. POEMS. (etc.) | thick-thin rule 22 | LONDON: | JOHN MURRAY, ALBEMARLE-STREET. | 1820.

To begin with this collection consisted of Hatchard's four volume works of 1816 (No. 35) and Murray's third edition of *Tales of the Hall*. These were issued with cancel-bifolia:

[i] half-title THE | WORKS | OF THE | REV. GEORGE CRABBE, LL.B. [ii] Printer's imprint LONDON: PRINTED BY THOMAS DAVISON, WHITEFRIARS [iii] title-page [iv] blank. It seems probable from machine collation that there were two separate settings of these bifolia.

Only half as many copies of Hatchard's 'sixth' edition of *Tales* as of the specially printed *Poems* and *The Borough* was sold to Murray when Crabbe transferred his work, and so Murray printed a new edition of *Tales* (for details see No. 30) to fill the gap. Only a very small number of this collection have been available for examination so the relative frequency of Hatchard and Murray *Tales* cannot be established.

The separate issues by Murray of each work are also found in a contemporary board binding with no other indication that they form part of a collection other than a paste-on label on the spine reading CRABBE'S | WORKS. | rule | SEVEN VOLS. | £2. 5s. | rule | VOL. (I.) (etc.). | *POEMS.* (etc.) The collection was also advertised at £2. 2s. though no copy so priced has been seen. In some cases both 'new edition' and 'works' title-pages are bound in to each volume.

Copies AbU B Bod OEF; FLU.

A44

WORKS

FIVE VOLUMES   1823

VOL. I POEMS

THE | WORKS | OF | THE REV. GEORGE CRABBE. | IN FIVE VOLUMES. | VOL. I. [etc] | LONDON: | JOHN MURRAY, ALBEMARLE-STREET. | 1823.

Collation Demy 8° [a]–b⁸ B–T⁸ = 160 leaves.

Pagination [i–ix] x–xii [xiii] xiv–xxxi [xxxii] [1–3] 4–17 [18–21] 22–30 [31] 32 [33–37] 38–73 [74–77] 78–102 [103–105] 106–147 [148–151] 152–181 [182–185] 186–206 [207–211] 212–227 [228–231] 232–236 [237–239] 240–260 [261–265] 266–271 [272–273] 274–280 [281–283] 284–286 [287–288] = 320 pages.

Contents [i] half-title WORKS | OF | THE REV. GEORGE CRABBE. [ii] printer's imprint LONDON: | PRINTED BY THOMAS DAVISON, WHITEFRIARS. [iii] title-page [iv] blank [v] Contents [vi] blank [vii] half-title POEMS. | rule 21 | Ipse per Ausonias . . . Mæoniumque . . . *Lucan.* [Otherwise as No. 8] [viii] blank [ix]–xii Dedication [xiii]–xxxi Preface [xxxii] blank [1]–286 text as of Poems No. 7 [287–288] blank.

Direction line signatures $ 1 and $ 2 signed on outer edge of direction line, with the exception of [a]; at gutter margin VOL. I.

Headline page numbers at outer margin, PART, BOOK numbers at gutter margin, running-title central.

Note on printing This edition has many of the footnotes as notes at the end of each poem.

Type page 133/4 by 83.5 approximately (prose 135 by 80).

Paper has wire lines, but no chain lines, no watermark, thus probably machine made. A superior quality to anything so far: at over £2 per ream it was the most expensive used by Murray for Crabbe's books.

Binding The usual grey-brown paper covered boards Labels WORKS | OF THE | REV. G. CRABBE | rule 7 | FIVE VOLS. | £2. 12s. 6d. | rule 7 | VOL. I. (etc) | POEMS. [etc]

Illustrations The 31 illustrations sometimes present were drawn by R. Westall R.A., and engraved by Charles Heath. All the engravings were published by John Murray in January 1822; they were sold separately on three different sizes of paper, quarto at four guineas, octavo at three pounds, and foolscap octavo at two guineas. Westall was paid ten guineas for each of the thirty-one drawings, Heath £42 for each engraving, and £51 was spent on advertising the plates.

The Village Book II Near her the swain, about to bear for life | One certain evil, doubts 'twixt war and wife; | But, while the falt'ring damsel takes her oath, | Consents to wed, and so secures them both. Normally placed as frontispiece tipped to [a]2^r.

The Parish Register Baptisms, 'Then sits and gazes, but with viewless look, | As gilds the moon the rimpling of the brook. Normally tipped to D3^r; note that in the text in this edition 'rimpling' is altered to 'rippling'.

The Hall of Justice "Oh! by the GOD who loves to spare | Deny me not the boon I crave; | Let this lov'd child your mercy share, | And let me find a peaceful grave'. Normally tipped to T1^r.

VOL. II THE BOROUGH

Title-page As Vol. I.

Collation Demy 8° [a]–b^{8}c^4 B–BB^{8}CC^6 = 218 leaves.

Pagination Two pages not reckoned in pagination [i–ix] x–xii [xiii] xiv–xxxviii [1–3] 4–15 [16–21] 22–31 [32–33] 34 [35–37] 38–50 [51–53] 54–73]74–75] 76 [77–79] 80–87 [88–93] 94–107 [108–111] 112–122 [123–125] 126–133 [134–135] 136 [137–139] 140–150 [151] 152 [153–155] 156–170 [171–172] 174–185 [186–189] 190–203 [204–207] 208–220 [221–223] 224–231 [232–235] 236–243 [244–247] 248–256 [257–259] 260–269 [270–273] 274–288 [289–293] 294–304 [305–307] 308–320 [321–325] 326–337 [338–339] 340 [341–343] 344–358 [359–361] 362–374 [375–377] 378–395 [396] = 436 pages.

Contents one leaf not reckoned in pagination, recto and verso blank. [i] half-title as Vol. I [ii] printer's imprint as Vol. I [iii] title-page [iv] blank [v] Contents

[vi] blank [vii] half title THE BOROUGH. | rule 21 | PAULO MAJORA CANAMUS. – *VIRGIL.* [viii] blank [ix]–xii Dedication [xiii]–xxxviii Preface [1]–395 text as No. 15 [396] printer's imprint as Vol. I.

Typography As Vol. I with the obvious changes. i.e. letter number, Vol. II in gutter margin. Also many letters have notes at the end of the letter instead of as footnotes.

Illustrations
Letter 2: "I go," he said; but as he spoke, she found | His hand more cold, and fluttering was the sound! | Then gazed affrighten'd; but she caught a last, | A dying look of love, – and all was past! Normally tipped to [a]2^r as frontispiece.

Letter 7: "I feel it not;" – 'Then take it every hour:' | "It makes me worse;" – 'Why then it shows its power.' Normally tipped to H8^r.

Letter 9: For lo! a lady sage, who pac'd the sand | With her fair children, one in either hand, | Intent on home, had turn'd, and saw the boat | Slipp'd from her moorings, and now far afloat. Normally tipped to K6^r.

Letter 10: "There, there's your money; but, while I have life, | "I'll never more sit down with man and wife." Normally tipped to L6^r.

Letter 16: "I go," he said, "but still my friends shall say, | "'Twas as a man – I did not sneak away; | "An honest life, with worthy souls I've spent, – | "Come, fill my glass;" – he took it and he went. Normally tipped to R4^r.

Letter 18: mends her meshes torn, and pours her lay | All in the stifling fervour of the day. Normally tipped to T1^r.

Letter 22: But new to danger on the angry sea, | He clung affrighten'd to his master's knee. Normally tipped to Z4^r.

Letter 24: Though deaf, she sees the rebel-heroes shout, – | Though lame, her white rod nimbly walks about; | With band of yarn she keeps offenders in, | And to her gown the sturdiest rogue can pin. Normally tipped to BB5^r.

VOL. III TALES

Title-page As Vol. I.

Collation Demy 8° [a]^8 b^4 B–FF^8 = 236 leaves.

Pagination [i–ix] x–xi [xii–xiii] xiv–xxiv [1–5] 6–23 [24–27] 28–45 [46–49] 50–69 [70–73] 74–86 [87–89] 90–117 [118–121] 122–140 [141–143] 144–159 [160–163] 164–177 [178–181] 182–194 [195–197] 198–211 [212–215] 216–233 [234–237]

238–251 [252–255] 256–275 [276–279] 280–298 [299–301] 302–317 [318–321]
322–344 [345–347] 348–366 [367–369] 370–380 [381–383] 384–401 [402–405]
406–421 [422–425] 426–446 [447–448] = 472 pages.

Contents [i] half-title as Vol. I [ii] printer's imprint as Vol. I [iii] title-page [iv]
blank [v] Contents [vi] blank [vii] half-title TALES. [viii] blank [ix]–xi Dedication
[xii] blank [xiii]–xxiv Preface [1] TALES. [2] blank [3]–446 text as first edition
(No. 22) [447] blank [448] printer's imprint as Vol. I.

Typography signatures as Vol. I but b2 not signed. TALE numbers in headline,
otherwise all typography as Vol. I (the prose is 137 by 80).

Illustrations

Tale 2: Beneath yon tree, observe an ancient pair – | A sleeping man; a woman
in her chair, | Watching his looks with kind and pensive air. Normally tipped to
[a]2ʳ as frontispiece.

Tale 4: To vary pleasures, from the lady's chest | Were drawn the pearly string
and tabby vest; | Beads, jewels, laces, all their value shown, | With the kind
notice – "They will be your own." Normally tipped to F5ʳ.

Tale 7: "For my small farm what can the damsel do?" | He said – then stopp'd
to take another view. Normally tipped to K8ʳ.

Tale 8: While quickly thus the mortal part declin'd, | The happiest visions fill'd
the active mind; | A soft, religious melancholy gain'd | Entire possession, and
for ever reign'd. Normally tipped to M2ʳ.

Tale 13: The mother smiling whisper'd – "Let him go | "And seek the licence!"
Jesse answer'd, "No:" | But Colin went. Normally tipped to R8ʳ.

Tale 15: "There are for all things time and place; appear | "Grave in your
pulpit, and be merry here: | "Now take your wine, for woes a sure resource, |
"And the best prelude to a long discourse." Normally tipped to U7ʳ.

Tale 17: "he fell | "Close at the door where he was wont to dwell; | "There his
sole friend, the ass, was standing by, | "Half dead himself, to see his master die."
Normally tipped to Z6ʳ.

Tale 20: "I'll shake you from the bed, | "You stubborn dog – Oh God! my
brother's dead!" Normally tipped to DD3ʳ.

VOL. IV and V TALES OF THE HALL

Title-page As Vol. I.

Collation Demy 8° *Vol. IV* [A]⁴ B–Y⁸Z⁴ = 176 leaves.

        Vol. V [A]⁴ B–Z⁸AA¹ = 181 leaves.

Pagination Vol. IV: [i–v] vi–viii [1–3] 4 [5] 6–15 [16–19] 20–35 [36–39] 40–49 [50–53] 54–73 [74–77] 78–99 [100–103] 104–123 [124–127] 128–144 [145–147] 148–185 [186–189] 190–231 [232–235] 236–252 [253–255] 256–289 [290–293] 294–342 [343–344] = 352 pages.

      Vol. V: [i–v] vi–viii [1–3] 4–47 [48–51] 52–88 [89–91] 92–111]112–115] 116–136 [137–139] 140–185 [186–189] 190–214 [215–217] 218–234 [235–237] 238–271 [272–275] 276–294 [295–297] 298–326 [327–329] 330–353 [354] = 362 pages.

Contents Vol. IV: [i] half-title as Vol. I [ii] Printer's imprint, as Vol. I [iii] title-page [iv] blank [v]–viii Contents [1] TALES OF THE HALL. [2] blank [3]–4 Dedication [5]–15 Preface [16] blank [17]–342 text as Vol. I first edition [343–344] blank or [343] blank [344] Printer's imprint as Vol. I.

Vol. V: [i] half-title as Vol. I [ii] printer's imprint as Vol I. [iii] title-page [iv] blank [v]–viii Contents [1]–353 text as Vol. II of first edition [354] printer's imprint as Vol. I.

Typography As Vol. I except TALES OF THE HALL is on the verso of each leaf and the tale title on the recto in centre of direction line. Vol. I Z2 not signed.

Illustrations Vol. IV.

Vol. IV Book 3 And while th'admiring people stood to gaze, | He, one by one, committed to the blaze, | Smiling in spleen; This is tipped to E3ʳ, though it comes before the following entry; It should perhaps be the frontispiece.

Book 3   "While the rough husband, yielding to the pay | "That buys his absence, growling stalks away." Tipped to [a]2ʳ as frontispiece; see previous entry.

Book 4   "With what strong interest looks she at the waves, | "Meeting and clashing o'er the seamen's graves: | "'Tis a poor girl betroth'd – a few hours more, | "And *he* will lie a corpse upon the shore." Normally tipped to F7ʳ.

Book 7   "The fair ones took me at my sign, and flew, | "Each like a dove, and to the stile withdrew." Normally tipped to L2ʳ.

Book 9   "And would the butler and the cook surprise, | "Who listen'd to his Latin exercise." Normally tipped to Q6ʳ.

Book 10   "My father's look was one I seldom saw, | "It gave no pleasure, nor created awe; | "It was the kind of cool contemptuous smile | "Of witty persons overcharged with bile." Normally tipped to R8ʳ.

Vol. V Book 12 "At the bed's feet the man reclined his frame: | "Their chairs were perished to support the flame | "That warm'd his agued limbs." Normally tipped to [a]2^r as frontispiece.

Book 13   "Think you, you walk'd unseen? There are who bring | "To me all secrets – O, you wicked thing! Normally tipped to E2^r.

Book 18   – there she oped her door, | Her heart, her purse, and comforted the poor, | The sick, the sad, – Normally tipped to P5^r.

Book 19   – He went, and he return'd, – | And in his look the pair his tale discern'd; | Stupid in grief, it seem'd not that he knew | How he came home, or what he should pursue. Normally tipped to Q7^r.

Book 20   "– It turn'd, and I beheld | An hideous form, that hope and zeal expell'd." Normally tipped to T2^r.

Book 21   "Who is there?" she cried, | "A dying wretch!" – was from the earth replied. | It was her lover – Normally tipped to U5^r.

Note This is a resetting of every text. Though dated 1823 Murray's ledger suggests that the 1,500 copies were ready by September 1822. Advertisements say that the retail price was £2 12 6; by March 1829 Murray had sold 778 sets at prices ranging from a guinea to two pounds, and the last 722 were then sold by Tegg for 10/– the set. It made a profit of just under £8! Of all Crabbe's books published by Murray [before 1834] it was the most expensive to print, at 1*s* 5*d* per volume. It has been suggested that Crabbe saw this edition through the press[9]. I have been able to discover no evidence for this, internal or external, though the internal evidence could only be of value if a complete collation of the texts were done, and this is the province of the editor rather than the bibliographer. In a sample collation no variants that might be called authorial have been found.

Copies B(3) P ReU.

A45

WORKS

EIGHT VOLUMES   1823

THE | WORKS | OF | THE REV. GEORGE CRABBE. | IN EIGHT VOLUMES. | VOL. I. (etc) | LONDON: | JOHN MURRAY, ALBEMARLE-STREET. | 1823.
VOL. I POEMS

Collation Foolscap 8° [a]–b^{8}B–R^{8}S^4 = 148 leaves.

Pagination [i–ix] x–xii [xiii] xiv–xxxii [1–3] 4–16 [17–19] 20–27]28–29] 30 [31–35] 36–68 [69–71] 72–94 [95–97] 98–135 [136–139] 140–166 [167–169] 170–188 [189–193] 194–207 [208–211] 212–215 [216–219] 220–238 [239–243] 244–248 [249–251] 252–258 [259–261] 262–264 = 296 pages.

Contents [i] half-title WORKS | OF | THE REV. GEORGE CRABBE. [ii] printer's imprint LONDON: | PRINTED BY THOMAS DAVISON, WHITEFRIARS. [iii] title-page [iv] blank [v] Contents [vi] blank [vii] half-title for Poems [viii] blank [ix]–vii Dedication [xiii]–xxxii Preface [1]–264 text as first edition of Poems. (N . 7).

Printer's Imprint p[ii] above and p264 LONDON: | PRINTED BY THOMAS DAVISON, WHITEFRIARS.

Direction line signed $ 1 and 2 except [a] and $ 2; VOL. I at gutter margin except [a].

Headline running title central; numerals at outer margin; where appropriate Book or Part number, roman, at gutter margin. Running title where appropriate, Part title recto, Poem title verso.

Notes the format is an inference from pinhole positions in observed copies; they are present roughly in the centre at the foot of $ 2 and 3. Further evidence is offered by the following pattern noted for the presence of ‡ in each gathering:

B2ᵛ	Ba Bb Bc D La Pa Pb CtY	B7ʳ	Le C
C2ᵛ	Ba Bb Bc C D La Le Pa Pb CtY		
D2ᵛ	Ba Bb Bc C D La Le Pa Pb CtY		
E2ᵛ	Ba Bb Bc C D La Le Pa Pb CtY		
F7ʳ	Ba Bb Bc C D La Le Pa Pb CtY		
G2ᵛ	Bb C D La Le Pa Pb CtY	None	Ba Bc
H8ᵛ	Ba Bb C Pb		Bc D La Le Pa CtY
I2ᵛ	Bb C Le Pa CtY		Ba Bc D La Pb
K2ᵛ	Bb D La Pb CtY		Ba Bc C Le Pa
L8ᵛ	Ba C La Pb		Bb Bc D Le Pa CtY
M8ᵛ	Ba Bb D La Le Pa CtY		Bc C Pb
N2ᵛ	Ba Bb C D Le Pa		Bc La Pb CtY
O2ᵛ	Ba Bb Bc C D CtY		La Le Pa Pb
P8ᵛ	Ba Bb Bc C D La Pa CtY		Le Pb
Q2ᵛ	Bb Bc C D CtY		Ba La Le Pa Pb
R8ᵛ	Bb Bc C D Pa Pb CtY		Ba La Le
S4ʳ	Bb Bc D La Pa Pb CtY		Ba C Le

This pattern may indicate that the volume (and Vols II and III) were printed by double octavo imposition, printing the same types of two gatherings twice, and the double dagger inserted for the second pull, for it appears from a Hinman collation that the copies with and without the symbol are identical. The alternative pattern in B is not so explicable.

Binding Probably the primary binding was in dark blue-grey paper-covered boards, with a label that reads CRABBE'S | WORKS. | WITH | 31 *Engravings* | rule | EIGHT VOLS. | rule | £4. 10s., with the volume number in arabic numberals blind-stamped beneath the label (though it is difficult to know whether this was a part of the trade binding). Copy B(3).

Two cloth bindings, one shiny olive-green cloth (DuU copy), the other similar plum cloth have also been noted, and if they are contemporary with the printing of this edition, then they must be reckoned early examples of the use of cloth. The second however, (Copy B(2)), may well be much later, for not only are the labels different, reading CRABBE'S | WORKS. | 8 VOLS. – 48s. | VOL. I. (etc) | POEMS. (etc), but bound in with volume I (sewn in), are advertisements for the publications of T Tegg dated 1831; presumably indicating that it is one of the copies remaindered in 1829 by Murray. This edition was also published without engravings, and this is the reason for the lower price; the difference is the cost of the engravings when bought separately. The engravings are actually present in this copy; they may have been purchased separately and added privately, though examination of this copy suggests that they were added before the volumes were sewed.

Illustrations The illustrations sometimes found are as the Five Volume edition of the same year.
The Village normally placed as a frontispiece tipped to [a]2^r.
The Parish Register normally tipped to D2^r.
The Hall of Justice normally tipped to R2^r.

VOL. II and VOL. III THE BOROUGH

Title-page As Vol. 1.

Collation Foolscap 8° *Vol. II* [a]–c^{8}B–M^{8}N^{4}O^2 = 117 leaves.
              Vol. III. [A]^{4}B–O^{8}P^2 = 109 leaves.

Pagination Vol. II [i–ix] x–xiii [xiv–xv] xvi–xlviii [1–3] 4–15 [16–21] 22–31 [32–33] 34 [35–37] 38–50 [51–53] 54–73 [74–75] 76 [77–79] 80–87 [88–93] 94–108 [109–111] 112–122 [123–125] 126–133 [134–135] 136 [137–139] 140–150 [151] 152 [153–155] 156–170 174–185 [186] = 234 pages.

Vol. III [i–viii] [1–3] 4–17 [18–21] 22–34 [35–37] 38–45 [46–49] 50–57 [58–61] 62–70 [71–73] 74–83 [84–87] 88–102 [103–107] 108–118 [119–121] 122–134

[135–139] 140–151 [152–153] 154 [155–157] 158–172 [173–175] 176–188 [189–191] 192–209 [210] = 218 pages.

Contents Vol. II [i] half-title as Vol. I [ii] printer's imprint at Vol. I [iii] title-page [iv] blank [v] Contents [vi] blank [vii] half-title for The Borough [viii] blank [ix]–xii Dedication [xiv] blank [xv]–xlviii Preface [1]–185 text of The Borough Letters 1–11 as first edition (No. 15) [186] printer's imprint as Vol. I.

    Vol. III [i–viii] as Vol. II [1]–209 text of The Borough Letters 12–24 as first edition (No. 15) [201] printer's imprint as Vol. I.

Typography and Paper As Vol. I except that the letter numbers in headline are arabic, and there is Vol. II. (III.) in direction line. The pattern of ‡ is also different.

Vol. II

a8^r	C Bc La Pb CtY	None	Ba Bb D Le Pa
B8^v	Ba Bb Bc D		C La Le Pa Pb CtY
c7^r	Ba Bb Bc D Le CtY		C La Pa Pb
B2^v	Bc C D		Ba Bb La Le Pa Pb CtY
C7^r	Ba Bc Le CtY		Bb C D La Pa Pb
D7^r	Ba C La Le Pb CtY		Bb Bc D Pa
E7^r	Ba Bb C Le Pa Pb CtY	None	Bc D La
F2^v	Ba Bb C Le		Bc D La Pa Pb CtY
G8^v	Bc D La Le Pa Pb CtY		Ba Bb C
H8^v	Bb C La Pa Pb		Ba Bc D Le CtY
I8^v	Bb Bc C D La Pb CtY		Ba Le Pa
K8^v	Ba Le Pa CtY		Bb Bc D C La Pb
L7^r	Bb Bc D La Le Pa CtY		Ba C Pb
M8^v	Ba C D La Le Pa Pb		Ba Bc CtY
N			all copies
O			all copies

Vol. III

B7^r	Ba La Pa Pb	Bb Bc D CtY
C8^v	Ba D Pa	Bc Bb La Pb CtY
D8^v	Bb La Pa Pb	Ba Bc D CtY
E2^v	La Pb CtY	Ba Bb Bc D Pa
F8^v	La Pb CtY	Ba Bb Bc D Pa
G8^v	Ba La Pa CtY	Bc Bb D Pb
H8^v	Ba Bc D La Pa	Bb Pb CtY
I8^v	Ba D La CtY	Bb Bc Pa Pb
K7^r	Ba Bb Bc D La	Pa Pb CtY

L8ᵛ Ba Bb Bc La	D Pa Pb CtY
M8ᵛ Ba La CtY	Bb Bc D Pa Pb
N8ᵛ Bb D La Pb	Ba Bc Pa CtY
O8ᵛ Ba Bb Pa	Bc D La Pb CtY

Illustrations Vol. II
Letter 2 normally tipped to [a]2ʳ as frontispiece.
Letter 7 normally tipped to H8ʳ.
Letter 9 normally tipped to K6ʳ.
Letter 10 normally tipped to L6ʳ.

Illustrations Vol. III
Letter 16 normally tipped to π2ʳ.
Letter 18 normally tipped to G4ʳ.
Letter 22 normally tipped to N8ʳ.

VOL. IV and V: TALES

Title-pages As Vol. I.

Collation Foolscap 8⁰ Vol. IV [a]–b⁸B–P⁸Q² = 130 leaves.
Vol. V [A]⁴B–R⁸S¹ = 133 leaves.

Pagination Vol. IV [i–ix] x–xi [xii–xiii] xiv–xxi [xxxii] [1–5] 6–25 [26–29] 30–48 [49–51] 52–73 [74–77] 78–92 [93–95] 96–126 [127–129] 130–150 [151–153] 154–171 [172–175] 176–190 [191–193] 194–207 [208–211] 212–226 [227–228] = 260 pages.
Vol. V [i–viii] [1–5] 6–25 [26–29] 30–44 [45–47] 48–69 [70–73] 74–94 [95–97] 98–115 [116–119] 120–145 [146–149] 150–170 [171–173] 174–186 [187–189] 190–208 [209–211] 212–229 [230–233] 234–257 [258] = 266 pages.

Contents Vol. IV [i] half-title as Vol. I [ii] printer's imprint as Vol. I [iii] title-page [iv] blank [v] Contents [vi] blank [vii] half-title for Tales [viii] blank [ix]–xi Dedication [xii] blank [xiii]–xxxi Preface [xxxii] blank [1] second half-title for Tales [2] blank [3]–226 text of Tales 1–10 as first edition (No. 22) [227] Note [228] Printer's imprint as Vol. I.
Vol. V [i–viii] as Vol. I [1] second half-title for Tales [2] blank [3]–257 text of Tales 11–21 as first edition (No. 22) [258] printer's imprint as Vol. I.

Typography and Paper As Vol. I except tale numbers in headline are arabic, and VOL. IV. (V.) in direction line. Also the pattern of daggers is different (not noted).

Illustrations Vol. III
Tale 2 normally tipped to [a]2ʳ as frontispiece.

Tale 4 normally tipped to F7^r.
Tale 7 normally tipped to L5^r.
Tale 8 normally tipped to M8^r.

Illustrations Vol. V
Tale 13 normally tipped to [A]2^r as frontispiece.
Tale 15 normally tipped to H1^r.
Tale 17 normally tipped to L3^r.
Tale 20 normally tipped to P2^r.

VOLUMES VI, VII and VIII: TALES OF THE HALL

Title-pages As Volume I.

    These are sheets of the third edition of *Tales of the Hall* No. 33, with new preliminary gatherings; Vol. VI has VOL. VI. at the gutter margin of b1^r, but VOL. I. in every subsequent gathering, while Vols. VII and VIII have VOL. II. and VOL. III. They are in every other way identical to the third edition of *Tales of the Hall*. For further confirmation of this *see* Appendix.

There are no daggers in the direction line.

The differences from No. 33 are as follows:

Vol. VI
Contents [i] half-title as Vol. I [ii] printer's imprint as Vol. I [iii] title-page as Vol. I [iv] blank [v]–vii Contents [viii] blank [ix] second half-title [x] blank [xi–xii] Dedication [xiii]–xxiii Preface [xxiv] blank; otherwise as No. 33.

Vol. VII
Contents [i–iv/ as Vol. I [v]–vii Contents [viii] blank otherwise as No. 33.

Vol. VIII as Vol. VII.

Illustrations Vol. VI
Book 3 Tipped to [a]2^r as frontispiece; though textually it comes after the second illustration (as in the Five Volume Works).
Book 3 This is tipped to D1^r.
Book 4 normally tipped to E4^r.
Book 7 normally tipped to K6^r.

Illustrations Vol. VII
Book 9 normally tipped to [A]2^r as frontispiece.
Book 10 normally tipped to C4^r.
Book 12 normally tipped to I1^r.
Book 13 normally tipped to I8^r.

Illustrations Vol. VIII
Book 18 normally tipped to [A]2^r as frontispiece.
Book 19 normally tipped to I5^r.
Book 20 normally tipped to L7^r.
Book 21 normally tipped to N2^r.

Note The first five volumes of this collection were printed in a run of 1500 each volume apparently by January 1823; by March 1829 677 sets had been sold, 573 as Coffee House Sales, 25 as 24 at 15/–, and 104 in other ways at 19/2. The remainder was then sold by Tegg for 10/– a set. The *Tales of the Hall* volumes were reckoned separately in Murray's ledgers, under the third edition heading; between June 30 1822 and 1829 (March?) 502 copies were sold in Coffee House sales, and the rest (1104) were then remaindered to Tegg. The discrepancy of 175 between the five volumes and *Tales of the Hall* may be accounted for by booksellers making up sets with already purchased copies of the latter – on the other hand it may indicate that the five vols were sold to the public as a separate issue. Such a set has not been found. See Appendix for further details.

Copies B(3) DuU LaU LeU P(2) UWC; Cty.

A46

POETICAL WORKS

THE FIRST ONE VOLUME COLLECTED WORKS 1829

THE | POETICAL WORKS | OF | GEORGE CRABBE | COMPLETE IN ONE VOLUME. | VIGNETTE DESIGN | PARIS | PUBLISHED BY A. AND W. GALIGNANI, | N° 18, RUE VIVIENNE. | rule 11.5 | 1829.

Collation $\pi^2 2\pi^1$ a^2 1–40^4 = 165 leaves.

Pagination 6 pages not reckoned in pagination [i] ii–iii [iv] [1] 2–319 [320] = 330 pages.

Contents π1^r half-title THE | POETICAL WORKS | OF | GEORGE CRABBE. π1^v printer's imprint rule 66.5 | PRINTED BY JULES DIDOT, SENIOR, | PRINTER TO HIS MAJESTY, RUE DU PONT-DE-LODI, N°6. frontispiece recto blank verso portrait of Crabbe by PICKERSGILL with Crabbe's facsimile autograph below. π2^r titlepage π2^v blank 2π1^r Contents 2π1^v blank [i]–iii Memoir of the Rev. George Crabbe. [iv] blank [1]–319 text; Poems, The Borough, Tales and Tales of the Hall as in their respective first editions [320] blank. [in some copies 2π1 is bound at the end of the volume] [Contents page indicates inaccurately that the Memoir begins on page v].

Each type page is surrounded with a rule: there are two columns of type, also divided by a rule.

Direction line signatures at foot of the second column within the ruled border, $ 1 signed.

Headline recto of leaf running title of poem, verso CRABBE'S POETICAL WORKS. Page numbers at outer margin. Headline separated from the text by a rule.

Type-page (between ruled margins) p99 132^r 196.5 by 117.5

p173 223^r 197 by 118

p241 311^r 197.5 by 118.

Paper White laid watermark a flower and some script but never sufficiently visible to identify either, at the outer edge of $ 3 and $ 4. Chainlines, run vertically 28 apart average, wire lines 0.95 apart average. I do not know what imposition would produce this combination of characteristics, though the vertical chainlines may indicate 8° in 4s. (the size of the leaf is 228 by 140).

Copies B BL Bod.

A47

SECOND IMPRESSION UNDATED

Title-page variants: . . . | GEORGE CRABBE. | decorative rule | COMPLETE IN ONE VOLUME | decorative rule | PARIS | PUBLISHED BY A. AND W. GALIGNANI AND CO., | N° 18, RUE VIVIENNE.

No Printer's imprint on verso of half-title.

Otherwise identical including paper. Without machine collation this may be issue or impression – not edition, I think.

Copy BL.

A48

WORKS

EIGHT VOLUMES   1834

Note In this collection the various volumes of Crabbe's verse are not published separately, and in addition to the posthumous poems in Volume VIII and the Life which makes up Volume I, there are a large number of miscellaneous Works added at various places throughout the collection.

VOL. I

THE | POETICAL WORKS | OF THE | REV. GEORGE CRABBE: | WITH | HIS LETTERS AND JOURNALS, | AND HIS LIFE, | BY HIS SON. | rule 25.5 | IN EIGHT VOLUMES. | VOL. I. | rule 25.5 | LONDON: | JOHN MURRAY, ALBEMARLE STREET. | MDCCCXXXIV.

Collation Double foolscap 16⁰ in 8s (two signatures) A⁶ B–X⁸ Y² = 168 leaves.

Pagination [i–vii] viii [ix] x–xi [xii] [1] 2–322 [323–324] = 336 pages.

Contents frontispiece recto blank verso Aldborough, Suffolk. Vignette title-page LIFE AND POEMS | OF THE | REV. GEORGE CRABBE. | VOL. I. | Engraving of the house of Crabbe's father | LONDON: | JOHN MURRAY, ALBEMARLE STREET. | 1834. [i] titlepage [ii] printer's imprint LONDON: | Printed by A. SPOTTISWOODE | New-Street-Square. [iii] half-title LIFE | OF THE | REV. GEORGE CRABBE, LL.B. | BY HIS SON, | THE REV. GEORGE CRABBE, A.M. [iv] blank [v] Dedication [vi] blank [vii]–viii Preface [ix]–xi Contents [xii] blank [1]–322 text [323–4] advertisements.

Printer's Imprint p.[ii] above, p322 LONDON: | Printed by A. SPOTTISWOODE, | New-Street-Square.

Direction line $ 1, 2, 3 and 4 signed, except A1, A4 and Y2; VOL. I. on $ 1 in gutter margin, except A1.

Headline running title central; recto refers to contents of page, verso LIFE OF CRABBE. Numerals at outer margin except on recto pages where a new chapter begins, then the running-title is omitted and numerals centred.

Paper cream wove, no mark.

Type-page C2ᵛ p 20 124 by 70.5
          I3ᵛ p118 125 by 71
          Q2ᵛ p228 124 by 71
          U8ᵛ p304 123 by 71.

Binding This edition is at the beginning of cloth-bound editions, and very early gilt stamping sand-grain Yellowish-Brown cloth with blind stamping front and back, spine blind stamped pattern, gold stamped within decorative border CRABBE'S | LIFE | AND | POEMS. | I.

VOL. II.

Title-page As Vol. I.

Collation Double foolscap 16⁰ in 8s (two signatures) [A]⁴ B–Y⁸ = 172 leaves.

Pagination [i–v] vi [vii] [viii] [1–3] 4–6 [7] 8–23 [24–26] 27–69 [70–72] 73–88 [89–90] 91–99 [100] 101–105 [106–108] 109–113 [114] 115–138 [139–140] 141–172 [173–174] 175–195 [196–198] 199–235 [236–238] 239–252 [253–254] 255–258 [259–260] 261–278 [279–280] 281–296 [297–298] 299–335 [336] = 344 pages.

Contents [i] half-title POETICAL WORKS | OF THE | REV. GEORGE CRABBE. | VOL. II. [ii] printer's imprint LONDON: | Printed by A. SPOTTISWOODE, New-Street-Square. frontispiece recto blank verso engraving of Slaughden; vignette title-page recto as Vol. I engraving of Burke's House (Beaconsfield). [iii] title-page [iv] blank [v]–vi Advertisement. [vii]–viii Contents [1] half-title POEMS. | rule 19 | Ipse etc, . . . mæonumque . . . | LUCAN. *Paneg. ad Pisones.* | rule 19.5 [2] blank [3]–6 Dedication [7]–23 Preface to Poems 1807 [24] blank [25]–69 THE LIBRARY [70] blank [71]–99 THE VILLAGE BOOKS I and II [100] blank 101–105 Appendix [106] blank [107]–138 THE NEWSPAPER (including Dedication and To the Reader omitted from previous editions of Poems) [139]–235 THE PARISH REGISTER Parts I, II and III [236] blank [237]–252 THE BIRTH OF FLATTERY [253]–258 REFLECTIONS [259]–278 SIR EUSTACE GREY [279]–292 THE HALL OF JUSTICE Parts I and II 293–296 WOMAN [297]–335 APPENDIX No. I. INEBRIETY. No. II FRAGMENTS: YE GENTLE GALES; MIRA; HYMN; THE WISH; THE COMPARISON; GOLDSMITH TO THE AUTHOR; FRAGMENT; THE RESURRECTION; MY BIRTH-DAY; TO ELIZA; LIFE; THE SACRAMENT; NIGHT; FRAGMENT, WRITTEN AT MIDNIGHT; TIME; THE CHOICE. No. III THE CANDIDATE [376] printer's imprint LONDON: Printed by A. SPOTTISWOODE, New-Street-Square.

Direction line $ 1, 2, 3, and 4 signed except A. VOL. II. on $ 1 in gutter margin.

Headline running title centre; where appropriate, recto has part or book title, verso general title of poem, and gutter margin part or book number in roman numerals. Page numbers at outer margin except on recto of first page of poem or part when it is centred.

Type-page H1ᵛ p98 121 by 71
             N1ᵛ p178 126 by 72
             R2ᵛ p224 125 by 72

Notes Poems rearranged to make chronological order; many notes added by his son, including an appendix to The Village and a selection of previous uncollected or unpublished poems in appendices to the volume.

VOL. III

Title-page As Vol. I.

Collation Double foolscap 16° in 8s (two signatures) A⁴ B–U⁸X⁴ = 160 leaves.

Pagination [i–iii] iv–viii [1–3] 4–6 [7] 8–13 [14–16] 17–30 [31–32] 33–45 [46–48] 49–61 [62–64] 65–73 [74] 75–97 [98–100] 101–108 [109–110] 111–125 [126–128] 129–141 [142–144] 145–153 [154–156] 157–168 [169–170] 171–185 [186–188] 189–200 [201–202] 203–217 [218–220] 221–232 [233–234] 235–243 [244–246] 247–255 [256–258] 259–267 [268–270] 271–280 [281–282] 283–298 [299–300] 301–311 [312] = 320 pages.

Contents frontispiece recto blank verso engraving ORFORD; vignette title-page recto as Vol. I engraving of Parham Mill verso blank [i] title-page [ii] printer's imprint as Vol. II [iii]–viii Contents [1] half-title THE BOROUGH. [2] blank [3]–6 Dedication [7]–13 Preface [14] blank 15–311 text of Letters I–XIX as first edition of The Borough (No. 15), including, however as an Introduction to Letter IV a part of the original preface now moved to pp. 65–73. [312] printer's imprint as Vol. II.

Direction line $ 1, 2, 3, 4 signed except A1, 3 and 4 and X3 and 4. VOL. III. at gutter margin.

Headline running title is letter title, letter numbers in roman at gutter margin, numerals as Vol. II.

Type page D5ᵛ p 42 121 by 71
K5ᵛ p138 124 by 71
Q3ᵛ p230 125 by 72.5

VOL. IV

Title-page As Vol. I.

Collation Double foolscap 16° in 8s A⁴B–X⁸ = 164 leaves.

Pagination [i–iii] iv [v]–viii [1–5] 6–19 [20–22] 23–35 [36–38] 39–53 [54–56] 57 [58] 59–71 [72–74] 75 [76] 77–96 [97–98] 99–128 [129–131] 132–133 [134–135] 136–149 [150–154] 155–172 [173–174] 175–192 [193–194] 195–213 [214–216] 217–230 [231–232] 233–261 [262–264] 265–283 [284–286] 287–302 [303–304] 305–317 [318–320] = 328 pages.

Contents Frontispiece recto blank verso engraving The Town Hall of Aldborough; vignette title-page as Vol. I, engraving of Woodbridge [i] title-page [ii] Printer's imprint as Vol. II [iii]–iv Advertisement [v]–viii Contents [1] half-title for THE BOROUGH [2] blank [3]–96 text; letters XX–XXIV as first edition (No. 15), adding further extracts from the original preface before letters XXIII and XXIV [97] half-title OCCASIONAL PIECES [98] blank 99–115 text: THE LADIES

OF THE LAKE; INFANCY – A FRAGMENT; THE MAGNET; STORM AND CALM; SATIRE; BELVOIR CASTLE; 116–128 THE WORLD OF DREAMS [129] half-title TALES. [130] blank [121]–133 Dedication [134] blank [135]–149 Preface [150] blank [151] half title TALES. [152] blank [153]–317 text of TALES I–VIII as first edition (No. 22) [318] printer's imprint as Vol. II [319–320] Advertisements.

Direction line: $1, 2, 3, 4 signed except A1, 3, 4. VOL. IV at gutter margin.

Headline BOROUGH as Vol. III. OCCASIONAL PIECES have recto individual poem title, verso OCCASIONAL PIECES. THE WORLD OF DREAMS, and TALES as BOROUGH.

Type page E6ᵛ p60 124.5 by 72
O4ᵛ p200 125 by 72
R8ᵛ p256 121.5 by 72

VOL. V

Collation Double foolscap 16° in 8s (two signatures) [A]^4 B–U^8 = 156 leaves.

Pagination [i–vii] viii [1–5] 6–17 [18–20] 21–35 [36–38] 39–56 [57–58] 59–72 [73–74] 75–94 [95–96] 97–116 [117–118] 119–133 [134–136] 137–159 [160–162] 163–181 [182–184] 185–196 [197–198] 199–217 [218–220] 221–236 [237–238] 239–261 [262–264] 265–281 [282–284] 285–297 [298–304] = 312 pages.

Contents [i] half-title as Vol. II [ii] printer's imprint as Vol. II frontispiece recto blank verso engraving Orford-ness Light-House; Vignette title-page recto as Vol. I Engraving The Lover's Journey. [iii] title-page [iv] blank [v] Advertisement [vi] blank [vii]–viii Contents [1] half-title TALES. [2] blank [3]–261 Text of Tales IX–XXI as first edition (No. 22) [262] blank [263] half title FLIRTATION, | A DIALOGUE. | [WRITTEN IN MAY, 1816, AND NOW FIRST PUBLISHED.] [264] blank 265–281 text 282 blank [283] half title OCCASIONAL PIECES. [NOW FIRST PUBLISHED.] [284]–297 text LINES IN LAURA'S ALBUM; LINES WRITTEN AT WARWICK; ON A DRAWING OF THE ELM TREE; ON RECEIVING FROM A LADY A PRESENT OF A RING; TO A LADY, WITH SOME POETICAL EXTRACTS; TO A LADY ON LEAVING HER AT SIDMOUTH; TO SARAH, COUNTESS OF JERSEY, ON HER BIRTHDAY; TO A LADY WHO DESIRED SOME VERSES AT PARTING [298] printer's imprint as Vol. II [299–304] Advertisements.

Direction line as Vol. II.

Headline as Vol. IV.

Type page H4ᵛ p104 120.5 by 71.5
M8ᵛ p176 124 by 71.5
Q3ᵛ p230 125 by 71

VOL. VI

Title-page As Vol. I.

Collation Double foolscap 16⁰ in 8s (two signatures) [A]⁴ B–U⁸ = 156 leaves.

Pagination [i–v] vi–viii [1–4] 5–16 [17–18] 19–32 [33–34] 35–43 [44–46] 47–65 [66–68] 69–89 [90–92] 93–110 [111–112] 113–130 [131–132] 133–164 [165–166] 167–202 [203–204] 205–219 [220–222] 223–251 [252–254] 255–295 [296–304] = 312 pages.

Contents [i] half-title as Vol. I [ii] printer's imprint as Vol. II frontispiece recto blank verso engraving Belvoir Castle; vignette title-page as Vol. I engraving Beccles Church [iii] title-page [iv] blank [v]–viii Contents [1] half-title TALES OF THE HALL. [2] blank [3] information concerning publication of Tales of the Hall [4] blank [5]–6 Dedication 7–16 Preface [17]–295 text of Books I–XI as first edition (No. 31). [290] printer's imprint as Vol. II [297–304] Advertisements.

Direction line as Vol. II.

Headline as Vol. IV.

Type page G1ᵛ p82   124 by 71.5
          P1ᵛ p210 124 by 71.5
          V1ᵛ p290 124 by 71.5

VOL. VII

Title-page As Vol. I.

Collation Double foolscap 16⁰ in 8s (two signatures) [A]⁴ B–U⁸ = 156 leaves

Pagination [i–v] vi–viii [1–4] 5–40 [41–42] 43–73 [74–76] 77–95 [96–98] 99–115 [116–118] 119–156 [157–158] 159–181 [182–184] 185–198 [199–200] 201–228 [229–230] 231–247 [248–250] 251–275 [276–278] 270–298 [290–304] = 312 pages.

Contents [i] half title [ii] printer's imprint as Vol. II frontispiece recto blank verso Holland House; vignette title-page recto as Vol. I engraving of Trowbridge verso blank [iii] title-page [iv] blank [v]–viii Contents [1] half-title TALES OF THE HALL [2] blank [3]–298 text of Tales XII–XXII as first edition (No. 31), but including in a footnote on p. 275 "Lines on the death of Sir Samuel Romilly" [299–304] Advertisements.

Headline: Direction line as Vol. VI.

Type page D2ᵛ p36   124   by 72
          H7ᵛ p110 120   by 72
          Q4ᵛ p232 124.5 by 71.5

VOL. VIII

Title-page As Vol. I

Collation Double foolscap 16º in 8s (two signatures) A⁴ B–X⁸ = 164 leaves.

Pagination [i–v] vi [vii] vii [1–4] 5–34 [35–36] 37–75 [76–78] 79–90 [91–92] 93–99 [100–102] 103–120 [121–122] 123–129 [130–132] 133–136 [137–138] 139–145 [146–148] 149–155 [156–158] 159–166 [167–168] 169–174 [175–176] 177–181 [182–184] 185–190 [191–192] 193–199 [200–202] 203–208 [209–210] 211–224 [225–226] 227–240 [241–242] 243–254 [255–256] 257–265 [266–268] 269–278 [279–280] 281–294 [295–296] 297–305 [306–309] 310–317 [318–320] = 328 pages.

Contents Frontispiece recto blank verso portrait of Crabbe by T Phillips RA; vignette title-page as Vol. I recto engraving of Hampstead Heath verso blank [i] title-page [ii] printer's imprint as Vol. II [iii] Dedication [iv] POSTHUMOUS TALES. [2] blank [3]–305 text: TALE I SILFORD HALL; OR, THE HAPPY DAY; TALE II THE FAMILY OF LOVE; TALE III THE EQUAL MARRIAGE; TALE IV RACHEL; TALE V VILLAS; TALE VI THE FAREWELL AND RETURN; TALE VII THE SCHOOL-FELLOW; TALE VIII BARNABY; THE SHOPMAN; TALE IX JANE; TALE X THE ANCIENT MANSION; TALE XI THE MERCHANT; TALE XII THE BROTHER BURGESSES; TALE XIII THE DEAN'S LADY; TALE XIV THE WIFE AND WIDOW; TALE XV BELINDA WATERS; TALE XVI THE DEALER AND CLERK; TALE XVII DANVERS AND RAYNER; TALE XVIII THE BOAT RACE; TALE XIX MASTER WILLIAM; OR, LAD'S LOVE; TALE XX THE WILL; TALE XXI THE COUSINS; TALE XXII PREACHING AND PRACTICE [306] blank [307]–317 Index [318] printer's imprint as Vol. II [319–320] blank.

Direction line as Vol. I except sig Y.

Headline as Vol. VII except on first page of Index.

Type page I3ᵛ p118 124 by 72.5
O1ᵛ p194 124.5 by 72.5
S1ᵛ p258 124 by 72

The advertisement on p. [iv] says that "SELECT SERMONS AND ESSAYS" will be published on 1st of December next, in 2 vols uniform with his life and poems. (*see* appendix II for further information.)

Notes on Composition and Publication (i) *Vol. VIII.*

Though he had referred to *Tales of the Hall* as "most assuredly my last work" (letter to Elizabeth Charter; 15 April 1818), Crabbe was at work on a new volume soon after publication of *Tales of the Hall*. Huchon, (p. 440) cites evidence that he was writing hard between 1822 and 1824; Mrs Leadbeater Crabbe confessed that his increasing infirmities distracted him, though he offered her several reports on his writing:

> I have some not perfectly formed intention of publishing three or
> four pieces of versification, but I want exertion. I have a
> tale related by a gentleman who writes poetry himself, Mr Henry
> Gally Knight........I cannot relate the story, but if printed,
> you shall have it if I can send it. With it will be two or
> three other attempts; one more essay at the description of a
> kind of hallucination or insanity'[10]. With these are some trifles
> which certain friends...........permit me to think of publishing....
>
> [25 Nov 1822]
>
> I have been compelled to attend so much to my infirmities and
> my pain, that I have gone on slowly with my intended little
> book of scraps.......
>
> [7 April 1823]
>
> If my health will allow me, I will endeavour to make a few things
> I have by me more fit for the press. I have some friends whom
> I consult[11], and having their sanction I should preceed to my *last*
> trial – for so I must consider it – with some alacrity....... the
> poems are in that kind of state which will not demand a great share
> of any man's attention, and my sons, if they please, may do what
> I leave undone.....My longest attempt I have called "The Deserted
> Wife". (or "Family").....when I speak of this as the longest, I
> mean as a single narrative, for there are connected stories or rather
> incidents brought together in this manner. It may be called, taken
> together, "A Farewell and Return". I suppose a young man leaving his
> native place, where he has hitherto resided, to go into the world at large
> and previously taking leave of whomsoever he thinks right; and here I
> have opportunity to introduce as many characters as I conceive I can
> best manage, these and their situations being briefly told. My youth
> returns – a youth no more –after twenty years; and the interest of the
> poem, if there be any, consists in the completion of the events,
> and the then state of the persons to whom he had bidden farewell.
>
> [26 March 1824]

Near the end of his life Crabbe wrote to his eldest son about ... "a recess at home ... (containing) ... another series of ... stories". (October 24 1831), and it was from this material that the *Posthumous Poems* were selected. The material comprised two parts: there were some tales which had been worked on before *Tales of the Hall* was published. Some of the posthumous poems were in fact material rejected from the earlier volume. There were also the 17 poems of the Farewell and Return. Several smaller pieces were rejected by George Crabbe junior, and were not published until Pollard's *New Poems*.

Notes on Composition and Publication (ii).

Franklin P Batdorf in an article entitled 'The Murray Reprints of George Crabbe: a Publisher's record' summarises the various impressions of this edition. Approximately 8,000 copies of the set were eventually sold. George Crabbe was paid £207 as an estimated half-share in the profits, and Lockhart was paid £300 to revise the manuscript of the biography. It was published one volume each month from February to September 1834, as the Prospectus foretold, at the retail price of 5/- per volume. Murray sold it at 3/4 per volume, 25 as 24. Of 7,000 copies printed of Vol. I, 526 were presentation, official or review copies, and the proportion remained substantially the same for the 5,000 copies printed of the first impression of the other volumes. *See* appendix for further details.

Copies B BL Bod CUL NUU P.

A49

SINGLE POEMS

POEMS etc, in *THE LADY'S MAGAZINE* (Published by J. Wheble) 1772.

THE | Lady's Magazine; | OR, | ENTERTAINING COMPANION | FOR THE | FAIR SEX, | Appropriated folely to their USE and AMUSEMENT | rule 103 | VOL. III. | thick-thin rule 101 | LONDON: | Printed for JOHN WHEEBLE, No. 24, in Pater-nofter Row, and fold | by C. ETHERINGTON and J. WILSON at York; FLETCHER and | HODGSON at Cambridge; and by all the bookfellers in Great-Britain | and Ireland.

Contributions generally recognized to be by Crabbe are:

September

p. 247
i POETICAL ESSAY ON HOPE.
Come mufing melancholy maid.
Signed C.
This poem won Wheble's prize for a poem on a set subject.

p. 430
ii TO MIRA.
Doubt not, lovely fair, my paffion
Signed Woodbridge, Suffolk. C.

November

p. 518
iii The ATHEIST RECLAIMED,
AN ANECDOTE.
Ned was one who diſbelieved the Omnipotent attributes of the Deity
Signed C.
This prose piece may have been encouraged by a notice that appeared in the
preceding month's issue and may relate to him; it is under the heading
OBSERVATIONS *on our* CORRESPONDENTS:
We mean not to diſcourage C. from his poetical purſuits, when we aſſure him that his
prose *contributions will be highly acceptable.*

December

p. 574
iv THE BEE.
An ESSAY, by the Author of the ATHEIST RECLAIMED.
Turn Infidel! 'tis reason's voice commands
Signed Woodbridge, Suffolk. G.C.

p. 575
v An ALEGORICAL FABLE.
A Youth unskill'd in folly's lore
Signed Woodbridge Suffolk, Oct. 15. G.C.

p. 576
vi On MELANCHOLY.
In a dark cave which never feels a ray
Signed Woodbridge. C.

Copy Bod.

A49a

POEMS in *THE LADY'S MAGAZINE* (Published by G. Robinson) 1772.

The | Lady's Magazine [in ornamental script] | OR, | ENTERTAINING COMPANION,
| for the [ornamented gothic script] | FAIR SEX, | Appropriated ſolely to their |
USE and AMUSEMENT. | rule | VOL. III, for the YEAR 1772. | rule | LONDON: |
Printed for G. ROBINSON, | № 25, Paternoſter-Row.

Contributions generally recognized to be by Crabbe are:

September

pp. 422–3
i SOLITUDE.
Free from envy, ſtrife, and ſorrow

p. 423
ii *A* SONG.
I
As Chloe fair, a new-made bride
Both signed G. EBBARE.

October

p. 469
iii *To* EMMA.
View, my fair, the fading flower
Signed Suffolk, Oct 15, 1772. G. EBBAAC.

November

pp. 517–8
DESPAIR.
iv TYRSIS *and* DAMON
Signed G. EBBARE.
It is interesting to note that the subject of Wheble's prize poem for the month of October was DESPAIR.

p. 518
v CUPID.
"Whoe'er thou art, thy master know
Signed G. EBBARE.
Between this and the following signed poem on p518 are two brief pieces which are not signed; there is no stylistic indication that they are by Crabbe, but equally there is no reason for the interpolation of two poems by another hand between those of G. EBBARE. The full text is given of these pieces.

vi SONG.
Ye rusticks and ye ſilvan crew,
Who never ſtrife or envy knew,
Intreat the gods that they will bleſs
This virtuous, lowly ſhepherdeſs:
As fam'd as Helen, who, of old,
From Greece was ſtole by Paris bold.

vii AIR.

Beauty and youth, are blended with truth,
    Poffeft of them all is my fair;
Genteel in her gait, that cedar more straight,
    No nymph can e'er with her compare.

p. 518

viii SONG.

Cease to bid me not to fing etc.

Signed G. EBBARE.

The signed works were first published in Adolphus Ward's edition of Crabbe's Poems. They are discussed together with those under no (49) above in G Pollard's article in *The Bodleian Library Record* Vol. V 1954–5, pp. 149–156.

Note

On p. 423 there is also a poem signed GC entitled *On the* WONDERS OF CREATION
    As in my journeyings thro' this *vale of tears*
Adolphus Ward dismisses this [and some others signed simply C] as obviously not by Crabbe. There appear, however to be no stylistic or external features which permit of such certainty.

Copies B Bod.

A50

A POEM FOR THE ANNIVERSARY OF THE LITERARY FUND

1809

In *THE GENTLEMAN'S MAGAZINE* for April 1809 p350–351 with the following introduction;

A POEM | *For the Anniversary of the* LITERARY FUND, | *April 20, 1809. Written by the Rev.* | GEORGE CRABBE, B.D. *and recited by* | MATTHEW BROWNE, ESQ. | ** The founder of this society having | intimated a hope that, on a Plan which he | has already communicated to his particu- | lar Friends, its Funds may be sufficiently | ample to afford assistance and relief to | learned Officiating Clergymen in distress, | though they may not actually have com- | menced Authors – the Author, in allusion | to this hope, has introduced into a Poem | which he is preparing for the press the fol- | lowing character of a learned Divine in | distress.

This is a version of Crabbe's portrait of the Curate in Letter III of *The Borough*. There are a number of differences.

A51

VERSES

1817

In *THE LITERARY GAZETTE* No. XXX of August 16 1817. On p104 under the heading ORIGINAL POETRY appears the following poem:

VERSES

BY THE REV. G. CRABBE;

Written on the Night of the 15th of April, 17**, immediately before the perusal of a Letter then received.

Through many a year the Merchant views
With steady eye his distant gains
etc.

A52

HOPE AND MEMORY

1823

A | COLLECTION | OF | POEMS, | CHIEFLY MANUSCRIPT, | AND | *FROM LIVING AUTHORS.* | rule 29.5 | EDITED FOR THE BENEFIT OF A FRIEND, | BY JOANNA BAILLIE. | rule 30 | *LONDON:* | PRINTED FOR | LONGMAN, HURST, REES, ORME, AND BROWN, | PATERNOSTER-ROW. | 1823.

Crabbe's contribution to this is:

pp. 56–64 HOPE AND MEMORY

Copies B CUL.

A53

LINES, ADDRESSED TO THE DOWAGER DUCHESS OF RUTLAND IN *THE CASKET*

1829

THE CASKET, | A MISCELLANY, | CONSISTING OF | UNPUBLISHED POEMS. | [. . .] LONDON: | JOHN MURRAY, ALBEMARLE-STREET. | MDCCCXXIX.

Crabbe's contribution to this was:

p. 142–3 LINES, | ADDRESSED TO THE | DOWAGER DUCHESS OF RUTLAND

Notes Other contributors include Byron, Wordsworth, Wm Praed, Samuel Rogers, Miss Mitford, Thomas Moore, The Ettrick Shepherd, the first appearance of Edward Fitzgerald etc. The volume was published for charity.

A54

EPITAPH ON WILLIAM SPRINGALL LEVETT

in THE | HISTORY, TOPOGRAPHY, | AND ANTIQUITIES, | OF | FRAMLINGHAM AND SAXSTED, | IN THE | COUNTY OF SUFFOLK, | [. . .] | LONDON: | MESSRS. WHITTAKER, TREACHER, AND CO. AVE-MARIA-LANE: | SOLD ALSO BY | THE AUTHOR, CHURCH-STREET, FRAMLINGHAM; J. LODER, WOODBRIDGE; | J. RAW, IPSWICH; T. C. NEWBY, BURY ST. EDMUND'S; | AND J. STACY, NORWICH. | MDCCCXXXIV.

On p163 (Y2^r) is the following:

Levett, William Springall, surgeon, 2nd Oct. 1774, 21 years.

> What! tho' no trophies peer above his dust,
> Nor sculptur'd conquests deck his sober bust;
> What! tho no earthly thunders sound his name,
> Death gives him conquest and our sorrows fame;
> One sigh reflection heaves, but shuns excess,
> More should we mourn him, did we love him less.★

★ This is from the pen of the late Rev. George Crabbe, L.L.B. formerly of Aldeburgh, Suffolk, and afterwards rector of Trowbridge, Wilts; the stone has been broken and the epitaph is buried in the soil.

SEPARATE PROSE WRITINGS

A55

CHARACTER OF LORD ROBERT MANNERS

1785

THE | ANNUAL REGISTER, | . . . | for the YEAR 1783. | vignette design | LONDON: Printed for J. DODSLEY, in Pall-Mall, 1785.

Crabbe's contribution to this is:

Character of Lord Robert Manners, | *late Commander of his Majesty's Ship the* Resolution, *of* 74 *Guns.*

There is no note of Authorship.

A DISCOURSE

A | DISCOURSE, | READ IN | THE CHAPEL AT BELVOIR CASTLE, | AFTER THE | FUNERAL | OF HIS GRACE THE DUKE OF | RUTLAND, | LATE LORD LIEUTENANT OF THE KINGDOM OF IRELAND, | &c. &c. | diamond rule 53 | By the Reverend GEORGE CRABBE. | Diamond rule 53 | LONDON: | PRINTED FOR J. DODSLEY, IN PALL-MALL. | diamond rule 28 | M.DCC.LXXXVIII. | diamond rule 30.5 | Price 1s.

Collation Medium 4° A–B⁴ = 8 leaves.

Pagination [1–7] 8–15 [16].

Contents [1] title-page [2] blank [3–5] Dedication [6] blank [7]–15 text [16] blank.

Direction line signatures A2^r, B1^r and B2^r signed in centre; catchwords on every page, all are accurate.
Press-figures: 3 A2^v; 4 B3^v.

Headline numerals central in square brackets.

Type page variation B3^r 175.5–176 by 122.5–124
$\qquad\qquad\qquad$ B3^v 174–175 $\quad$ by 122–123.5

Binding No information.

Notes on Composition and Publication

There are several letters between Crabbe and Dodsley about this publication suggesting the care Crabbe took over it. The Duke died suddenly in Ireland 24 October 1787. The sermon was dedicated to the Duchess and is dated Belvoir, January 31st 1788.
The print run is not known.

Copies Bod BL(2) CUL; TxU.

A57

A DISCOURSE

SECOND EDITION

A | DISCOURSE, | READ IN | THE CHAPEL AT BELVOIR CASTLE, | AFTER THE | FUNERAL | OF HIS GRACE THE | DUKE OF RUTLAND, | LATE LORD LIEUTENANT OF THE KINGDOM

OF | IRELAND, &c. &c. | diamond rule 45.5 | By the Reverend GEORGE CRABBE. | thick-thin rule 84.5 | *DUBLIN:* | PRINTED BY P. BYRNE, No. 108, GRAFTON-STREET. | diamond rule 24 | M.DCC.LXXXVIII.

Collation Demy 8⁰ in 4s A–B⁴ = 8 leaves.

Pagination [i–iii] iv–v [vi] [7] 8–15 [16] = 16 pages.

Contents [i] titlepage [ii] blank [iii]–v Dedication [vi] blank [7]–15 text [16] blank.

Direction line A2ʳ B1ʳ B2ʳ signed in centre, catchwords accurate.

Headline numerals in parentheses in centre.

Type page B3ʳ 154.5 by 85
          B3ᵛ 149.5 by 85.

Paper white laid chainlines 26.5–28; vestiges of watermark on top edge of B1, B4. The single copy examined quite severely cut down (leaf size 191 by 113) in binding.

Notes on Publication This is not a line by line reprint of the first edition. The text has not been checked for variant readings.

Copy BL.

A58

NATURAL HISTORY OF THE VALE OF BELVOIR

1795

THE | HISTORY AND ANTIQUITIES | OF THE | COUNTY OF LEICESTER. | . . . | LONDON: | PRINTED BY AND FOR JOHN NICHOLS, | PRINTER TO THE SOCIETY OF ANTIQUARIES. | MDCCXCV.

Crabbe's contribution to this is:
Vol. 1 pp. cxci–cii.
THE NATURAL HISTORY | OF | THE VALE OF BELVOIR. | By the Rev. GEORGE CRABBE, B.D. Rector of Muston.

    "—— Do but compare the country where I lye
    My *Hill* and *Oulds* will say, they are the Island's eye.
    Consider . . .
                      DRAYTON, *Poly-olbion*, Song XXVI

It is simply an annotated list of species and fossils.

A59

THE | HISTORY | OF | FRAMLINGHAM, | IN THE COUNTY OF SUFFOLK | . . . | BEGUN | *By the late* ROBERT HAWES, *Gent.* | STEWARD OF THE MANORS OF FRAMLING-HAM AND SAXSTED. | WITH CONSIDERABLE ADDITIONS AND NOTES, | BY ROBERT LODER. | . . . | WOODBRIDGE: | PRINTED BY AND FOR R. LODER | 1798.

On pp. 449–453, as the last appendix is:

A CATALOGUE OF PLANTS | GROWING IN, AND NEAR THE PARISH OF FRAMLINGHAM, with a prefatory note signed G.C.

His name also appears in the list of subscribers as from Great Glemham.

A60

THE | BOTANIST'S[12] GUIDE | THROUGH | ENGLAND AND[12] WALES. | BY | DAWSON TURNFUR, P.R.S.A. S. & L.S. | . . . | AND | LEWIS WESTON DILLWYN, F.R.S. & L.S. | VOL. I. (II.) | diamond rule | LONDON: | PRINTED AND SOLD BY | *PHILLIPS AND FARDON,* | GEORGE YARD, | LOMBARD STREET. | rule | 1805.

Apparently Crabbe contributed locations for the entry under SUFFOLK only, where his name is frequently found; pp536–576. (Vol. II.)

A61

Memoir.

The New Monthly Magazine January 1816.

A biography of Crabbe reputedly written by himself. It was reprinted in The Annual Biography and Obituary for 1833.

A62

SERMON

1817

The Variation of public Opinion and Feelings | *considered, as it respects Religion.* | thick-thin rule 24.5 | A | SERMON, | PREACHED BEFORE | THE RIGHT REVEREND THE | LORD BISHOP OF SARUM, | *ON HIS VISITATION,* | 𝔥𝔢𝔩𝔡 𝔞𝔱 𝔇𝔢𝔳𝔦𝔷𝔢𝔰, | *On Friday*

the | 5th of August 1817. | rule 35 | BY THE | REV. G. CRABBE, L.L.B. | RECTOR OF
TROWBRIDGE, IN THE DIOCESE OF SARUM. | rule 35 | LONDON: | PRINTED FOR
J. HATCHARD, | BOOKSELLER TO THE QUEEN, | NO. 190, OPPOSITE ALBANY, PICCA-
DILLY. | 1817.

Collation Demy 8º A–B⁸C⁴ = 20 leaves.

Pagination [1–5] 6–36 [37–40]. = 40 pages.

Contents [1] title-page [2] printer's imprint rule 57 | S. Gosnell, Printer, Little
Queen Street, London. [3] Dedication [4] blank [5]–36 text [37–40] Hatchard's
Advertisements.

Printer's Imprint Above p[2] and p36 rule 59 | Printed by S. Gosnell, Little Queen
Street, London.

Direction line signatures A2, 3, 4; B1, 2, 3, 4; C1, 2. B7ʳ has press figure 4.

Headline numerals central.

Type page B1ʳ 143.5 by 76
B1ᵛ 145 by 80.

Copy Bod.

AMERICAN EDITIONS

A63

THE VILLAGE

1791

THE | VILLAGE: | A | POEM, | IN TWO BOOKS. | diamond rule | BY | THE REVᴰ.
GEORGE CRABBE, | CHAPLAIN TO HIS GRACE THE LATE DUKE OF RUTLAND, *&c.* |
rule | THE FOURTH EDITION. | double rule | LONDON: PRINTED. | NEW-YORK:
RE-PRINTED FOR BERRY AND ROGERS, | NO. 35, HANOVER-SQUARE, | AND SOLD BY
THOMAS AND ANDREWS, BOSTON. | — 1791. —.

Collation 12º A–C = 18 leaves.

Contents [1] title-page [2] blank [3]–36 text = 36 pages.

Direction line Catchwords on each page are correct; signed $ 1, 2, 3, except A1.

Headline Pages numbered centrally within parentheses.

Paper Cream laid; chain lines 28, wire lines 1. No watermark.

Binding No information.

Notes Evans' Catalogue of early American imprints lists what is perhaps an earlier edition of this under 1790, but the information was taken from an advertisement and no copy is known to have survived.

There is no information about the date of the first edition of this printing.

Copy MWA.

A64

POEMS

1808

POEMS | BY THE | REV. GEORGE CRABBE, LL.B. | diamond rule 7 | Ipse [etc as Poems 1807 (No. 7)] LUCAN. | thin-thick rule 17 | NEW YORK: | PUBLISHED BY INSKEEP & BRADFORD. | PRINTED BY ROBERT CARR. | dotted line 11 | 1808.

Collation Royal or Medium 12° in 6s A–Y⁶ = 132 leaves.

Pagination [i–iii] iv–v [vi–vii] viii–xxi [xxii–xxiv] [1–3] 4–15 [16–19] 20–26 [27–29] 30–59 [60–63] 64–84 [85–87] 88–121 [122–125] 126–149 [150–153] 154–171 [172–175] 176–188 [189–191] 192–195 [196–199] 200–216 [217–219] 220–223 [224–225] 226–231 [232–233] 234–235 [236–240] = 264 pages.

Contents [i] title-page [ii] blank [iii]–v Dedication [vi] blank [vii]–xxi Preface [xxii] blank [xxiii] Contents [xxiv] blank [1]–235 text (as No. 7) [236] Printer's imprint double rule 36.5 | PRINTED BY ROBERT CARR. | double rule 36.5 [237–240] blank.

Direction line $ 1 so signed, $ 3 signed $ 2 (except A1) to right of centre of direction line.

Type-page D1ʳ 131.5 by 77.5
D4ʳ 131.5 by 81
F1ʳ 131.5 by 80.

Paper wove.

Binding No evidence.

Copies B Bod.

A65

POEMS

SECOND ISSUE 1808

POEMS. │ BY THE │ REV. GEORGE CRABBE, LL.B. │ diamond rule 8.5 │ Ipse [etc as No. 7]
LUCAN. │ thin-thick rule 17.5 │ PHILADELPHIA: │ PUBLISHED BY BRADFORD &
INSKEEP, │ NO. 4, SOUTH THIRD STREET │ dotted rule 10.5 │ 1808.

Otherwise the sheets are identical with the New York issue. Since Robert Carr's
imprint survives on p236 of the Philadelphia issue, it is possible that all the
sheets were printed in New York; on the other hand, this is no evidence as to
which of the two was issued first, or if simultaneously. The title-page in this issue
is also integral, so presumably sig A must have been printed in two separate
states. The collating machine showed up no differences in any leaf of A so it is
probable that the title-page of one (i.e. A1r) was substituted for the other at some
point during the print run, and otherwise the type remained more or less un-
disturbed.

Copies B Bod; MWA.

A66

THE BOROUGH

1810

THE BOROUGH: │ A POEM, │ IN │ TWENTY-FOUR LETTERS. │ BY │ THE REV. G. CRABBE,
LL.B. │ PAULO MAJORA CANAMUS. *Virgil.* │ PUBLISHED │ BY BRADFORD AND INSKEEP,
PHILADELPHIA; │ Inskeep and Bradford, Newyork; and Wm. M'Ilhenny,
Boston. │ 1810.

Collation Royal 12° in 6s [A]² B–Gg⁶ Hh⁴ = 180 leaves.

Pagination [i–v] vi–vii [viii–ix] x–xxv [xxvi–xxviii] [1–3] 4–13 [14–17] 18–26
[27–29] 30–40 [41–43] 44–60 [61–63] 64–70 [71–73] 74–85 [86–89] 90–98 [99–
101] 102–108 [109–111] 112–121 [122–125] 126–137 [138–141] 142–151 [152–
155] 156–167 [168–171] 172–182 [183–185] 186–192 [193–196] 197–202 [203–
205] 206–212 [213–215] 216–223 [224–227] 228–240 [241–243] 244–253 [254–
257] 258–268 [269–271] 272–281 [282–285] 286–297 [298–301] 302–311 [312–
315] 316–330 [331–332] [Printing 279 as 272 and 289 as 982] = 360 pages.

Contents [i] half-title THE BOROUGH. [ii] blank [iii] title-page [iv] blank [v]–vii Dedication [viii] blank [ix]–xxv Preface [xxvi] blank [xxvii] Contents [xxviii] blank [1]–330 text; (as first edition) [331–2] blank.

Direction line $ 1 and $ 3 signed ($ 3 signed $ 2), except L3 not signed, U3 signed U.

Headline running title central; page numbers at outer margin; no running letter number.

Type-page K4ᵛ   p80   135.5 by 78.5
       O6ᵛ   p132 133   by 76.5
       U4ᵛ   p200 133.5 by 78.5
       Cc4ᵛ   p272 133.5 by 77.5

Paper wove, dingy white, no mark.

Binding Blue paper covered boards: front has an exact replica of the title-page within ruled border; back has advertisements for Bradford and Inskeep and Moses Thomas within a similar ruled border; spine reads wavy rule | THE | BOROUGH. | wavy rule.

Copy Bod; MWA.

A67

TALES

1813

TALES. | BY | THE REV. GEORGE CRABBE, LL.B. | thick-thin rule 13 (14) | VOL. I. (II.) | diamond rule 9.5 (9) | *NEW-YORK*: | PUBLISHED BY JAMES EASTBURN, 86, BROADWAY, | CORNER OF WALL-STREET. | dotted rule 7 dots (8) | 1813.

Collation Demy 12° in sixes Vol. I   A–U⁶X³ = 123 leaves
               Vol. II π² A² B–X⁶ = 124 leaves.

Pagination Vol. I [i–ix] x–xxii [xxiii–xxiv] [1–5] 6–25 [26–29] 30–48 [49–51] 52–72 [73–75] 76–89 [90–93] 94–122 [123–125] 126–146 [147–149] 150–167 [168–171] 172–185 [186–189] 190–203 [204–207] 208–222 = 246 pages.
Vol. II [i–iv] [1–3] 4–22 [23–25] 26–40 [41–43] 44–64 [65–67] 68–87 [88–91] 92–107 [108–111] 112–135 [136–139] 140–158 [159–161] 162–173 [174–177] 178–195 [196–199] 200–215 [216–219] 220–242 [243–244] = 248 pages.

Contents Vol. I [i] half-title thick thin rule 73 | TALES. | thick-thin rule 73 [ii]

blank [iii] title-page [iv] blank [v–vii] Dedication [viii] blank [ix]–xxii Preface [xxiii] Contents [xxiv] blank [1]–222 text of Tales 1–10 as first edition.
Vol. II [i] title-page [ii] blank [iii] contents[iv] blank [1]–242 [243–244] blank text of Tales 11–21 as first edition, though numbered 1–11.

Printer's Imprint Only on Vol. II p242 rule 27 | *John Forbes, Printer.*

Direction line \$1 and 3 signed (\$ 3 signed \$ 2) except Vol. I A1, C1 and S3 (Vol. I E1 signed in centre of almost blank leaf), centrally. Vol. I. (II.) at gutter margin.

Headline running title centre, page numbers outer margin, TALE 1.] etc. gutter margin.

Note on Printing Error on p227 Vol. II last line 'And took his place withing the evening coach'; does not have Tales I's error on p275 (Vol. II p99).

Type page Vol. I p63 H2ʳ 135.5 by 77
Vol. II p92 I2ᵛ 144 by 72.

Paper wove, no mark, white.

Binding Brown paper over boards; front has a variation on title-page within a decorative border; back has publisher's advertisements within a similar border (Vols. I–II have different advertisements); spine reads TALES, | by the | *Rev. G. Crabbe* | VOL. I (II.)

Copies BrU; CtY MWA.

A68

TALES OF THE HALL

1819

𝕿𝖆𝖑𝖊𝖘 𝖔𝖋 𝖙𝖍𝖊 𝕳𝖆𝖑𝖑 | rule 23 | BY | THE REV. GEORGE CRABBE, LL.B. | rule 23 | *IN TWO VOLUMES.* | VOL. I. (II.) | FROM THE LONDON EDITION. | thick-thin rule 6.5 | BOSTON: | WELLS AND LILLY, COURT-STREET. | rule 6 | 1819.

Collation Demy 12° in sixes A⁶B[6] (one leaf used in Vol. II π) 1–21₆
π⁴2π¹ (printed as part of Vol. I B) 1–22₆23₂.

Pagination Vol. I [i–v] vi [vii] viii–xvi [xvii] xviii–xxi [xxii] [1–3] 4–14 [15–17] 18–24 [25–27] 28–41 [42–45] 46–62 [63–65] 66–81 [82–85] 86–98 [99–101] 102–129 [130–133] 134–164 [165–167] 168–180 [181–183] 184–209 [210–213] 214–250.
Pagination Vol. II [i–v] vi–ix [x] [1–3] 4–35 [36–39] 40–66 [67–69] 70–84 [85–87]

88–102 [103–105] 106–138 [139–141] 142–159 [160–163] 164–175 [176–179] 180–204 [205–207] 208–222 [223–225] 226–246 [247–249] 250–267 [268].

Contents Vol. I [i] [ii] [iii] title-page [iv] blank [v]–vi Dedication [vii]–xvi Preface [xvii]–xxi Contents [xxii] blank [1]–250 Text of Books I–XI ([251–252] blank).

Vol. II [i] [ii] [iii] title-page [iv] blank [v]–ixC ontents [x] blank [1]–267 text of Books XII–XXII [268] blank.

Direction Line $ 1 and 3 signed, $ 3 with numeral and asterisk; at gutter margin is VOL. I. (II.)

Headline Follows English first edition implicitly, having on Books I–VIII TALES OF THE HALL. on both verso and recto, while Book IX onwards have the Book title on the recto, and the general title on the verso, except XVI, which has LADY BARBARA, verso and OR, THE GHOST. recto. At the gutter margin is Book I. etc. It does correct the error found in some copies of the English edition on Vol. I p. 223.

Type-page Vol. I p87 8$_2$^{r} 120 by 68
Vol. II p121 111^r 116 by 68.

Paper poor quality, cream.

Binding No information.

Copies MH MWA.

A69

CRABBE'S LIFE

1834

THE LIFE | OF THE | REV. GEORGE CRABBE, LL.B. | BY HIS SON, | THE REV. GEORGE CRABBE, A.M. | rule 26 | CAMBRIDGE & BOSTON: | JAMES MUNROE AND COMPANY. | MDCCCXXXIV.

Collation 12° in 6s a⁶ 1–26⁶ = 162 leaves.

Pagination [i–vii] viii [ix] x–xi [xii] [1]–311 [312] = 324 pages.

Contents [i–ii] blank [iii] title-page [iv] printer's imprint CAMBRIDGE PRESS: | METCALF, TORRY, AND BALLOU. [v] Inscription [vi] blank [vii]–viii Preface [ix]–xi Contents [xii] blank [1]–311 text [312] printer's imprint as [iv] above.

Direction line signatures $ 1 and $ 3 (as $ *) signed.

Headline recto descriptive title, verso running title LIFE OF CRABBE.

Paper white, wove, no mark.

Binding Brown pebbled cloth, on spine [within decorative border] 𝕷𝖎𝖋𝖊 | 𝖔𝖋 | 𝕮𝖗𝖆𝖇𝖇𝖊 | rule | 1834 | rule.

Copy B.

A70

CRABBE'S LIFE AND NEW POEMS

1835

VOL. I
LIFE | OF THE | REV. GEORGE CRABBE, LL.B. | WITH HIS LETTERS AND JOURNALS. | BY | THE REV. GEORGE CRABBE, A.M. | HIS SON. | PHILADELPHIA: | CAREY, LEA & BLANCHARD. | 1835.

Collation Royal 12° in 6s [A]–2B⁶2C³ (including V and W) = 165 leaves.

Pagination [i–vii] viii [ix–x] xi [xii] [13] 14–330 = 330 pages.
Contents [1] half-title LIFE OF THE REV. GEORGE CRABBE. [ii] Printer's imprint Philadelphia: | Printed by James Kay, Jun. & Co. | Race Street above 4th. [iii] title-page [iv] blank [v] Inscription [vi] blank [vii]–viii Preface [ix]–xi Contents [xii] blank [13]–330 Life (as Vol. I of 1834).

VOL. II POSTHUMOUS POEMS | OF THE REV. GEORGE CRABBE. | EDITED | BY HIS SON. | PHILADELPHIA: | CAREY, LEA & BLANCHARD. | 1835.

Collation Royal 12° in 6s [A]⁶[–A6 = Z1) B–Y⁶ Z¹(=A6) 2A⁶ (including V and W) = 150 leaves.

Pagination leaf not reckoned in pagination [i–v] vi [vii] viii [9–11] 12–297 [298] = 300 pages.

Contents leaf not reckoned in pagination recto half-title CRABBE'S POSTHUMOUS POEMS. verso printer's imprint Philadelphia: | Printed by James Kay, Jun. & Co. | Race Street, above 4th. [1] title-page [ii] blank [iii] Inscription [iv] blank [v]–vi Advertisement [vii]–viii Contents [9]–297 text as Vol. VIII of 1834 [298] blank.

Direction line signatures in centre $ 1 and $ 3 (signed as $ 2).

Paper white wove, no mark.

Binding Irregular pebbled cloth, brown. On spine is stamped:

C R A B B E , S

LIFE

AND

N E W P O E M S

Copy P.

1(2)

APOCRYPHAL WORK

A71

THE SKULL

1783

THE | SKULL: | A | TRUE BUT MELANCHOLY TALE. | INSCRIBED TO THE | PRETTIEST WOMAN IN ENGLAND. | diamond rule 48 | LONDON: | PRINTED BY MILLAN AND RAE, HENRIETTA-STREET, COVENT-GARDEN; | AND | SOLD BY J. BOWEN, NEW-BOND-STREET; T. EGERTON, CHARING-CROSS; | AND MESS. RICHARDSON AND URQUHART, ROYAL-EXCHANGE. | MDCCLXXXIII. | [PRICE TWO SHILLINGS.].

Collation Demy 4° in 2s, 2 sigs

either $\pi^2a^2B-E^2F[^2]$
or $a^4B-E^2F[^2]$ $=$ 15 or 16 leaves.

Pagination Two leaves not reckoned in pagination [i] ii–iv [v–vi] 1–18 ([19–20]) = 30 or 32 pages.

Contents $\pi 1^r$ title-page $\pi 1^v$ blank $2\pi 1^r$ pictorial title-page: in an ornamental script The | SKULL, | A True, but Melancholy Tale | Inscrib'd | To the Prettiest WOMAN | in | England. | drawing of a skull on a catafalque | "Tho' once the Toast of all the Routs and Drums | At last to this complexion Chloe comes." $2\pi 1^v$ blank [i]–iv Address to the prettiest woman in England, dated May 19 1783 $\pi 2^r$ or [v] The Argument $\pi 2^v$ or [vi] blank [1]–18 text ([19–20] blank).

Direction line Signed on $ 1; the third leaf is signed a, so it is possible that the title-page and the leaf with The Argument on it are conjugate and separate from a. There are no physical details in either copy which illuminate this matter. Accurate catchwords on every page.

Headline Numerals central within parentheses.

Paper White, laid, chainlines horizontal 27, wire lines vertical 1.25, watermark fleur-de-lys.

cf above, direction line. In fact the leaf with The Argument on it has a different watermark in DFo copy, while in CtY copy it has apparently the fleur-de-lys as all the others. In CtY copy D2 has the bottom of what DFo Argument leaf is top. In both copies some gatherings appear to have no watermark at all.

Binding No information, but perhaps issued in wrappers.

Copies CtY DFo.

A72

THE SKULL

SECOND EDITION   1783

THE | SKULL; | A | POEM. | INSCRIBED TO THE | PRETTIEST WOMAN IN ENGLAND. | "Tho' once the Toast of all the Routs and Drums, | "At last to this Complexion CHLOE comes!" | THE SECOND EDITION. | diamond rule 60 | LONDON: | PRINTED BY MILLAN AND RAE, HENRIETTA-STREET, COVENT-GARDEN; | AND | SOLD BY J. MURRAY, FLEET-STREET; J. DEBRETT, PICCADILLY; J. BOWEN, | NEW-BOND-STREET; MESS. RICHARDSON AND URQUHART, | ROYAL-EXCHANGE; T. EGERTON, CHARING-CROSS; | AND J. SOUTHERNE, ST. JAMES'S-STREET. | MDCCLXXXIII. | [PRICE TWO SHILLINGS.]

Collation As first edition, though F2 is clearly present.

Pagination As first edition without parentheses round F2 leaf.

Contents As first edition except [19] Advertisement for Richardson and Urquhart [20] blank.

Typography and Paper As first edition.

Copy MH.

ADDENDUM

A72a

THE VILLAGE

                                                                          1833

THE VILLAGE AND OTHER POEMS.
London: Jones & Co 1833 pp. viii + 86 16mo.

Appendix I

i PROSPECTUS FOR WORKS

EIGHT VOLUMES

1834

PROSPECTUS | OF THE | FIRST COMPLETE AND UNIFORM EDITION | OF THE | POETICAL
WORKS | OF | THE REV. GEORGE CRABBE: | WITH HIS | LETTERS AND JOURNALS, |
AND | A MEMOIR OF HIS LIFE, | BY HIS SON AND EXECUTOR. | rule 23.5 | "Though
Nature's sternest painter, yet the best." – BYRON. | rule 23 | LONDON: | JOHN
MURRAY, ALBEMARLE STREET. | MDCCCXXXIII.

Collation π⁴.

Pagination [1–3] 4–7 [8].

Printer's Imprint p[2] LONDON: | Printed by A. SPOTTISWOODE, | New-Street-
Square.

Binding Green paper covers.

Notes Dated on p[3] Albemarle Street, October 1833. Extract from p. 7.
III. Each *vol.* will contain a Frontispiece and Vignette Title-page, engraved by
the Findens, from original drawings, illustrative of the actual scenery of the
Poet's life, and the localities from which he drew his pictures of Nature, – all
taken on the spot, during the present autumn, and expressly for this work, by
Clarkson Stanfield, A.R.A.
IV. The price of each *vol.*; neatly bound in cloth boards, will be only Five
Shillings.
V. The publication will commence on the first of February, and be completed
on the first of September 1834; and with the last *vol.* will be given a copious
Index to the names of the persons, places and subjects referred to in the Life and
Works.

Copies Bod BL.

Appendix II BALANCE SHEET FOR CRABBE'S WORKS

CRABBE'S WORKS (General Account)

1) Dec 10 1818

	£	s	d			£	s	d
To acceptance for Copyright	3000			June 30 1822	By Balance Tales otH flscp 8°	1584	14	11
Cheque for Stamp	35				[2 vols] 8°	16	9	0
					[flscap 8°]	33	0	0
	3035				5 vols 8°	406	12	0
					5 vols flscp	7	19	7
						299	11	7
				Dec 31 1829	Balance being loss	686	12	11
						3035		

2) 1819

Tales of the Hall 2 Vols 8°

Mar 18	£	s	d			£	s	d
250 Rms Demy 35/-	437	10	0	June 30 1822	By sale of Copies rec from			
Entering at S Hall	2	2	0		Hatchard and son	458	19	6
BM Copies					By 3000 Copies first edition			
Paper 154 Rms 35/-	269	10	0		1500 2nd edition			
Law expenses	2	13	4		4500			
Paid Hatchard and Son	420	6	0		330 on hand			
Printing	339	9	0		4170 sold as follows: at 14/-	2919	0	0
,, 2nd edn	194	7	6			3377	19	6
Printing Titles etc	18	4	9					
Advertising	111	2	0					
Balance carried up	1584	14	11					
	3377	19	6	July 1822	By 330 copies on hand sold at 2/-	33	0	0
To Amount carried up	33	0	0					

BALANCE SHEET FOR CRABBE'S WORKS

3)

Foolscap 8vo

April 14 1820	To 267 Rm fcap 27/6	367	2	6	1820 April	By 3000 Copies			
	Printing	275	8	6	1822 June 30	1606 on hand			
	Advertising	10	10	0		1394 Sold 25 as 24 at 10/-	669	10	0
	Balance Profit carried up	16	9	0	1822 June 30	By 1606 copies on hand sold as follows			
		669	10	0		502 as C H Sales 25 as 24 at 10/-	241	0	0
1829 [and 30]	Balance profit on this edition	406	12	0		1104 to T Tegg 25 as 24 for 3/-	165	12	0
							406	12	0

4)

Illustrations

1820							
1821 July	Drawing	325	10	0	1822 Octr	By 50	
	Engraving C Heath	1302	0	0			
	Working McQueen	339	10	8			
	Advertising	50	0	0			
		2017	0	8			

BALANCE SHEET FOR CRABBE'S WORKS

5) Crabbe's Works 5 Vols 8vo

		£	s	d
1820 June 30	To Printing	529	16	3
	365 Rms Demy	739	10	0
	Advertising	30	5	2
1822 Sept		1299	11	5
	Balance Profit Carried fwd	7	19	7
1829 March		1307	11	

Mr M		£	s	d
By 1500 copies sold as follows				
C H Sale 185 25 as 24 at 30/-		267	0	0
do 511 do 21/-		515	11	0
82 various 40/-		164	0	0
722 to T Tegg 5 vols at 2/-		361	0	0
		1307	11	0

March 31 1829		£	s	d
By Balance Profit brought forward		7	19	7

6) Foolscap 5 Vols

		£	s	d
1823 Jany	To Printing (Davison)	280	8	9
	248 Rms fcap 26/-	322	8	0
	Advertising	22	0	0
1829 Mar		624	16	9
1829 Dec 31	Balance Profit carried forward	299	11	7
		924	8	4

Mr M		£	s	d
By 1500 copies sold as follows				
573 as C H Sales (25 as 24 at 15/-)		413	5	0
104 various at 19/2		99	13	4
823 to T Tegg at 10/-		411	10	0
		924	8	4

		£	s	d
By balance profit brought forward		299	11	7

BALANCE SHEET FOR CRABBE'S WORKS

7)

Crabbe's Tales 2 Vols fcap Mr M

		£ s d			£ s d
1820	To Printing	86 12 0	1820	By 750 Copies	
	Paper 48 rms 27/6	66		518 on hand June 30 /22	
		152 12 0		232 sold at 5/-	58 0 0
	To Loss	94 12 0		Loss	94 12 0
					152 12 0
			1822 June 30	By 518 on hand & sold at 2/-	51 16 0
				Loss	42 16 0
					94 12 0

8)

Dr Crabbe's Sermons

		£ s d			£ s d
1835 Dec 31	Engrav of Head of Crabbe Messrs Finden	37 5 6	1838 Nov	By Balance not proceeded with	75 1 6
1837 April 7	Do Monument & Writ,,	37 16 0			
		75 1 6			

The above is a copy of the balance-sheet for Crabbe's works published by John Murray made in 1830. It is on folios 85–6 of the Copies Ledger B, still in the archives of John Murray.

The first entry is a cumulative analysis of Tales of the Hall and the collected works; it shows on the debit side the money paid to Crabbe for the copyright of his poems, plus the official stamp for the contract, and on the credit side the profit made by each edition. Evidently Murray had not yet been able to recoup the money he paid for the copyright; and further, the small printing of Tales, entry no. 7 (which is on folio 263 of the same Ledger), shows a further small addition to the loss, bringing it to £729 8s. 11d. for the period to 1830. This sum also takes into account the small profit (£38 13s 6d) made on the '2426'[13] copies sold by Hatchard to Murray. Whether this loss was offset by a profit on the illustrations by Westall is not related, for the entry in the ledger (no. 41) is not completed. The expenditure was large, but the income may have been larger, since the cheapest price at which the sets were available was £2. There are too many imponderables even to guess at the likely financial outcome: the numbers printed (the enigmatic 50 on the credit side may indicate 5,000 copies or 500; it is impossible to tell), whether Murray sold them wholesale, as with all the volumes, or retail, and whether they were all sold at the first rate, or whether they had to be remaindered.

The last full quotation (no. 8) is from Copy Ledger C folio 96 and relates to the advertised, but not printed volume of Crabbe's sermons: it appears that two engravings were made for this, and their cost would undoubtedly be set down by Murray as loss against the Crabbe account.[14]

Finally there follows a summary of some interesting details from the accounts for the Works of 1834. Franklin P. Batdorf has given an analysis of the number of copies printed (in SB), but he does not deal with the financial side of the edition; this has its interest in the light of Murray's letter to George Crabbe the younger in which he claims that there is still a debt of nearly £200 (Huchon p. 521).

The figures show that in 1845 the approximate situation (which is impossible to guage precisely since Vols. II to VII were accounted separately from Vol. I and Vol. VIII) was that the edition as a whole showed a profit of £625 though Vol. I and Vol. VIII both lost money, because of the advances paid to the Crabbes.

When the loss incurred over the two sets of abandoned illustrations are taken into account – £180, then the overall loss to Murray on Crabbe's works, (excluding the illustrations that *were* proceeded with) was in 1845 approximately £220.

NOTES AND REFERENCES

1 Neither copy consulted has the hypothetical $\pi 1$; it may not have existed.

2 BL copy does not have E2, which may not have existed.

3 John Nichols: *Literary anecdotes of the Eighteenth Century*: Nichols, Son & Bentley, London 1812–15 Volume 8 page 90.

4 R. L. Chamberlain: *Unpublished poems of Crabbe in the Murray Manuscript Collection*: Ann Arbor Xerox series, 1967.

5 René Huchon; (translated by Frederick Clarke): *George Crabbe and his Times 1754–1832*: London, John Murray 1907, page 115.

6 '*The Public Advertiser* July 24 1781, though Crabbe's son in his biographical memoir and, presumably following him, Alfred Ainger in *George Crabbe*: English Men of Letters series, London, Macmillan 1903, say it appeared in June of that year. Neither authority quotes any source for the June date. *The Advertiser* states quite clearly 'this day appeared a poem entitled *The Library*.'

7 Cf. No 18.

8 In TxU(3) – (the Bowles copy) it is clear that the P6 cancellans was pasted on before the volume was sewn. It may have been quired merely.

9 In *Tales* 1812, ed. M. Mills CUP 1967, p. xxxvi.

10 It is tempting to speculate that this is the poem eventually published by Pollard in *New Poems of George Crabbe* as 'The Insanity of Ambitious Love'. If so then Crabbe was re-working material written much earlier, for 'The Insanity of Ambitious Love' is found in a notebook dated May 1816 (Pollard p2)

11 The family of Samuel Hoare the banker. Crabbe was a frequent visitor to the Hoares in his later years.

12 S and AND appear in slightly smaller type capitals.

13 The figure quoted in *A Publisher and his Friends*, Samuel Smiles LLD (condensed and edited by T. Mackay) London 1911 p. 210 'Crabbe had some difficulty in getting his old poems out of the hands of his previous publisher, who wrote to him in a strain of wildest indignation, and even threatened him with legal proceedings but eventually the stock, consisting of 2,426 copies, was handed over by Hatchard and Colburn to Mr. Murray, and nothing more was heard of this controversy between them and the poet.' There is some conflicting evidence in a letter published in NQ. A letter of 1819 from Crabbe to Murray suggests that twice this number of copies remained in Hatchard's stock.

14 Detailed discussion of the other entries may be found under the relevant entry in the check-list.

A II

Subsequent Editions
of Crabbe's Work

A II

A IIa   *Editions published after the 8 volume set of 1834.*

As in section **AI** British and American editions are listed separately. All items are listed in strict chronological order, not grouped by volume title. The selections tend to be published with very misleading titles, 'Poems of George Crabbe', or 'Works' being used to describe compilations which bear no relationship to the original volumes which had these titles. This alone would make a chronological list justifiable. It has the added advantage of giving an untrammeled idea of the number of issues of Crabbe which have taken place since his death. Essays introducing editions are described in section F.

Square brackets [ ] surround dates which are supplied from sources other than title-pages. Where these are followed by a query [ ]? it indicates that some doubt remains about the date which has been conjecturally attributed to the volume. Some title-pages of American editions transcribed from *The National Union Catalog* may not be full and complete citations of the original. Subsequent issues or impressions of any edition are distinguished by separate numbers only where they embody alterations to the title-page(s). Where publishers records have revealed issues for which no title-page variations can be discovered, these have been listed for statistical interest but not separately numbered.

There are, of course, numerous anthologies which have included excerpts from Crabbe. These have been recorded only where entire and unedited poems are printed.

A IIb   *Letters, Sermons, Etc.*

Section **A11b** lists letters, sermons, etc. published posthumously; and poems making their first appearance in print subsequent to the eight volume edition of 1834.

A IIa

EDITIONS OF CRABBE PUBLISHED SUBSEQUENT TO THE EIGHT
VOLUME SET, EDITED BY THE POET'S SON AND ISSUED BY JOHN
MURRAY IN 1834

I BRITISH EDITIONS

1835

A73 *The poetical works of the Rev. George Crabbe LL.D.* London: Allman, 1835.
pp. xxiii + 192. 16mo. The second title-page cites the publishers as T. Allman &
E. Spettigue. The volume prints only the contents of *Poems* 1807, despite calling
itself 'poetical works'. There is no introduction and no indication of an editor.
The volume was part of Spettigue's 'Standard Edition of the British Poets'.

A73a 1836. *The poetical works of George Crabbe LL.D.* The edition seems to
have been copied from that of 1835. Printing of legend is slightly larger type.
There is only one t.p.: the portrait, unsigned in 1835 is now signed "J. Newman
Sc" and is a close but not exact copy of 1835.
The imprint is London: | Somers & Co. | No. 7 Mitre Square, | Aldgate. |
[Short rule] 1836.
Contents are the same but page contents vary due to larger type.

A74 There was a re-issue in [1850]? B.M. Catalogue says "previous edition
1816". No trace of this has been found.

[1837]

A75 *The poetical works of the Rev. George Crabbe. LL.D.* With an essay on his
genius and writings. With a portrait. London: Charles Daly, [1837]. pp. 213.
8vo. The date is given on the portrait, not on the title-page itself.

A76 There was a re-issue in 1840.

1838

A77 *The Village, The Parish Register & other poems.* Edinburgh: William &
Robert Chambers, 1838. pp. 32. 8vo. Sub-heading 'The people's edition'. No
introduction or indication of an editor.

A78 *The Borough. A poem.* London: W. Smith, 1838. pp. 74. 8vo.

A79 Re-issued in 1840 in 'Smith's Standard Library'. (see also item 81).

1839

A80 *The Borough: a poem by the Rev. George Crabbe. LL.B.* London: Charles
Daly, 14 Leicester Street, Leicester Square, 1839. pp. xxxii + 256. 32mo.
Crabbe's own Preface is re-printed, but there is no other introduction, and no

indication of an editor. This may be from Daly's 'Classical Library' – see item (A82) below.

There is no date on the title-pages of the University of New Brunswick copy. In this copy the first title-page has "19 Red Lion Square" as Daly's address, whilst the second reads "17 Greville Street, Hatton Garden". Daly's various addresses are listed below, and suggest that this copy was issued some time after the initial date of publication.

The New Brunswick copy is also incorrectly bound as follows: pagination runs viii, x, xi, ix, xii, xiii.

1840

A81 *George Crabbe's Tales.* London: Smith, 1840. pp. 81. 'Smith's Standard Library.' Re-issued 1846.

[1844/55]?

A82 *George Crabbe's poetical works.* Preface to the Tales. Life by A. C. Cunningham, Esq. And illustrations. London: Charles Daly, 17 Greville Street, Hatton Garden, [n.d.] pp. xvi + 523. 12mo.

Omits *Tales of the Hall* and *Posthumous Poems*. The 'Life' is entirely derivative biography.

Daly did not move to premises in Greville Street until 1844. His premises were as follows, according to P. A. H. Brown; *London Publishers and Printers*:

14 Leicester Street, Leicester Square: 1835–1839.
19 Red Lion Square: 1840–1841.
17 Greville Street, Hatton Garden: 1844–1855.

There is no other evidence to help date this edition. There are advertisements at the back of one copy examined, which refer to Daly's 'Classical Library' – "embellished with beautiful frontispieces and vignette titles . . . Uniformly and correctly printed in Medium 32mo . . . The Borough 2/–. Miscellaneous Poems 1/6." This description of *The Borough* would fit item (A80) above. No copy of a volume titled 'Miscellaneous Poems' has come to light.

The same advertisement lists the following: "Royal 18mo. Crabbe's Poetical Works – Tales of the Hall, Borough, Village, Minor Poems etc., Illustrations . . ." No edition published by Daly which includes *Tales of the Hall* has in fact come to light. There is no means of telling whether the advertisement refers to an intended edition which never materialized, or to a volume which has disappeared from notice.

1845

A83 *The Tales and miscellaneous poems of the Rev. George Crabbe.* A new edition. London: John James Chidley, 1845. pp. xii + 384. 8vo. Prints *Tales*, plus 'The

Birth of Flattery', 'Reflections', 'Sir Eustace Grey', and the other occasional pieces from *Poems* 1807. There is no introduction or indication of an editor.

1846

A84 *The Rev. George Crabbe's poems.* Containing *The Library, The Village, The Newspaper,* 'The Parish Register', *The Borough.* A new edition. London: John James Chidley, 1846. pp. iv + 359. 8vo. There is no introduction, or indication of an editor. Re-issued the following year.

1847

A85 *The Tales and miscellaneous poems of The Rev. George Crabbe.* London: H. G. Bohn, 1847. pp. xii + 384. 8vo. This seems to be a re-issue of Chidley's edition – (A83) above –, the only difference being that the ruled frames, which surround the text in Chidley, have disappeared in this issue.

A86 *The Life and Poetical Works of the Rev. George Crabbe,* Edited by his son. Complete in one volume. With portrait and vignette. London: John Murray, 1847. pp. xii + 587. 8vo. Murray decided on this edition after the 8 volume set of 1834 had come to a halt in its sales. It reprints all the material of the 8 volume set.

A87, A88, A89, A90, A91, A92, A93 There were re-issues in 1851, 1853, 1854, 1860/61, 1866, 1901 and 1932. In these the title-page has: "A new edition with portrait and engravings" added to it. Frequently the date of the portrait and that of the title-page got "out of step" in these re-issues. The composition is pp. viii + 584.

[1854]

A94 *Tales.* By the Rev. George Crabbe LL.B. London: Nathaniel Cook, Milford House, Strand. [n.d.] pp. 82. "The Universal Library". (See also next item).

A95 *The Borough.* A poem. By the Rev. George Crabbe LL.B. And the poems of Gray and Collins. London: Nathaniel Cook. etc. [n.d.] paginated 83–156. This is also part of Cook's "Universal Library". These little volumes – the copy inspected had blue paper covers, presumably as issued – came out in parts. Both these Crabbe items are in the third volume of "Poetry", and were issued sequent to each other, as may be inferred from the pagination. The conjectural date is that of the B.M. Catalogue. Cook seems to have spelt his name both with and without a final 'e'.

1854/55

A96 *The poetical works of George Crabbe.* With Life. Eight engravings on steel. Edinburgh: Gall & Inglis. London: Houlston & Stoneman. [n.d.] pp. xvi + 496. 8vo. The anonymous 'Life' is dated Edinburgh, 1854, though the B.M.

Catalogue gives 1855 as the date of the edition. First issue was in fact in December 1854. Omits *Tales of the Hall*.

Gall & Inglis' records for the printing of this edition are still extant. The first impression was one of 3,092 copies. There were further issues virtually every subsequent year up to 1874, about 13,000 copies being printed in all.

A97 In 1874 the same work was issued with red rules surrounding the text – 3092 copies being printed.

A98 In July 1881 the text was issued in a new format: printed on larger paper with tinted marginal illustrations of landscape scenes, in 'The Landscape Poets' series. Between 1881 and 1884 1500 copies of this were printed.

In the course of the various issues of the 1854 edition the following alterations were made:

  a) The number of the steel engravings was reduced from eight to six. The second title-page is altered accordingly.

  b) The various changes of address of the firm, were recorded on the title-pages. These moves were as follows:

    1841–1857. 38 North Bridge, Edinburgh.

    1857–1878. 6 & 13 George Street, Edinburgh.

    1878 onwards 20 Bernard Terrace, Edinburgh.

  The following related volume has been noted:

  With second title-page reading:

A99 *The poetical works . . .* etc. London: Published by Thomas Holmes, Great Book Establishment, 76 St Paul's Churchyard. [n.d.] (Harvard University). In this copy the first title-page is that of Gall & Inglis, 38 North Bridge, with eight engravings.

It is possible that other such variations exist. They may assist in identification of editions which otherwise appear to be omitted from this list.

1858

A100 *The poetical works of George Crabbe*. A new edition, illustrated. With a life. London: G. Routledge & Co., 1858. pp. xx + 466. 8vo. The illustrations are by Birket Foster, the life is signed 'W.R.' Part of the 'Routledge's British Poets' series.

[1863]

A101 *The Parish Register, & other poems*. By The Rev. George Crabbe, LL.B. and *The Sabbath, & other poems*. By The Rev. James Grahame. With memoirs of the authors. London & Edinburgh: William & Robert Chambers, [n.d.]. 8vo. The Crabbe section is pp. xiv + 128 of pp. 223. The date is supplied by the publisher's records.

1867

A102 *Summer Scenes*. By Birket Foster. A series of photographs, from some of his choicest water-colour drawings, with appropriate selections from the poems ... of Crabbe ... etc. London: 1867. 4to.

The British Library copy has been destroyed. No other copy has been available for inspection.

[1873]

A103 *The poetical works of the Rev. George Crabbe* . . . illustrated, with plates including a portrait. London: James Blackwood & Co., [n.d.]. 8vo. In two parts, the first of which contains *The Library*, *The Village*, 'The Parish Register', *The Borough*, etc., the second contains *Tales*, and "miscellaneous poems." Part 1 is paginated iv + 130, and Part II iv + 384. The date is that of the B.M. Catalogue.

[1874]

A104 *The poetical works of Geoffrey Chaucer and George Crabbe*. Illustrated. London: James Blackwood & Co. [n.d.] pp. 403. "Blackwood's Universal Library of Standard Authors". The Crabbe section occupies pp. 293–403. It comprises *Tales* and *The Borough*. The conjectural date is that of the entry in the *National Union Catalog*, for the American issue of the same work, though in America it was issued from New York: G. Routledge & Sons. It is entered under 'Chaucer'.

1879

A105 *The Village*. With prefatory and explanatory notes. London: Blackie, 1879. pp. 32. 8vo. 'Blackie's School Classics' series. The biographical note is of no intrinsic value, and the notes to the text are elementary in the extreme.

A106 *Readings in Crabbe, Tales of the Hall*. (Abridged and adapted, with an introduction, by Edward Fitzgerald.) Guildford, Surrey. Billing & Son, 1879. pp. 242. 8vo.

Published by Fitzerald privately. Billing was the printer.

A107, A108 Repeated, with pp. xiv of introduction, in 1882 and 1883. Fitzgerald felt Crabbe to be over-full of longeurs in *Tales of the Hall*, and he provided prose bridges of his own to sustain the narrative flow of the poem between the sections he felt to be Crabbe at his best.

[1886]

A109 *Poems by George Crabbe*. London: Cassell & Co., (n.d.) pp. 192. 8vo. Volume 20 of 'Cassell's National Library'. There is a biographical sketch, pp.

5–8, not very accurately transposed from other sources. This is signed 'H.M.' Contents: *The Village*, *The Library*, *The Newspaper*, 'The Parish Register.'

1888

A110 *The poetical works of George Crabbe* selected, with prefatory notice, biographical and critical, by Edward Lamplough. London: Walter Scott, 1888. pp. xxiii + 255. Part of 'The Canterbury Poets' series. Comprises extracts from from 'The Parish Register', *The Newspaper*, *The Village*, *The Borough*, and *Tales*.

A111 *The Library*. In Henry Morley: *A Miscellany*. London: Routledge & Co., 1888. pp. 251–272.

1891

A112 *The Poets and Poetry of the Century*: volume 1. George Crabbe to Samuel Taylor Coleridge. London: Hutchinson & Co., 1891. 8vo.

A113, A114, A115 Re-issued in [1898], [1899] and 1905. pp. 1–84 contain Crabbe. Prints excerpts from *The Village*, 'The Parish Register', *The Borough*, *Tales*, and *Tales of the Hall*; and 'The Hall of Justice' and 'Sir Eustace Grey' in full. There is an introduction by A. H. Miles.

A116 *Crabbe's Tales*: Edited, with an introduction by Henry Morley LL.D. London: Routledge & Co., 1891. pp. xii + 192. 12mo. **A116a** There was a new edition in 1898. This is volume 8 of Routledge's 'Companion Poets' series.

1899

A117 *The Poems of George Crabbe*: A selection. Arranged and edited by Bernard Holland. London: Edward Arnold, 1899. pp. xvi + 389. 8vo.

A118 This selection was re-issued in 1909.

1903

A119 *Selections from the poems of George Crabbe*. With an introduction and notes by Anthony Deane. London: Methuen, 1903, pp. xxxii + 251. 8vo. 'The Little Library' series.

A120 Re-issued, with a new introduction in 'The Gateway Library' series in 1932.

A121 *The Borough. A poem by the Rev. George Crabbe*. London: J. M. Dent & Co., 1903. pp. viii + 339. 8vo. 'The Temple Classics' series. A note on p. 331 reads: "This edition has been edited by Mr. Henry Williams, M.A. who has collated the text, supplied the marginalia, and added the notes . . ."

1905–1907

A122 *George Crabbe. Poems*. Edited by Adolphus William Ward . . . Cambridge: The University Press, 1905–1907. (3 volumes). 8vo. Several pieces of juvenalia and ephemera made their first appearance in this edition, which remains the most complete text of Crabbe available. It was also the first time that the complete text of *Inebriety* had been reprinted. The volume was re-issued in a xerographic reprint in 1963, and by AMS Press Inc. of New York in 1976.

[1908]

A123 *George Crabbe. Selections from Poems.* Arranged A. T. Quiller-Couch. Oxford: The Clarendon Press, [1908]. pp. 32. 8vo.

A124 Re-issued in [1912] in the series 'Select English Classics', with title-page reading . . . 'arranged with an introduction by A. T. Quiller-Couch.' The introduction is fragmentary, and of no critical significance. Dates from B.M. Catalogue.

A125 *The poetical works of George Crabbe.* Edited by A. J. & R. M. Carlyle. London: Oxford University Press, 1908. pp. xxii + 600. 8vo. 'The Oxford Edition'.

A126 Re-issued in 1914 in the 'Oxford Standard Authors' series.

A127 and again in 1932.

1930

A128 *The Library*: with drawings in black and white by E. J. G. Ardizzone. London: Alexander Moring Ltd., The De La More Press, 1930. pp. 31. 8vo. 'The St. George' series. There is no indication of an editor.

[1932]

A129 *The Augustan Books of Poetry: George Crabbe.* London: Benn & Co., (n.d.) pp. iv + 31. 8vo. Extracts from *The Village*, 'The Parish Register,' *The Borough*, *Tales*, plus one lyric. The introduction is not signed.

1933

A130 *George Crabbe. An anthology.* Chosen by F. L. Lucas. Cambridge; The University Press, 1933. pp. xxxii + 227. 8vo. In the 'Poets in brief' series. The introduction is a repeat of Lucas's essay in *Life and Letters*, (q.v. in the 'Criticisms' section).

A131 Republished New York: Octagon Books Ltd., 1974.

1946

A132 *George Crabbe's poems.* Selected with an introduction and notes by Philip Henderson. London: Lawson & Dunn, 1946. pp. xxii + 134. 8vo.

1950

A133 *George Crabbe: poems.* Selected and edited by Geoffrey Grigson. London: Grey Walls Press, 1950. pp. 64. 8vo. 'The Crown Classics' series.

A134 *The Village*: with Introduction and notes by Arthur Sale. University Tutorial Press, 1950. pp. xiv + 41.

1955

A135 *George Crabbe: Selections from his poetry*. Edited with an introduction and notes by Frank Whitehead. London: Chatto & Windus, 1955. pp. 204. 8vo. 'Queens Classics' series.

1960

A136 *New poems of George Crabbe*. Edited with an introduction by Arthur Pollard. Liverpool: The University Press, 1960. pp. 189. 8vo. (Details under the section 'Poems published for the first time since 1834'.)

1967

A137 *George Crabbe: Tales 1812, with other selected poems*. Edited with an introduction by Howard Mills. Cambridge: The University Press, 1967. pp. xxxviii + 444. 8vo.

A138 *A Crabbe selection*. Edited with an introduction and notes by Geoffrey Newbold. London: Macmillan, 1967, pp. xxv + 174. 8vo. 'Macmillan's English Classics' series.

1973

A139 *The Borough*. A facsimile of the first edition, edited by J. Lucas. The Scholar Press, 1973.

A140 *Crabbe*. Selected by C. Day Lewis. London: Penguin Books, 1973. pp. 159. 8vo. 'Poet to Poet' series.

II   AMERICAN EDITIONS.

These are almost invariably related to previously published British editions.

1839

A141 *The poetical works of Crabbe, Heber, and Pollok. Complete in one volume.* Philadelphia: Grigg & Elliot. 1839. Crabbe is pp. v–396. Composition of vol. runs viii [9]–396, [2], [v]–xxvii, 43, 79. There is a front plate of the three authors. Reprints *Poems, The Borough, Tales, Tales of the Hall* and *Posthumous Poems*. The unsigned memoir is, in its first and last three paragraphs an unacknowledged repeat of 'C.T.' from the Galignani edition of 1829, though the tenses are altered from present to past. The remainder is biography derived directly from the memoir Crabbe himself wrote, or from the son's *Life*, 1834. There were re-issues as follows:

A141a, A142, A143, A144, A145, A146, A147 By Grigg & Elliott in 1843, 1844, 1845, 1846, 1847, 1848, 1849.

A148, A149, A150, A151, A151a Philadelphia: Lippincott, Grambo & Co. 1850, 1852, 1853, 1854, 1855.

A152, A153 Philadelphia: J. B. Lippincott & Co. 1856, 1857.

1844

A154 *The Tales of the Hall*, a poem, by Rev. George Crabbe. New York: Burgess, Stringer, & Co., 222 Broadway, corner of Ann Street, 1844. Title-page, 1–129 [130] = 132 pages. Decorated paper wrappers with facsimile of title-page; added here below Ann Street are the following: Redding & co., Boston. – G. B. Zieber & Co., Philadelphia. – Wm. Taylor, Baltimore. – Bravo & Morgan, New Orleans. The price was twenty-five cents.

[1853]

A155 *George Crabbe's poetical works*. Preface to the Tales. Life by A. C. Cunningham, Esq.

Substantially item [A82] from the British list.

This edition of *Poetical Works*, with the Life by Cunningham went through a series of re-issues in America as follows:

A156 Boston: Phillips, 1853[?].

A157 Boston: Phillips, Sampson, and Company; New York: J. C. Derby, 1855.

A158 Boston: Phillips, Sampson, 1857.

A159 Boston: Crosby, Nichols, Lee & Co., 1860.

A160 Boston: Crosby & Nichols, 1863. This edition had an added t.p. illustrated in color.

(The University of Virginia copy has errors in printing and binding as follows: pp. xiv–xv are in reverse order, and xvi is printed on the verso of xiii.)

A161 Boston: Crosby & Nichols, 1865.

A162 Boston: Crosby & Ainsworth: New York: O. S. Felt, 1866. The illustrated t.p. for both locations has the imprint of the Boston publishers.

A163 New York: T. Y. Crowell. 1877.

A164 New York: J. W. Lovell Co. [188?] "Red Line" edition.

A165 New York: J. B. Alden, 1883.

A166 New York: R. Worthington. 1884.

In many or all of the American issues the following physical changes have taken place from the London edition by Daly: the colophon "J. Davy & Sons, Printers, 137 Long Acre" is removed from the verso of the t.p., and the colophon "stereotyped by T. Caldwell, 19 Charterhouse Lane" disappears from the verso of p. 525. Despite the claim of the original edition that this came "with illustrations", the only illustration present in copies inspected was the portrait frontispiece.

[1855]?

A167 *The poetical works of George Crabbe.* With Life . . . Philadelphia, J. B. Lippincott & Co. [n.d.] pp. xvi + 496. 'Cabinet edition' inscribed on back of spine, but nowhere inside the volume. Prefatory matter misbound. (Washington & Lee University.)

This is the edition first issued by Gall & Inglis: item (A96) in the British list. Both title-pages have the American publisher's imprint.

1855

A168 *The poetical works of the Rev. George Crabbe* LL.D. With an essay on his genius and writings. Philadelphia: J. B. Perry, 1855. pp. 213 +[1](index).

The contents are of 'Poems, 1807'. This is a re-issue of the edition published by Daly in 1837, item (A75) in the British list.

A169 Perry's edition was re-issued in 1856.

A170 *The Borough; a poem*, by the Rev. George Crabbe . . . Philadelphia: J. B. Perry, 1855. pp. xxxii + 256. This is bound with item (A168) in the copy at the University of Texas, and appears to have been issued with it. This edition of *The Borough* is a re-issue of the one by Daly in 1839, item (A80) in the British list.

1856

A171 *The Rural Poetry of the English Language* illustrating the Seasons and Months of the Year, their Changes, Employments, Lessons, and Pleasures, Topographically Paragraphed; with a complete index: by Joseph William Jenks M.A., Boston: John P. Jewitt & Co., 1856. 4to.

Prints the following Crabbe poems:

The Village, (complete) – pp. 255–260.

'The Parish Register,' (in sections) – "Baptisms", pp. 315–322: "Marriages", pp. 369–374: "Burials", pp. 407–415.

[1879]?

A172 New York: Clark & Maynard. [n.d.].

The Village. With prefatory and explanatory notes. *See* British list item [ ].

A173 Idem dated 1861.

A174 New York: Maynard, Merrill & Co. 1898. 'Maynard's English Classics' series, no. 10.

1886
A175 *Poems by George Crabbe*. London & New York: Cassell & co., 1886. See item (A109) of the British list.

1910
A176 *The borough: a poem, in twenty four letters*. By the Rev. G. Crabbe. . . . Philadelphia: Bradford & Inskeep, 1910. pp. xxv + 330.

1966
A177 *The Library*. A facsimile reprint of the first edition. Harvard College Library copy. Boston: G. K. Hall & Co., 1966.

A IIb

1837

A178 *Blackwood's Magazine*, vol. 41: April 1837. pp. 464–465. Prints 'Parham Revisited', and an alternative version of part of 'Woman'.

1839

A179 *The Sacred Casket*, (2nd edition): 1839. Prints a version of lines 348–371 of 'Sir Eustace Grey' as a hymn called 'The Christian Pilgrim'.

1850

A180 HASTINGS, J. D. (ed.) *Posthumous sermons of George Crabbe*. Hatchard: 1850. Re-issued by Ann Arbor, University Microfilms: 1974.

1860

A181 JACKSON, W. *Old fashioned wit and humour*; with a prefatory letter from Crabbe.

1862

A182 LEADBEATER, M. *The Leadbeater Papers*. Bell & Daldy: 1862. Volume 2 contains a transcript (not completely accurate) of the correspondence between Crabbe and Mary Leadbeater.

1891

A183 DOWDEN, E. *The Illustrated London News*: June 20, 1891. p. 818. Hitherto unpublished extracts: 'Midnight' and 'The deserted wife.'

1896

A184 NICOLL, W. R. & WISE, T. J. (eds.) *Literary anecdotes of the nineteenth century*, vol. 2. 1896. pp. 143–171. Two poetical epistles. 'From The Devil. An epistle-general', & 'From the author. To Mira.'

1904

A185 HUCHON, R. Two unpublished poems of Crabbe. *The Monthly Review*, vol. 14: 1904. pp. 117–139. The poems are taken from Sir John Murray's MSS collection. The first is about "a jealous squire" thwarted by his nephew in his quest for an inheritance.

> 'Twas in a country of so fair a kind
> The boast of all residing in the place . . .

The other comprises one of the early drafts for what eventually became one of the *Posthumous Tales*. It dates from about 1822 and is in stanzas beginning

> O give me the hour that I love to spend
> When the heart is quite warm and the words are all free.

1906

A186 JOURDAIN, M. Treasure trove: some unpublished verse by Crabbe. *Book Monthly*: May 1906. pp. 544–548.

'To a Lady on leaving her at –'

'The friend in love'.

Verse letter to the Duke of Rutland.

Verses to the Duchess of Rutland.

(These, unknown to Jourdain, had previously been published in *The Casket*, edited by Mrs Blencoe, Murray, 1829, pp. 142–143.)

1922

A187 *The London Mercury*, vol. 35: September 1922. pp. 465–466. 'To Miss E.V. in her tenth year'.

1924

A188 *Mental Hygiene*, vol. 8: January 24 1924. p. 105. "Man's Life." Although listed by one bibliography as an uncollected poem this is simply the first few lines of *Tales*, II. 'The Parting Hour'.

1932

A189 FORSTER, E. M. Crabbe on smugglers; an unpublished letter. *The Spectator*, vol. 148; February 20, 1932. p. 245. A letter of November 11, 1819 to Hatchard the publisher, commenting on the critique of 'Smugglers and Poachers' in the *Christian Observer*. The letter also implies the amicable termination of the business association between Crabbe and Hatchard.

A190 GRIERSON, H. J. C. Scott, Shelley and Crabbe. *The Times Literary Supplement*, September 15, 1932. p. 643. Includes a letter from Crabbe to Scott, showing that Crabbe was, under the slightly blasé front he put on, very sensitive to criticism of his work.

A191 BULLOUGH, G. A letter from Crabbe to Scott. *The Times Literary Supplement*, September 22, 1932. p. 666. Letter dated from Trowbridge, June 1815. Acknowledges the gift from Scott of his poem *The Lord of the Isles*.

1938

A192 DAVENPORT, W. H. An uncollected poem of George Crabbe. *Notes and Queries*, vol. 175: 1938. p. 471. Reports that *The Literary Gazette* for August 16, 1817 prints "Verses by the Rev. G. Crabbe; written on the night of the 15th April, 17**, immediately before the perusal of a letter then received".

A193 WECTER, D. Four letters from George Crabbe to Edmund Burke: *The Review of English Studies*, vol. 14: 1938. pp. 298–309. The letters are dated 1781, 1782, and 1785. They shed some new light on the circumstances and timing of publication of *The Library*, and on the verses on the death of Lord Robert Manners.

1941

A194 FELLOWES, E. H. & PINE, E. The Tenbury discoveries. *The Times Literary Supplement*, September 20, 1941. p. 476. (Repeated in *Tenbury letters*; Golden Cockerel Press 1942. Edited by Fellowes and Pine.) Includes a letter from Crabbe to Mrs Norris. Describes his fits of "giddyness" and informs his correspondent, "I have long been gathering verses and completing Tales. . . ." The letter is dated March 14, 1818, from Trowbridge.

1950

A195 LAWSON, S. Crabbe thanks Jeffrey. *Notes and Queries*, vol. 195: December 9, 1950. p. 538. Crabbe's acknowledgement of the favourable review Jeffrey had given to *Poems* in the *Edinburgh Review*. "Be assured that the present Edition of the work should have been made more worthy of your Acceptance had Mr. Hatchard allowed me time sufficient for the Correction of general defects, whereas he scarcely gave me enough for the Removal of particular Blemishes . . ."

1951

A196 POLLARD, A. Two new letters of Crabbe. *The Review of English Studies*: October, 1951. pp. 375–377. The first of these is now in the Wentworth Woodhouse collection at Sheffield City Library. It enables us to be exact about the date of Crabbe's appointment as domestic chaplain at Belvoir. The second concerns the date of publication of *The Library*, which it places at March 16, 1785.

1960

A197 POLLARD, A. *New Poems by George Crabbe*, edited with an introduction by Arthur Pollard. Liverpool University Press, 1960. Contains hitherto unpublished poems edited from the Murray MSS.

1961

A198 BRUMBAUGH, T. B. An unpublished Crabbe sermon. *Notes and Queries*, new series, vol. 8: 1961. pp. 20–21. Summarizes a sermon of about 1814. The mood of this is very sombre, despite being on the text, 'The ransomed of the Lord shall return'. Isaiah. 35.x.

1965

A199 LINK, F. M. Three Crabbe Letters. *English Language Notes*, vol. 2: March,

1965. pp. 200–206. Mainly domestic letters dated December 5, 1814; March 25, 1825; and February 4, 1831.

1975

A200 FAULKNER, T. C. Letters of George Crabbe and Thomas Fulford. *The Review of English Studies*, vol. 26: February 1975. pp. 56–62. The letters by Crabbe discuss his facial neuralgia, and offer some thoughts on Milton's prosody. Thomas Fulford, who was Crabbe's successor at Trowbridge, writes to his mother to complain of the filth left by the Crabbes in the rectory!

B

Bibliographical Notes and Articles

B

B1 Bobart, H. T. *Notes and Queries*, 1st series, vol. 9: January 14, 1854. p. 35. Reports a mention in a second-hand book catalogue of five volumes of Crabbe MSS including poems, prayers and letters. The contributor asks for information on the present whereabouts of this material.

1863

B2 Blair, D. *Notes and Queries*, 3rd series, vol. 4: November 7, 1863. p. 375. Calls attention to a version of 'Woman' which is different from that published in *Poems 1807*, and which appeared in *Blackwood's Magazine*, April 1837.

1891

B3 Dowden, E. Relics of Crabbe. *The Illustrated London News*: June 20, 1891. p. 818. Describes the fragment called 'Midnight', and a poem called 'The deserted wife' or 'The deserted family' which had come from the Dawson Turner MSS collection.

1903

B4 Huchon, R. A brief appreciation . . . of the George Crabbe collection . . . on view at the Guildhall, Bath . . . : September 2, 1903. A description of the exhibits for the Crabbe celebrations. Provides a useful *catalogue raisonée* of the location of Crabbe material available at the turn of the century.

1905

B5 Gantz, C. *Celebrations for the one hundred and fiftieth anniversary of the birth of Crabbe*, to be held September 16 & 18 (1905), at Aldeburgh. *and Souvenir of the Crabbe celebrations*, and a catalogue of the exhibits.
The prospectus lists some lectures given, but not apparently subsequently reprinted. The souvenir has a useful list of MSS exhibited, with some of the owners of Crabbeiana at the time.

1936

B6 Sparrow, J. Query no. 90 *Bibliographical Notes and Queries*, vol. 2 no. 1: January 1936.
Notes the issue of *Works*, 1823 with and without illustrations. Queries the relative dates on which each state may have been first issued.

1949

B7 Batdorf, F. P. An unrecorded edition of Crabbe. *Papers of the Bibliographical Society of America*, vol. 43: 1949. pp. 349–350.
Published by William and Robert Chambers in 1838, this edition of *Poems* had

hitherto escaped the attention of the bibliographers. It is "a small testimony to the reputation of the author in the years following his death".

1950

B8 Batdorf, F. P. Notes on three editions of Crabbe's *Tales in Verse*. *Papers of the Bibliographical Society of America*, vol. 44: 1950. pp. 276–279. A bibliographical description of the 3rd, 4th, and 7th editions of *Tales*.

1951

B9 Todd, W. B. Two issues of the *Works* of Crabbe. *Papers of the Bibliographical Society of America*, vol. 45; 1951.

Describes the differing states (with and without Westall's plates) of the five and eight volume sets of *Works* which Murray issued in 1823.

B10 Batdorf, F. P. Crabbe: an unrecorded early anthology. *Studies in Bibliography*, vol. 3: 1951. p. 266.

A description of the *Tales and Miscellaneous Poems* published by Bohn in 1847.

1952

B11 Batdorf, F. P. The Murray reprints of Crabbe: a publisher's record. *Studies in Bibliography*, vol. 4: 1952. pp. 192–199.

A statistical breakdown of the various issues of the eight volume set which was first issued in 1834. Provides a valuable source of information on the public demand for Crabbe during this period.

1954

B12 Prichard, M. F. L. Crabbe's first appearance in print? *Notes and Queries*, new series 1: June 1954. p. 263.

Suggests that Crabbe may be the "Master G.C. at Mr. Harvey's school in Bungay" who answered a mathematical problem set in the *Norwich Mercury* on August 16, 1766.

B13 [Anon] George Crabbe 1754–1832. *A catalogue of the exhibition of works and manuscripts held at the Moot Hall, Aldeburgh*. Aldeburgh Festival Committee: 1954. Detailed bibliographical accounts of a number of Crabbe books and MSS on display for the 200th anniversary of his birth.

B14 [Anon] Crabbe at Aldeburgh. *The Times Literary Supplement*: July 2, 1954. p. 431. A review of the exhibits at the bicentenary exhibition.

1955

B15 [Anon] Facsimilies of all the title-pages of first editions of Crabbe published during the poet's lifetime. In *Proceedings of the Suffolk Institute of Archaeology and Natural History*, Vol. 26, part 2: 1955. pp. 98–136. Re-publishes the exhibition material.

1956

B16 Pollard, G. The early poems of George Crabbe and the *Lady's Magazine*. *Bodleian Library Record*, vol. 5: 1956. pp. 149–156. Sorts out, once and for all, the mystery of the *Lady's Magazine*, for which Crabbe was claimed by his son to have written some of his earliest pieces. Though a *Lady's Magazine* had been discovered it did not contain the poems recorded by his son. Pollard reports that there were two magazines of this title, and that Crabbe in fact wrote for both of them.

C

Bibliographies of Crabbe

C

INTRODUCTORY NOTE

There has not previously been any attempt at an exhaustive bibliography of editions of Crabbe, nor at a check-list of critical articles on him. Partial bibliographies of texts and/or critical works exist in the following – (usually as reference lists of what the particular author has consulted):

1888
C1 Kebbel; *Life of Crabbe*.

1905/7
C2 Ward's edition of *Poems*

1907
C3 Clarke's translation of Huchon.

1965
C4 Sigworth; *Nature's sternest painter*.

C5 Chamberlain; *George Crabbe*.

1972
C6 Pollard; *Crabbe*; in "The Critical Heritage" series.

C7 Blackburne; *The Restless Ocean*.

1976
C8 New; *George Crabbe's poetry*.

C9 Hatch, *Crabbe's arabesque*.

By far the most complete list has been that in *The New Cambridge Bibliography of English Literature*, supplemented each year by the *Annual Bibliography*.

D

Contemporary Reviews
of Crabbe's Works

D

Section D is a chronological list of reviews of each of Crabbe's volumes in order of publication. The terminal date for this section is fixed at 1837 since the posthumous poems of the 1834 edition comprised the last appearance of any new poems authorized by Crabbe. Up to about 1837 the various issues of this edition continued to attract critics to assess the posthumous poems as new work. Reviews thereafter tend to be retrospective, and to deal with Crabbe's output *in toto*.

THE CANDIDATE

D1 (Anon.) *The Critical Review*, vol. 50: September 1780. pp. 233–235. A jocose piece of annihilation. Makes perfectly apposite objections to Crabbe's sense in places, and criticizes his use of compound adjectives.

D2 Cartwright, E. *The Monthly Review*, vol. 63: September 1780. pp. 226–227. "Besides some few other trifling innaccuracies, his rhymes are not always regulated by the purest standard of pronunciation." In one respect the poem is materially defective – "the want of a subject to make a proper . . . impression on the mind."

D3 (Anon.) *The Gentleman's Magazine*, vol. 50: October 1780. p. 475. Gives the poet not "much encouragement to stand a poll at Parnassus."

THE LIBRARY

D4 (Anon.) *The Critical Review*, vol. 52: August 1781. pp. 148–150. "A vein of good sense and philosophical reflection runs through this little performance." On the whole the review is much more favourable than any previous criticism Crabbe had met with in the press.

D5 (Anon.) *The Gentleman's Magazine*, vol. 51: October 1781. p. 474. Gives the poem a very tepid approval.

D6 Cartwright, E. *The Monthly Review*, vol. 65: December 1781. pp. 423–425. Calls the poem "the production of no common pen."

THE VILLAGE

D7 (Anon.) *The Critical Review*, vol. 56: July 1783. pp. 60–61.

The poem deserves much approbation both for language and sentiment. The reviewer notices the abrupt ending, but does not actually condemn it.

D8 (Anon.) *The British Magazine and Review*, vol. 3: August 1783. pp. 132–134.

The poem is "a formidable rival" to Goldsmith's *Deserted Village*. Its picture of rural life is gloomy, but not exaggerated. The panegyric on Robert Manners would have been better published separately. "We cannot too strongly recommend the perusal of Mr. Crabbe's *Village* to every reader of taste and sensibility."

D9 Cartwright, E. *The Monthly Review*, vol. 69: November 1783. pp. 418–421.

Thinks the poet may have erred as far in favour of the sordid side of village life as Goldsmith did in favour of the ideal. "The first part asserts as a general proposition what can only be affirmed by individuals, the second part contradicts the assertion of the first." Finds it a poem of good parts but defective in its overall plan.

D10 (Anon.) *The Gentleman's Magazine*, vol. 53: December 1783. pp. 1041–1042.

Criticizes the poet because he represents "only the dark side ... the poverty and misery attendant on the peasant."

THE NEWSPAPER

D11 (Anon.) *The Critical Review*, vol. 59: April 1785. pp. 345–348.

"His talents are ... more conspicuous in the pathetic and descriptive than in the satyric line." Despite blemishes of expression the poem is "entitled to rank in the first class of modern productions."

D12 Burney, C. *The Monthly Review*, vol. 73: November 1785. pp. 374–376.

This poem is not equal to *The Library*. Burney frowns on Crabbe's parodies of Pope, and finds his language not very poetical. Yet "the author is possessed of genius, taste, and imagination, and a manly vein of poetry."

POEMS, 1807

D13 (Anon.) *The Gentleman's Magazine*, vol. 77: November 1807. pp. 1033–1040, and vol. 78: January 1808. p. 59.

Finds the poet's judgement matured and recommends "a perusal of this interesting publication to the Amateurs of elegant Poetry."

D14 (Anon.) *The Critical Review*, 3rd series, vol. 12: December 1807. pp. 439–440.

Notes the force and truth of *Poems*. The reviewer still likes best the poems which had the approval of Burke, Fox and Johnson. Since they approved of the author, who are the present generation to carp about him!

D15 (Anon.) *The Anti-Jacobin Review and Magazine*, vol. 28: December 1807. pp. 337–347.

Crabbe is "entitled to rank with the first moral poets of the age" . . . "Few poems are better calculated to interest the feelings; to meliorate the heart, and to inform the mind." This is the first criticism to call him the "poet of Nature."

D16 [Anon.] *The Poetical Register*, vol. 6: 1807. p. 538.

Brief, but very enthusiastic, notice of *Poems*.

D17 [Anon.] *The Oxford Review*, vol. 3: January 1808. pp. 87–96.

Praises Crabbe's "talent for the pathetic," and is generally approving, though not of his tendency to introduce lines from other poets into his work.

D18 Jeffrey, F. *The Edinburgh Review*, vol. 12: April 1808. pp. 131–151.

Praises Crabbe's truth and force, joined to a power of selection. Calls him "one of the most original, nervous, and pathetic poets of the present century." Points to the "many gleams of gaiety and humour," contrasts him favourably with the Lake School, and coins the much-used phrase about Crabbe's "Chinese accuracy."

D19 Denman, T. *The Monthly Review*, vol. 56: June 1808. pp. 170–179.

Notes the all-round improvement in the new pieces included in this volume.

D20 [Anon.] *The British Critic*, vol. 31: June 1808. pp. 590–595.

Admires his "excursive fancy, judicious selection, and harmonious structure."

D21 [Anon.] *The Annual Review*, vol. 6: 1808. pp. 514–521.

Notes Crabbe's originality – both of virtues and of faults. Finds him "little formed to amuse or captivate; but powerful to strike . . . to instruct." Makes what is probably the first reference to Crabbe as "a kind of Dutch painter," a concept which later becomes standard currency in Crabbe criticism.

D22 [Anon.] *The Universal Magazine*, second series, vol. 10: November 1808. pp. 434–438. & pp. 513–518. Vol. 11: February 1811. pp. 39–45 & pp. 127–132.

Picks holes in Crabbe's grammar and syntax, but approves of his method and manner. Likens his humour and playfulness to that of Cowper. Deplores the sycophantic effusiveness of the Dedication.

D23 Montgomery, J. *The Eclectic Review*, vol. 5: January 1809. pp. 40–49.

Finds Crabbe has talents "of the middle order, without much fancy, fervour, grace, or feeling". His strengths are his "truth, spirit and discrimination". Remarks on his "Dutch drollery", and notes the originality of the topics he chooses.

THE BOROUGH

D24 Denman, T. *The Monthly Review*, vol. 61: April 1810. pp. 396–409.

Crabbe is the "Hogarth of poetry" – the first occasion this analogy is drawn, though it becomes a commonplace one. The new poem is merely *The Village* extended beyond all reasonable bounds." The structure is "without composition." *The Borough* presents "an unfavourable opinion of mankind and . . . (an) austere morality." Pleads with the author to undertake more correcting of his material before he releases it to the press.

D25 Jeffrey, F. *The Edinburgh Review*, vol. 16: April 1810. pp. 30–55.

Finds greater faults and fewer beauties in this than in any previous Crabbe volume. The two principal faults are in the description of things not worth describing, and in the excitation of disgust rather than pity. The disgust exercises Jeffrey a good deal. He is severe on 'The Parish Clerk', which he does not like at all.

D26 Montgomery, J. *The Eclectic Review*, vol. 6: June 1810. pp. 546–561.

As with his review of *Poems*, Montgomery takes Crabbe to task for his obsequious dedication. The poet is castigated for his attitude to sects in religion, but 'Peter Grimes' is singled out for particular praise. On the whole *The Borough* is found to be too long, too diffuse, and too full of lapses of taste. This is particularly true of 'The Parish Clerk.'

D27 [Anon.] *The Gentleman's Magazine*, vol. 80, part i: January–June 1810. pp. 445, 548, 633.

Brief notice, with quotation, suggesting that Crabbe's merits so far outweigh his faults that rehearsal of either is superfluous.

D28 [Anon.] *The Critical Review*, 3rd series, vol. 20: July 1810. pp. 291–305.

A succinct catalogue of Crabbe's merits and faults. The preface is disliked. Calls attention to his "Dutch minuteness." Reprobates the slovenly technical work by either proof-reader or publisher. The reviewer particularly admires 'The Parish Clerk.'

D29 [Anon.] *La Belle Assemblée*, n.s. vol. 2: July 1810. pp. 36–40, & Supplement for 1811. pp. 353–354.

"It really is a public acquisition when such a poet as Mr Crabbe appears"

". . . he is not only the first Poet now living of his kind, but . . . he is likewise the first, of his kind, of any that the country has ever produced. He is at the head of a new species of poetry, the comic-descriptive."

The Supplement declares Crabbe might be compared with Rowlandson, "whose roughest and rudest sketches preserve a likeness, and whose harshest lines produce a more striking effect than the *taille douce* of the best French engravers." Admits he dwells too much on the ugly aspects of life, and thus "he becomes prosaic."

D30 [Anon.] *The Monthly Mirror*, vol. 8: August 1810. pp. 126–134, & October 1810. pp. 280–284.

Speaks of "this frightful Preface." The poem is unbalanced because of the preponderant tone of gloom, as in 'Peter Grimes.'

D31 Gifford, W. *The Quarterly Review*, vol. 4: November 1810. pp. 281–312.

Designates Crabbe as "the poet of reality", for which it reprehends him, as being antipathetic to "fancy", and to the pleasure for which we normally turn to poetry. Offers a theory on contemporary thinking about the art of poetry. Asks whether there can legitimately be a "Dutch school" of poetry and lists the liabilities Crabbe's art suffers from in apparently making the assumption that there *can* be a "Dutch school". Complains that "he lives without an atmosphere". The poem is only good in parts because the author lacks a sense of governing taste.

D32 [Anon.] *The New Annual Register for 1810*. p. 368.
Brief notice of *The Borough*. Sings the praises of the volume.

D33 [Anon.] *The Poetical Register*, vol. 8: 1810. p. 554.
An adulatory review. Praises Crabbe's descriptive powers, and his "high poetry."

D34 [Anon.] *The British Critic*, vol. 37: March 1811. pp. 236–247.
Thinks *The Borough* is the best poetry Crabbe has published, but cannot see the excellence of 'Peter Grimes'.

D35 [Anon.] *The Christian Observer*, vol. 10: August 1811. pp. 502–511.
Begins the debate about Crabbe's treatment of Methodism in Letter IV of *The Borough*. For his handling of this topic, and for his portrait of the vicar in Letter III, the article takes him to task most severely. Some admiration for the poem is tempered by reproof of his emphasis on the sordid and the eccentric. Crabbe has "an ill-advised fondness for antithesis . . . and a slovenly system of versification."

TALES IN VERSE

D36 [Anon.] *The Scotish* (sic) *Review*, vol. 3, no. vii: September 1812. pp. 60–94.

The *Tales* are defective in their moral message and often in their structure. Claims to see a discrepancy between the Shakespearian mottoes and the poems Crabbe constructs upon them. The volume has too much "mere description," too few striking incidents, and is over-burdened with Crabbe's own conservative prejudices.

D37 [Anon.] *The British Review*, vol. 4: October 1812. pp. 51–64.

Finds the poet "too studious of simplicity". While he may be "happy at seizing the little peculiarities of mind", he presents things in too bare a manner and with too much emphasis upon pain. There is praise mingled with this general condemnation, particularly praise for his moral purity, but on the whole the reviewer feels the volume represents a falling-off in Crabbe's talents.

D38 [Anon.] *scourge* vol. 4: November 1812. pp. 386–394.

Castigates the poet for being impervious to criticisms made of his earlier volumes. Though there is much to praise, his tone is too gloomy.

D39 Jeffrey, F. *The Edinburgh Review*, vol. 20: November 1812. pp. 277–305.

Finds in this volume a slightly more "amiable and consoling" view of human nature, but the similarities with faults in his earlier volumes are too strong. *Tales in Verse* is more directly moral than Crabbe's previous volumes. He is praised for shifting his attention away from an exclusive account of the poor and towards "middling" people and common emotions.

D40 [Anon.] *The Critical Review*, 4th series, vol. 2: December 1812. pp. 561–579.

Notes how the debate on Crabbe's status divides the critical world into two radically opposed sides. Thinks this volume should have been called something like "Characteristic Sketches of Life" rather than *Tales in Verse*. The reviewer wonders if Crabbe has been altogether well-advised to start moving away from his concentration upon low life. His prosaic openings are strongly objected to. Whilst acknowledging that the poet does revise his work before publication, he is still found culpably careless in this matter.

D41 [Anon.] *The Eclectic Review*, vol. 8: December 1812. pp. 1240–1253.

Crabbe lacks "fancy", and he insists too much on painful reality. Imagination is fettered by this tendency, and his verse goes "jogging on a broken-winded Pegasus through all the flats and bogs of Parnassus".

D42 Denman, T. *The Monthly Review*, vol. 69: December 1812. pp. 352–364.
Much undiscriminating minuteness and coarse peculiarity spoil what would otherwise be a most enjoyable volume.

D43 [Anon.] *The Gentleman's Magazine*, vol. 82: July–December 1812. pp. 241–244 & 346–349.
Liberal quotation interspersed with highly enthusiastic comments. Speaks of "this accurate delineator of human nature."

D44 [Anon.] *The New Review*, vol. 1: February 1813. pp. 176–178.
Crabbe has the accuracy of a Chinese painter. Readers with a taste for epic will leave him alone; those who prefer minute descriptions of character will appreciate this volume.

D45 [Anon.] *The Universal Magazine*, vol. 19: March 1813. pp. 128–133 & 219–224.
Accords the *Tales* very high praise, liking even Crabbe's system of versification. His "naturalness" is much approved of. He is a master of the pathetic, and an inheritor of Dryden's manner. In making fiction the ally of truth he has performed a valuable service to literature.

D46 [Anon.] *The British Critic*, vol. 41: April 1813, pp. 380–386.
Sees so little change from previous work by Crabbe in this poem that the reviewer thinks the *Tales* "cut out from longer poems . . . (and) . . . primarily intended to figure . . . (there)." Crabbe is so strongly individual, his characteristics are so marked, that the faults themselves seem an ineradicable part of the whole. Despite such objections, the review is by no means all unfavourable.

D47 [Anon.] *The Country Magazine*, vol. 1: January–April 1813. pp. 48–54 & 146–156.
No copy available for inspection.

TALES OF THE HALL

D48 Wilson, J. ("Christopher North") *Blackwood's Magazine*, vol. 5: July 1819. pp. 469–483.
Sees Crabbe, Burns and Wordsworth as the three great poets of the day who have all chosen to limit themselves to "local" scenes and characters. Of the three, Crabbe is particular for his "almost miraculous" powers of describing common actuality. The plan of the new volume is approved, and the author is found to be "mellowed and softened" in his attitudes to life.

D49 [Anon.] *The Literary Chronicle and Weekly Review*, vol. 1: July 10 1819. pp. 113–115 & July 17 1819. pp. 133–134.

"Feeling, energy, originality, minute observation, an unrivalled vividness, and not infrequently a certain painful truth of painting, are the characteristics of Mr Crabbe's styles." His stories lack interest but have a unique gift for revealing character.

D50 [Anon.] *Green Man*, July 17, 1819. pp. 68–69.

Sees the same merits in this volume as in all Crabbe's previous ones. "The current of his mind still enjoys all its wonted serenity. His philosophy is as orthodox as usual, his sympathies as inflamed, and his lessons as wholesome and practical. As a poet he possesses a singular reverence for truth . . . he is ambitious of fidelity almost to excess."

D51 Jeffrey, F. *The Edinburgh Review*, vol. 32: July 1819. pp. 118–148.

Jeffrey puzzles over the alternating excellences and lapses which he has always found in Crabbe, and which he still discerns alongside each other in this volume. He believes the odd combination to spring from the "directness" of Crabbe's inspiration – "the courage to write from (his) own impressions . . . (not to) . . . fear the laugh or wonder of the more shallow and barren part of his readers." Crabbe draws men in "their true postures and dimensions, and with all the imperfections that actually belong to their condition". Though, in this sense, he is "satirical", he is not misanthropic, and Jeffrey defends his low-life subjects where these are still present in *Tales of the Hall*.

D52 [Anon.] *The British Critic*, 2nd series, vol. 12: September 1819. pp. 285–301.

Declares a dislike of Crabbe's "school", and attempts due praise despite this stumbling-block. Finds this volume alarmingly more variable in quality than anything prior to it. Crabbe describes "man in his working-day not his Sunday clothes". He is, metaphorically, "building pigstyes round the Parthenon". His sense of rhythm is defective and at best he is the "skilful anatomist of a diseased patient".

D53 [Anon.] *The Edinburgh Monthly Review*, vol. 2: September 1819. pp. 287–302.

This is the best volume Crabbe has produced. The critic offers a rather adulatory catalogue of Crabbe's merits.

D54 [Anon.] *The New British Lady's Magazine*, third series, vol. 3: September 1819. pp. 133–134.

The poetry of Crabbe is generally confined to the delineation of the British

Character; he views society with a scrutinizing not a lofty eye; he does not introduce us to the splendid tragic hero, but to a family circle in common life, wherein we are sure to recognize many characters who come under our daily observation, and in whose actions we rarely perceive any improbability.

D55 [Anon.] *The Monthly Magazine*, vol. 48: September 1819. p. 155.

Crabbe is "the inimitable poet of truth and nature". He is not depressing even though he is "moral" and writes of "Dutch" realities.

D56 [Anon.] *The New Monthly Magazine*, vol. 12: September 1819. pp. 198–205, & 324–328.

The poet has, to the gratification of the writer, meliorated his low-life studies with more benevolent glances at "middle-ranking" things and people. Crabbe's benign morality is praised.

D57 [Anon.] *The Christian Observer*, vol. 18: October 1819. pp. 650–668.

Likens Crabbe to Wilkie. He lacks the command of "great" (i.e. heroic) powers, virtues, and vices. Notes an almost deliberate attempt to eschew the epic style in this volume. The reviewer does not relish Crabbe's kind of Christianity. Instead of showing us the effect of good qualities on inherently bad ones, he perversely chooses to show the exact opposite.

D 58 [Anon.] *The Monthly Review*, vol. 90: November 1819. pp. 225–238.

Opens with the general proclamation that modern poetry has gone to the Dutch dogs! Crabbe, to his detriment, has forgotten Burke and Johnson, and he now writes far too laxly. Some of the connecting passages in *Tales of the Hall* are hopeless fustian. But his humour is praised, and the ending of the poem is found deeply moving.

D59 [Anon.] *The Gentleman's Magazine*, vol. 89: 1819. pp. 45–47.

An adulatory review, which even approves of "the manly and ingenous prose" of the Preface!

D60 [Anon.] *The Literary Gazette for 1819*. pp. 424–426.

Approves of the new volume, finding it to be entirely in the customary mould of Crabbe's work.

D61 [Anon.] *La Belle Assemblée* New series vol. 20, Supplement for 1819. pp. 343–344.

Mr. Crabbe is a peculiar kind of poet, but all his writings breathe a philanthropic love to the whole human race . . . when we close one of his unfinished volumes, we are in haste to take it up again.

D62 [Anon.] *The Eclectic Review*, second series vol. 13: February 1820. pp. 114–133.

Adopts a jocose tone about the Preface to this volume. Takes the poet to task seriously for his religious sentiments: the reviewer is saddened at Crabbe's refusal to indulge meliorating imagination in his admittedly well-observed accounts of actuality. Ends its rather pompous resume with a ringing affirmation of Crabbe's permanent value.

LIFE & POETICAL WORKS, 1834

Reviews of this edition concentrate on different volumes, since the *Life* of Crabbe by his son, which comprised volume 1, was a new work, and the *Posthumous Tales* which appeared a few months later as volume 8 had not hitherto been seen by the critics either, although all the material in volumes 2–7 had been.

D63 Lockhart, J. G. *The Quarterly Review*, vol. 50: January 1834. pp. 468–508 (general review) & vol. 52: August 1834. pp. 184–203. (On the *Posthumous Tales*.)

Expresses surprise that "the poet of the poor" is popular with the upper classes, but not with those who were his principal subjects. Denies emphatically the gloom which some critics ascribe to Crabbe. The posthumous poems are inferior to his earlier work, but still worth publishing: Lockhart finds them more "amusing" than some of the earlier series.

D64 [Anon.] *The Athenaeum*: 1834. pp. 81–84, 165, 328, 503, 568, 636.

(Reviewed each volume as it appeared.) Great enthusiasm for the *Life*, and admiration for the *Posthumous Tales*, where no real falling-off in quality is discerned. Of the other volumes the reviewer has mixed feelings, complaining that some of the familiar poems have been over-edited.

D65 [Anon.] *Tait's Edinburgh Magazine*, (new series), vol. 1: April 1834. pp. 161–168.

Crabbe has never been popular enough: "of late he has been undeservedly neglected." Finds him far less gloomy than his undeserved reputation makes him out to be. His "truth" is much praised, and his integrity as "poet of the poor."

D66 Peabody, O. W. B. *The North American Review*, vol. 39: July 1834. pp. 135–166.

Thinks Crabbe is "stern" because his life itself was stern, but his overall validity as a spokesman on the human lot transcends his moods of gloom.

D67 [Anon.] *The British Critic*, vol. 16: July 1834. pp. 56–70.

Gives a lengthy resumé of the *Life*. Of the poetry, finds *The Borough* to have some of Crabbe's finest touches because the background was immediate and real to the poet. "Paucity of incident" is the chief fault of his tales. His principal merit is vigour, though too often offset by a corresponding coarseness.

D68 [Anon.] *The Monthly Review*, n.s., vol. 3: September 1834. pp. 101–115.

Crabbe is a poet of character, not of externals. Stresses his moral intentions and praises him as an innovator.

D69 [Anon.] *The Eclectic Review*, 3rd series, vol. 11: March 1834. pp. 253–278. (*Life*) & 3rd series, vol. 12: October 1834. pp. 305–314. (*Posthumous Tales*).

Stresses Crabbe's benevolence which underlies "the lessons of a grey and reverend Moralist." Likens the poet to Teniers or Cuyp. Concurs with *The Quarterly Review* in finding the *Posthumous Tales* more cheerful, on the whole, than earlier volumes of Crabbe had been.

D70 [Anon.] *The Gentleman's Magazine*, n.s. vol. 1: March 1834. pp. 253–264. (*Life*) & n.s. vol. 2: December 1834. pp. 563–575. (*Posthumous Tales*).

Notes the differences of opinion between the critics who have written on Crabbe over the years, and finds praise for their general disinterest and impartiality. Believes Crabbe will last, despite the fact that his reputation was slow to rise. This was because his subjects and his manner were different from anything hitherto attempted. Over the years Crabbe changed: his last work is less "low" and less "harsh". His truth is praised. The tone of *Posthumous Tales* is described as one of "Evening-tide".

D71 Empson, W. *The Edinburgh Review*, vol. 60: January 1835. pp. 255–296.

The posthumous poems are markedly inferior to Crabbe's earlier work. Whilst "truth" is allowed to be one of his principal qualities, it is only a "partial truth." *Posthumous Tales* has too much material which repeats ideas Crabbe had already expressed, and the tone is too gloomy.

D72 [Anon.] *The New England Magazine*, vol. 8: March 1835. pp. 215–220.

Review of the American edition of the *Life*. Notes Crabbe's "Teniers-like" reality. He founded no new school, and wrote without a theory. His analyses of life emphasize his own early hardship. "The genius of Crabbe was severe, even to sternness", but he has "deep and tender sympathy with human suffering".

D73 [Anon.] *The London Review*, vol. 1: July 1835. pp. 316–341.

Crabbe never showed any intellectual powers, merely a talent for observation.

He lacks human sympathy, having been soured in his youth. The reviewer dislikes his "cold resignation to the existance of human suffering," and he finds the posthumous work to be "duplicates . . . (made) . . . with half-palsied hands and faded colours."

D74 [Anon.] *The New York Review*, vol. 1: March 1837. pp. 96–109.

Crabbe's reputation has been justifiably consistent. If the poet is gloomy, so is life itself, and this demonstrates his "truth". As "the first poet of the poor" Crabbe is unique. His kindliness is singled out for praise, with his strong religious feelings. Far from being "Pope in worsted stockings", he is not even of Pope's school.

The various re-issues of the 8 volume *Works* continued to elicit critical appraisals. Since these are not strictly "contemporary" criticisms, however, they will be found in the 'Critical Essays' section.

E

Full-Length Critical and Biographical Studies

E

Section E lists complete books which deal wholly or principally with Crabbe and which cover his entire literary career and range. Certain monographs seem to fall between this and the next category. Their insertion in section F is a reflection of their length rather than of their quality.

1834

E1 Crabbe, G. (Junior). *The Life of the Rev. George Crabbe, LL.B. by his son the Rev. George Crabbe, A.M.* Murray; 1834. pp. 322.

Comprises vol. 1 of the 8 vol. *Works*, edited by the poet's son. This remains the standard work on Crabbe's life, despite inaccuracies and a tendency to make him appear a more benign and equable man than he probably was. Often acclaimed as "a minor classic of Victorian biography." There have been re-issues and re-prints as follows:

E2 S. Spottiswoode, London; 1834. pp. 311. The t.p. of this edition has 'LL.D.' for 'LL.B.'

E3 James Munroe & Co., Cambridge and Boston; 1834. pp. xii + 311.

E4 Carey, Lee and Blanchard, Pennsylvania; 1835. pp. 330. The t.p. of this edition runs as follows: "Life of the Rev. George Crabbe with his letters and journals. By the Rev. George Crabbe, A.M. his son."

E5 G. Dearborn, New York; 1837. pp. xi + 311. 12mo.

E6 John Murray; 1847. (In the one volume edition of Crabbe's works. For further re-issues of this see the section on 'Editions published after 1834'.)

E7 Oxford University Press; 1932. 'The World's Classics' series. pp. xxiv + 324.

E8 The Cresset Press; 1947. 'The Cresset Library' series. pp. xxx + 280.

E9 Chanticleer Press, New York; (1947). pp. 286.

E10 Clodd, E. *George Crabbe: a biography*. Joseph Buck, Aldeburgh; 1865. Biographical fragments of no value except as a collector's curiosity item.

1888

E11 Kebbel, T. E. *The Life of George Crabbe*. Walter Scott; 1888; pp. 157. Contains a very incomplete bibliography. For the main part a superficial redaction of the *Life* by George Crabbe junior. Until the last chapter there are very few critical observations or judgements. (Facsimile reprint by the Kennikat Press; 1972).

1903

E12 Ainger, A. C. *Crabbe*. 'English Men of Letters' series. Macmillan; 1903. pp. viii + 210.

More humane, better informed, and more incisive than Kebbel, this still depends heavily on the *Life*, by Crabbe's son.

Reprinted by Gale Research Co. USA: 1970.

1906

E13 Huchon, R. *Un Poete Realiste Anglais. George Crabbe 1754–1832.* Paris: 1906. pp. xi + 688.

A monumental attempt at Crabbe scholarship. Minute and particular biographical detail is supplied from evidence not available to Crabbe's son. This is essential for anyone wishing to know Crabbe, though its insights and judgements are by no means reliable where criticism takes over from biography. (*See* E14 below for English translation.)

1907

E14 Clarke, F. (translator). *George Crabbe and his times, 1754–1832.* John Murray; 1907. pp. xvi + 561.

English translation of Huchon (above). Contains a bibliography.

1913

E15 Broadley, A. M. & Jerrold, W. *The Romance of an Elderly Poet: a hitherto unknown chapter in the life of George Crabbe revealed by his ten years correspondence with Elizabeth Charter from 1815–1825.* Stanley Paul; 1913. pp. xii + 309.

An account of Crabbe's extraordinary literary flirtations, particularly of the one with Elizabeth Charter. Poorly edited, and with flaccid commentary, this does not make edifying reading except for the Crabbe specialist.

1933

E16 Evans, J. H. *The Poems of George Crabbe: a literary and historical study.*
The Sheldon Press, London; Macmillan, New York; 1933. pp. 208.

A fanciful and amateur attempt to link passages in Crabbe's poetry with his various incumbencies. Of no critical value.

1955

E17 Haddakin, L. *The Poetry of Crabbe*. Chatto and Windus; 1955. pp. 176.

Makes a claim for taking Crabbe very seriously as an important poet – the first book to do this since Huchon, (q.v.) above. Whilst willing to acknowledge the limitations of his art, insists that he has been undervalued.

1965

E18 Chamberlain, R. L. *George Crabbe*. Twayne Publishers inc., New York; 1965. pp. 188.

A sympathetic study of Crabbe, which manages to make one admire the poet and brings the man to life as well.

E19 Sigworth, O. F. *Nature's sternest painter: five essays on the poetry of George Crabbe*. University of Arizona Press, Tucson; 1965. pp. viii + 191.

The five essays are entitled 'Crabbe and the eighteenth century', 'Crabbe in the Romantic Movement', 'Crabbe as nature poet', 'Crabbe as narrative poet', 'Criticism and critique'.

1972

E20 Blackburn, N. *The Restless Ocean: the story of George Crabbe the Aldeburgh poet 1754–1832*. Terence Dalton, Lavenham; 1972. pp. 236.

A very readable biography. Though offering some fresh biographical evidence, this never quite succeeds in replacing the earlier biography by Huchon. Its critical judgements are sometimes eccentric. Contains many illustrations.

E21 Pollard, A. (compiler). *Crabbe: the critical heritage*. 'The Critical Heritage' series. Routledge and Kegan Paul; 1972. pp. 495. (See heading to the "contemporary reviews" section).

Assembles most of the contemporary criticisms of Crabbe together with a representative selection of more recent views.

1976

E22 Jain, B. B. *The poetry of George Crabbe*. 'Salzburg studies in English literature: Romantic reassessment, No. 37'. Salzburg Institute fur Englische Sprache und Literature; pp. 336. (USA distributor, The Humanities Press).

Full of errors, of downright "howlers", and misguided in many of its judgements. Seems to add absolutely nothing to the canon of Crabbe criticism.

E23 New, P. *George Crabbe's poetry*. The Macmillan Press Ltd.; 1976. pp. 248.

Sets Crabbe's poetry in the literary and ethical context of his time. The core of his work belongs substantially between Johnson's Shakespeare and the major English novels of the following five decades. The general theses of the book are exemplified with some penetrating analyses of the poems, though Crabbe's humour may be undervalued.

E24 Hatch, R. B. *Crabbe's Arabesque. Social Drama in the Poetry of George Crabbe.* McGill-Queen's University Press; 1976. pp. 284.

Demonstrates Crabbe's development in the handling of dramatic structures in which conflicting questions clash or are reconciled. Concentrates upon social issues: workhouses, the game laws, social schism, art, etc. Finds *Tales of the Hall* to be the final summation of what Crabbe had been striving to say: "in *Tales of the Hall* Crabbe is able to combine his empirical view of man's imperfectibility with a sense of morality by creating in his poetry the machinery to accommodate his vision of the richness and complexity of the external world . . .'

1977

E25 Bareham, T. *George Crabbe.* Vision Press Ltd.; 1977. pp. 245.

Examines Crabbe's poetry in relationship to contemporary ideas on religion, law, politics, psychology and aesthetics.

F

Critical Articles

F

Section F contains magazine and review articles, learned notes, monographs, transcriptions of lectures, etc. Some extremely peripheral items from *Notes and Queries* have not been listed, and reviews of specific books are included only when they seem to make an individual statement about Crabbe as well as about the volume they are reviewing. Chapters from literary histories are listed where they add new light or information to Crabbe criticism. In all these cases the dividing lines are tenuous and the editor has exercised his personal judgement, for better or worse.

1815

F1 Talfourd, Sir T. N. An attempt to estimate the poetical talent of the present age, including a sketch of the history of poetry and the characters of Southey, Crabbe, Scott, Moore, Byron, Campbell, Lamb, Coleridge, and Wordsworth. *The Pamphleteer*, vol. 10: May 1815. The article occupies pp. 413–471; the Crabbe section is pp. 437–444.

Praises the moral basis of Crabbe's art. Argues that, since life itself is not all pleasant, art does not need to be either. Crabbe is "Hogarthian" in that he directs our attention, never merely to the sordid side of life, but to the implications of that aspect of things.

1816

F2 [Crabbe, G.] Memoirs of eminent persons: a biographical account of the Rev. George Crabbe, LL.B. *The New Monthly Magazine and Universal Register*, vol. 4: January 1816. pp. 511–517.

The only autobiographical account of Crabbe's life. The style is coy and stilted, and the poet reveals disappointingly little about himself which cannot be learned more fully elsewhere.

(Reprinted in *The Annual Biography*, vol. 17: 1833. pp. 11–32, and in The catalogue of works and MSS. exhibited at the bi-centenary exhibition at Aldeburgh . . . *The Proceedings of the Suffolk Institute of Archaeology and Natural History*, vol. 26: 1954. See also 1819 & 1832 below.)

1819

F3 Dana, R. H. Discussion of Crabbe in a review of Hazlitt's 'English Poets'. *The North American Review*, vol. 8: March 1819. pp. 276–322.

Crabbe, more than any other poet since Chaucer, can show "a variety of characters, with the growth and gradual change in each individual, the most secret thoughts, and the course of the passions". He also has a fine vein of "sarcastic humour".

F4 [Crabbe, G.] Memoir of Crabbe. *The European Magazine*, vol. 76: September 1819. pp. 195–200.

Substantially the same article as (2) above.

1820

F5 [Anon.] *The Pocket Magazine of Classic and Polite Literature*; with engravings illustrative of Crabbe. Vol. 6: 1820.

The illustrations are by Corbould. According to *The New Cambridge Bibliography*, these illustrations were "later published separately".

1821

F6 Hazlitt, W. Mr. Crabbe. *The London Magazine*, vol. 3: May 1821. pp. 484–490.

Hazlitt at his most destructive. He objects to the presentation of minute details of unpleasant reality in Crabbe, finding the poetry depressing and degrading. He does not, however, deny the importance of the position Crabbe has among contemporary poets, though he holds this rather due to the degeneracy of the times than the excellence of the poet.

(The essay was repeated, with substantial additions and alterations in *The spirit of the age*. London; Henry Colburn: 1825. pp. 185–205 under the chapter heading 'Mr. Campbell and Mr. Crabbe'.

1827

F7 Wilson, J. Discussion of Crabbe in a review of 'The Chronicles of the Canongate'. *Blackwood's Magazine*, vol. 22: November 1827. pp. 537–540.

An adamantly political view which argues that Tories are naturally more sympathetic to the poor than Whigs are, and since Crabbe is a Whig, his sympathy is thus limited. He is a "mere" delineator of natural and social phenomena, a "downright reality" man, who degrades life rather than exalts it.

1829

F8 C.T. Memoir of Crabbe in the Galignani edition of *Poetical Works*, 1829.

The biography is not entirely accurate. Critically, the article stresses Crabbe's current popularity. It praises his "originality of thought, force, precision, truth, depth, and pathos of description."

1832

F9 Bransby, J. H. *Brief notices of the late Rev. George Crabbe*. Caernarvon: R. M. Preece & Co. 1832. pp. 10.

A letter to the editor of the *Caernarvon Herald*. The author was at school with the poet's son. He had solicited money from Crabbe for a charity, and prints the poet's reply. Describes him as "indifferent to fame".

F10 [Anon.] The Rev. George Crabbe. *The Athenaeum*: 1832. p. 112.

A brief notice of Crabbe's death, with a highly pontifical account of his excessive bleakness as a poet. There are also biographical fragments about Crabbe on pp. 162 and 256.

F11 [Anon.] In "The Departed of XXXII". *Fraser's Magazine*, vol. 6: December 1832. pp. 751–752.

Thumbnail obituary appreciation. His matter lives on, though his manner was *passé*.

F12 Taylor, T. *Cullings from Crabbe: with a memoir of his life and notices of his writings*. Bath. Printed and published by T. Taylor: 1832.

Taylor also compiled the memoir and critical sketch. Much of the early part of the memoir is close précis of Crabbe's autobiographical sketch (1816). The later portions are personal reminiscence, and these are incorporated in the *Life* written in 1834 by Crabbe's son.

"His writings are most beautifully correct: and he of all poets has entirely confined himself to reality – laying bare the galling miseries of the suffering poor..."

F13 Duncan, S. J. 'Farewell, dear Crabbe'. Twenty-two lines of verse which conclude the memoir above. Repeated in the 'Life' by Crabbe's son.

Stresses the human sympathy, the moral rectitude, and the Hogarthian reality of Crabbe's view of the world.

F14 [Anon.] *Beauties of the Rev. George Crabbe. With a biographical sketch*. London: Effingham Wilson. 1832.

Appears to depend upon Crabbe's autobiographical sketch. Adds nothing new to the detail on his life.

1836

F15 [Anon.] British poetry at the close of the last century. Article in the *North American Review*, vol. 42: January 1836. pp. 63–69.

A response to Allan Cunningham's essay in his *Works of Burns*. Crabbe is seen as one of the three reformers of poetry in his period; – Cowper and Burns being the other two. Of them all, Crabbe is the most idiosyncratic, and has inspired least imitation. His work is limited because it over-emphasizes the gloom and reality of things, not allowing an escape into the domains poetry more normally inhabits. Crabbe's later work is slightly less marked by this tendency.

1837

F16 [Anon.] Essay on Crabbe's "genius and writings", in the *Poetical Works*, (Daly), 1837.

". . . truth is at once the actuating principle and the inevitable tendency . . . (of Crabbe's poetry). . . . (It) . . . imitates that quick, intuitive power . . . of laying us, as it were, open to ourselves; of tearing the sophisticated web, which human self-love draws over human frailty; of diving into the very heart of our mystery." Stresses the "prime wisdom" of Crabbe's morality, and the "searching keenness" of his satire. "Crabbe had perhaps a more distinct, yet general knowledge of human nature than any poet of the age." Also praises the "quickness of his intellect which . . . would render him, probably, an equal match for Coleridge and Wordsworth upon their own metaphysical grounds."

1839

F17 [Anon.] Memoir of Crabbe in *The Poetical Works of Crabbe, Heber, and Pollock*, 1839.

The first and last three paragraphs are unacknowledged repetition of 'C.T.' (item 8, above), though tenses are, where necessary, changed from present to past: the remainder is standard biography drawn from George Crabbe, junior.

1841

F18 [Anon.] The Life and Poems of Rev. George Crabbe, LL.B. *The Methodist Quarterly*, vol. 23: October 1841. pp. 514–534. (A 'sketch of Mr. Crabbe's literary life' is offered earlier in the same vol. – pp. 460–471.)

A general review of Crabbe's work. Of the early work the reviewer likes *The Library*, which "contains many commendable passages, much good sense, and the exhibition of a fine ear for polished versification." *The Village* may have had too much influence on judgements of Crabbe's customary tone. Its gloom is not his norm. Of *Poems* 'Sir Eustace Grey' is particularly admired, while 'The Parish Register' "may be considered as ranking Mr. Crabbe with the radical poets of England." *The Borough* was the most finished of his works. The review manages to be remarkably forbearing about Crabbe's anti-methodist bent. It has high praise for his versification: "extremely polished, and sometimes exquisitely musical".

[1844?–55?]

F19 Cunningham, A. C. Life of Crabbe. In the Daly edition of *Poetical Works* [1844–55].

Mainly biography derived from George Crabbe junior's *Life*. The critical comments reiterate the usual observations on Crabbe as poet of the poor.

1846

F20 Tuckerman, H. In *Thoughts on the poets*. New York: 1846. pp. 122–136.

In Crabbe's last work we find ..."a kind of Indian summer invading the winter of old age." Both his sphere of observation and his quality of vision make him remarkable. Though he lacks some of the normal "poetical" attributes he compensates by his honesty and integrity. He can be slipshod, and there is no element of "wonder" in his work. Dickens is the direct successor to Crabbe's indignation on behalf of the poor.

1847

F21 Howitt, W. In *Homes and haunts of the most eminent British poets*. Routledge: 1847. (2nd edition). pp. 350–368.

Crabbe freed poetry from "the false sublime ... Out of the scum and chaos of lowest life he has evoked the true sublime". Though mainly a description of a mid-century visit to Aldeburgh, the critical remarks are not without value.

F22 Gilfillan, G. George Crabbe. *Tait's Edinburgh Magazine*, vol. 14: March 1847. pp. 141–147.

Crabbe had a native taste for the sombre and the ugly. His gloom came from personal circumstances. His insistance upon truth limits the order of poetry he wrote. He lacks humour.

(Repeated in *A second gallery of literary portraits*. Edinburgh; James Hogg: 1850.)

1850

F23 Giles, H. In *Lectures and essays*. Boston: 1850. Vol. 1. pp. 45–92.

Crabbe wrote three kinds of poetry; tragic, moral, and satirical. His gloom is therefore natural, though sometimes too predominant. His truth, and his descriptive power are considerable, though he lacked the proper humour for a satirist.

1851

F24 Lawrence, F. *Sharpe's London Journal*, vol. 12: 1851. pp. 21–28.

Crabbe is "a mannerist ... but still a poet of high pretension." The freshness and vigour of his ideas took readers by surprise. Lists the defects in his work as flatness, coarseness and a taste for prosaic subjects.

F25 Frank, P. George Crabbe. *The People's Journal*, vol. 11: 1851. pp. 1–3.

Notes the considerable change in literary taste and manner during Crabbe's lengthy lifetime. He was "M.D. extraordinary to the human mind," though he suffered "a palpable deficiency of imagination."

1852

F26 Belfast, The Earl of. Essay on Southey, Crabbe and Campbell in *Poets, and Poetry of the nineteenth century*. Longmans: 1852. pp. 258–268.

Crabbe was not a realist: he depressed the status and condition of the poor in his poetry, knowing them not to be as miserable as he too often made them. His style is harsh, lacking all the qualities of music or painting, and having too much of the scientist about it. Reproves his excessive use of chiasmus and punning.

1854

F27 [Anon.] Life of Crabbe in the Gall & Inglis *Poetical Works*, [1854–55].

Crabbe is "the poet of common life . . . He scarcely groups his figures at all, but sets them on his page with the fidelity and everyday look which they wore . . ."

1858

F28 [Anon.] Publisher's Advertisement, and Life of Crabbe in the "Routledge's British Poets" edition of 1858.

The Advertisement is worth citation in full since it epitomizes Crabbe's standing – or the standing a publisher believed he should have – in the middle years of the nineteenth century:

> "Few poets have a claim to be more widely known than George Crabbe, for all he wrote has good as its basis. His poetry is healthy and fit to permeate through the hearts of a thinking people. No mysticism, no extravagant misleading theories, no unintelligible flights of imagination disfigure his manly verse; it is truth clothed in sense, and uttered in an impressive style, that fixes it in the memory of the reader. He is said to be "a stern painter", but his pictures of the class that formed the object of his writings are not such as to create antagonism between them and other classes; he can, as in his 'noble peasant' draw attractive pictures of the poor, as well as sketches to claim pity for their state.
>
> In fact we think it one of the strongest proofs of the advantages derived from the cheap circulation of good literature that there is sufficient demand for the Poems of Crabbe to induce us to publish all of them that are available . . ."

The unsigned Life declares him to be a severe but not a morbid writer of great originality.

1859

F29 [Roscoe, W. C.] *The National Review*, vol. 8: January 1859. pp. 1–32.

Ostensibly a review of the 1853 reprint of Murray's *Life and poetical works*. Crabbe is now less read than he should be, and "the times" are blamed for this, for there is now too much concentration upon ". . . . devotion to the affections." Crabbe had imagination, "even though within narrow limits." He is not unwarrantably stern, though his poetic texture is "sandstone" rather than "marble." His work is without real humour, and quite destitute of philosophical spirit. He does not "resonate" as Shakespeare or Wordsworth do. The author makes a useful contrast of Crabbe with Pope.

1860

F30 Clodd, E. A brief sketch of the life of Crabbe. *The Aldeburgh Magazine*: 1860.

A rudimentary and derivative biographical sketch. (Enlarged and augmented in his *Life of Crabbe* (q.v. in Complete Books section.)

F31 [Anon.] *Notes and Queries*, 2nd series, vol. 10: July–December 1860. pp. 123 & 178.

P. 123 queries an anecdote in Timbs's *Anecdote Biography*. This anecdote purports to be about Crabbe at a conversatzione at Beccles. He there professed to own a pen-and-ink sketch of Burke impeaching Warren Hastings. Crabbe's family know nothing of such a sketch. p. 178 responds that 'Beccles' should read 'Bristol'.

1862

F32 Williams, S. F. In *Essays*, 1862. pp. 161–190.

Uses Crabbe's "stern morality" as an excuse for his own tumid periods. Remarks on Crabbe's "winteriness of temper."

[1863]

F33 [Anon.] Memoir of Crabbe in the Chambers edition of *The Parish Register* ... [1863].

Crabbe is distinguished by his realism, and the unflattering truth of his representation. He should be brought back to the attention of his "neglectful countrymen" as a true classic.

1864

F34 [Anon.] George Crabbe. *The Saturday Review*, vol. 18: September 24, 1864. pp. 394–396.

Tales of the Hall is the summation of what he thought and felt. Deceit, error and silliness are what Crabbe sees all around him rather than great crimes, though bright spots frequently intervene. "He saw the oddities, the queerness, the little ludicrous follies and vanities of ordinary people, and he loved to laugh at them in a shrewd, gentle way". Affirms that he is not generally read nor is likely ever to be.

1865

F35 Hall, S. C. Memories of the authors of the age: George Crabbe. *The Art Journal*, vol. 17: 1865. pp. 373–374.

Thumbnail biography and brief reminiscences of one who had met Crabbe in London in 1826. Stresses the benignity which impressed those who came into contact with the elderly poet.

F36 [Anon.] The turning point of a poet's life. *The Leisure Hour*, vol. 14: 1865. pp. 396–399.

Recounts, without addition to the facts, the story of Crabbe's decision to quit Aldeburgh and seek his poetical fortune in London.

1869

F37 Fitzgerald, E. Sea words and phrases along the Suffolk coast. Appendix 1, Crabbe's Suffolk. *East Anglian Notes and Queries*, January 1869.

Picks out characteristic Suffolk idioms in Crabbe, but the scantness of the examples seems rather to prove his independence of local speech patterns than his adherence to them.

(Repeated in The Works of Edward Fitzgerald. Macmillan: 1887. (2 vols.) and in *Notes for a bibliography of Edward Fitzgerald* by F. W. Prideaux. Frank Hollings: 1901. pp. 75–88.)

F38 [Anon.] *The St. James's Magazine*, n.s. vol. 2: February 1869. pp. 677–688.

Written on the fiftieth anniversary of the publication of *Tales of the Hall*. Crabbe is not in the first flight of poets, but he has an undeniable power of imagination and honesty of purpose. Within his limits he is "a true artist". His "human living interest" may bring him back to popularity after a period when he has been out of favour with the reading public.

1872

F39 Sheldon, F. Crabbe. *The North American Review*, vol. 115: July 1872. pp. 48–65.

Crabbe has great vitality, but is not in the first rank of poets because he has "but one string to his lyre". He was deeply scarred by his experiences in youth. He lacks imagination, and his strength does not lie in satire. His humour is excellent, and his realism provides a capital antidote to "the vapoury verse" of the nineteenth century. Much of his best work is in *Tales of the Hall*.

1873

F40 Devey, J. "The Realistic School." A chapter on Crabbe and Browning in *A Comparative Estimate of Modern English Poets*. London: Moxon, 1873. chapter 14, pp. 368–375.

Crabbe labours under the disadvantage of his profession. He has no sense of beauty. Wanting in all the qualities of first class poetry, he is now virtually laid on the shelf.

F41 [Anon.] *Notes and Queries*, 4th series, vol. 12: July–December 1873. pp. 67, 96, 178. p. 67 has a query about the continuation of the poem

> O man of the sea
> Come listen to me . . .

which Crabbe liked to quote to children. (*Life*, p. 86) p. 96 answers this query. p. 178 provides further material on it.

1874

F42 Stephen, Sir L. Crabbe's Poetry. *The Cornhill Magazine*, vol. 30: 1874. pp. 454–473.

Crabbe was writing at the nadir of English poetry. He chose to describe the baser elements of human nature, whilst his style is gauche, has no lyrical power, and lacks Pope's terseness and polish. Despite all these limitations "he bears the essential marks of genius. . . . Nobody describes better the process of going to the dogs." Stephen contrasts Crabbe, (unfavourably), with Balzac.

The essay is repeated in *Hours in a library*, 2nd series. Smith, Elder & Co.: 1876.

1876

F43 [Anon.] *Notes and Queries*, 5th series, vol. 6: July–December 1876. p. 440.

A note on the reported exhumation of the poet's skull during repairs to Trowbridge church.

1880

F44 Woodbury, G. E. A neglected poet. *Atlantic Monthly*, vol. 45: May 1880. pp. 624–629.

Crabbe has much more than merely historical interest and importance. Limitations were imposed on him as an artist by his "almost perfect physical vision", and his consequent insistence upon reality keeps him at an imaginative level below that of Burns or Wordsworth.

(Repeated in *Studies in letters and life*. Boston: 1890. pp. 29–46.)

1882

F45 Fitzgerald, E. Introduction to *Readings in Crabbe: Tales of the Hall*. Quaritch: 1882.

"The mingled yarn of grave and gay" is what Fitzgerald likes best in Crabbe, and he finds more of it present in *Tales of the Hall* than elsewhere in the poet's work. The poem deals mainly with the follies rather than the vices of men, and with the comedy rather than with the tragedy of life. Because Crabbe learned life from experience and not from books, he should endure as a spokesman on the human lot, despite his diffuseness, and the occasional coarseness of his style and manner.

F46 Oliphant, Mrs M. George Crabbe. pp. 184–216 of *The Literary History of the nineteenth century*. Macmillan. 1882.

Deals cogently with the work up to *The Borough*, but adds nothing new.

1887

F47 Patmore, C. Crabbe and Shelley. *The St. James's Gazette*, vol. 14: February 16, 1887. p. 6.

Shelley the atheist had a delicate, radiant and pious imagination; Crabbe the Christian had a coarse and mundane one. Shelley was fine, Crabbe gross; Shelley was a singer, Crabbe a proser who insisted too much upon reality.

(Repeated in *Principle in art*. G. Bell & Sons: 1889.)

F48 Rae, W. F. George Crabbe. *Temple Bar*, vol. 80: July 1887. pp. 327–340.

Suggests there are three kinds of poetry; Nature poetry, psychological poetry, and the work of pretty rhymsters. Crabbe is neglected because he fits no category at all. He can be too literal and his sense of duty compels him to moralize his tales. His humour is stressed. Perhaps he is a novelist manqué, not a poet at all.

F49 [Anon.] *Notes and Queries*, 7th series, vol. 3: January–June 1887. pp. 306 & 460.

The first of these is a query about Crabbe's birthplace, which is answered by the second entry.

1888

F50 Lamplough, E. Introduction to 'The Canterbury Poets' edition, Walter Scott: 1888.

A recorder of the temporal and actual, Crabbe lacks high imagination. As a portrayer of character "his success is beyond denial eminent."

F51 [Anon.] *Notes and Queries*, 7th series, vol. 6: July–December 1888. p. 506.

Provides background information about 'Lady Barbara or the ghost' (*Tales of the Hall*, XVI).

F52 [Anon.] Review of Kebbel. *The Athenaeum*, 1888. p. 478.

Crabbe is "one of the most original writers in the language," though he suffers from "an incurable want of taste." He owes a far smaller debt to Pope than is usually suggested. The writer stresses Crabbe's sincerity and "manliness."

F53 [Anon.] Review of Kebbel. *The Saturday Review*, 13 October 1888. pp. 438–439.

Crabbe is certainly a great observer and describer, but this may not make him a great poet.

1889

F54 [Anon.] *Notes and Queries*, 7th series, vol. 7: January–June 1889. pp. 114, 214, 373, 511.

p. 114 reminds readers who think Crabbe neglected that not only has a selection of his work recently appeared, together with Kebbel's *Life*, but that many people who knew the poet are still alive and can be met with!

p. 214 raises questions about the morality of the punishment meted out in 'The Learned Boy', (*Tales*, XXI).

pp. 373 & 511 pursue the topic of Crabbe's cruelty and his morality in this poem.

F55 Saintsbury, G. Crabbe. *Macmillan's Magazine*, June 1889. pp. 99–110.

Notes the absolute decline in Crabbe's reputation. Though the tone of his late work is slightly less harsh, his themes remain essentially the same. Crabbe's is "the style of drab stucco." Agrees with Hazlitt that Crabbe lacks "poetical point of view." There is no "transport" in him because there is no music. He may be a great writer, but he is not a great poet.

(Repeated in *Essays in English literature* 1780–1860: Percival & Co 1890)

F56 [Anon.] *Notes and Queries*, 7th series, vol. 8: July–September 1889. pp. 116 & 298.

Further discussions of the poem above, one of them arguing that there is tenderness in the poem to offset its ostensible cruelty.

1890

F 57 [Anon.] *Notes and Queries*, 7th series, vol. 9: January–June 1890. p. 71.

Further discussion of 'The Learned Boy'.

F 58 [Anon.] *Temple Bar*, vol. 90: September–December 1890. pp. 270–279.

Clearly hostile to Crabbe's kind of work. Is not surprised that his fame is quite gone, though there is some merit in attempting to get people to re-read him. Questions the reasons for his pessimism, since his life was essentially so sunny and fortunate!

1891

F59 Morley, H. Introduction to "Routledge's Companion Poets" edition: 1891.

Crabbe . . . "has a distinct place among the poets who have written tales in verse. Out of the troubles of his own life came a keen, observant interest in all the knots and problems that make interesting stories . . ."

F60 Miles, A. H. Introduction to *The Poets of the Century*, 1891.

After a biographical account, the article stresses Crabbe as a bridge figure, admired by conservatives and *avant garde* alike. He is *not* "Pope in worsted stockings", having a coarser versification but a more refined morality. "He had vigorous creative skill, remarkable facility of expression, a wonderful knowledge of human nature, and an extraordinary insight into character . . ."

1896

F61 Holgate, C. W. The skull of Crabbe. *Wiltshire Archaeological and Natural History Magazine*, vol. 29: 1896.

Describes the theft of Crabbe's skull, during renovations at Trowbridge parish church, and the eventual recovery and reburial of it.

1897

F62 [Anon.] *Notes and Queries*, 8th series, vol. 12: July–December 1897, p. 308.

Questions the usual affirmation that 'Lady Barbara' is based on an old Wiltshire legend.

F63 Hillier, A. C. Jane Austen's husband. *Temple Bar*, vol. 112: November 1897. pp. 350–361.

Discerns a significant development from the early Crabbe to the work he wrote after 1805. He is an innovator; and very much a late developer, for *Tales*, and *Tales of the Hall* are his best work. In these poems he truly finds his gift for "getting at the determining kernel of a character".

1899

F64 Prower, M. George Crabbe. *The Gentleman's Magazine*, vol. 286: April 1899. pp. 356–367.

Crabbe is denied imaginative force by some critics because of his "realism". But he intensely imaginative on *human* nature whatever his treatment of inanimate objects. Claims that much of his verse has "a scholarly precision" when contrasted with that of Wordsworth.

F65 Holland, B. Introductory essay to the Edward Arnold edition of *Poems of George Crabbe*: 1899.

Makes the familiar comparison of Crabbe with Wordsworth. Also affirms that, as a narrative poet, nobody since Chaucer has been Crabbe's peer, though he can be careless, disorderly and diffuse. His reputation may well be on the increase again, after reaching its lowest point in the 1870's.

1900

F66 [Anon.] Edward Fitzgerald's 'Great Gun'. *Academy*, vol. 58: 14 April 1900. p. 311.

In reviewing Bernard Holland's selection of Crabbe, asks if the poet has "quite the stuff to live". He justifies the "sternest" of Byron's tag, but not "The best", for his light shines on too many "dead dogs". He does have "Truth, power and pathos".

1901

F67 Statham, H. George Crabbe. *The Quarterly Review*, vol. 193: January 1901. pp. 21–43.

Crabbe is unjustly neglected. Perhaps he brought the eighteenth century too close: his form and content seem to suggest he was born too late. He produced "a gallery of portraits such as very few writers in our language have equalled in variety, keenness of insight and power of delineation". Makes an interesting comparison of Crabbe with Jane Austen.

F68 [Anon.] Publisher's announcement in *Literature*, vol. 8, no. 180: March 30, 1901. pp. 231–232.

Announces the forthcoming re-print of Murray's *Life and works*, (1847). Claims that among more discerning readers Crabbe's status is still high, though he may have lost popular appeal.

F69 Hutton, W. H. Some memories of Crabbe. *The Cornhill Magazine*, vol. 83: June 1901. pp. 750–758.

Stresses Crabbe's failure to hold attraction for the literary generation at the turn of the century, but notes a possible renewal of interest. A pleasant, if slightly chatty, article stressing Crabbe's realism, and glancing at the records of some of the parishes he served. (Repeated in *Burford Papers*. Constable: 1906.)

F70 Gribble, F. Crabbe's Aldeburgh. *Literature*, vol. 8: September 28, 1901. pp. 295–298.

Suggests that Crabbe's roots in Aldeburgh are shown throughout his strange career. He came from a backwater where minding your neighbour's business was still acceptable. The pursuit of a career by means of patronage would not be strange to a lad from such an environment. It also explains the personal interest which comes through the stories he chooses to tell.

F71 More, P. E. A plea for Crabbe. *Atlantic Monthly*, vol. 88: December 1901. pp. 850–857.

Defends the ethical, and anti-Romantic Crabbe. It is no surprise that readers demanding the "rapturous liberties of Shelley and Keats" are repulsed by Crabbe's "clean good sense." His ability to wed science to human interest, and his stern judicial piety are praised, while 'Peter Grimes' gives him a station among "the fewer master poets of human passion".

(Reprinted in *Shelburne Essays*, 1. Putnam: 1904.)

1902

F72 Hutton, W. H. Crabbe as parish priest. *The Guardian*, no. 2957: Wednesday, August 6, 1902, p. 1129.

An article stimulated by the recent re-issue of *Life and Works*, and the promise of Canon Ainger's forthcoming volume on Crabbe in the 'English Men of Letters' series. (q.v.) Pleads that Crabbe's seriousness as a priest can only be understood in terms of the period he lived in. He was a devoted pastor, even though he may have lacked theological sophistication.

1903

F73 Deane, A. C. Introduction to the "Little Library" edition, Methuen: 1903.

Suggests a recent resurgence of interest in Crabbe. He attempted to interpret nineteenth century life in terms of eighteenth century verse, but despite obvious limitations he has enough real excellences to impress any intelligent reader.

F74 [Anon.] A review of Murray's 1901 re-issue of *Works*, of Holland's selection, and of the Dent re-issue of *The Borough*. *The Edinburgh Review*, vol. 198: July–October 1903. pp. 30–51.

Crabbe's popularity has increased in recent years. But why, when he was able to write so well, did he often write so badly? He was a "middle aged" poet, and his hard-headed approach chimes with the "present" rather un-poetical times. *Tales of the Hall* was his most pleasant volume: usually there is more salt than honey in him.

F75 [Anon.] George Crabbe. (Ostensibly a review of Canon Ainger's book) *The Spectator*, vol. 91 December 5, 1903. pp. 343–344.

There has been a steady revival of interest in Crabbe over the past twenty five years. Notes his "sombre but minute realism". "In many of the characteristics of his art he resembles Emile Zola".

F76 [Anon.] Review of the 1903 issue of *The Borough*. *The Saturday Review*, 25 April 1903. pp. 520–521.

An almost vitriolic denunciation of Crabbe. "We have got far beyond him, and, to speak frankly, we do not need him any longer."

F77 [Anon.] Review of Canon Ainger's book. *The Athenaeum*, 1903. p. 573.

Possibly the first time that the debate about Crabbe's use of opium is given a serious and extended airing. He has "an eye only for the follies, the frailties and vices, the afflictions, the mischances and the disappointments of the human family".

F78 Lawson, J. *The Gentleman's Magazine*, n.s. vol. 71 : 1903. p. 23.

A fairly standard rehearsal of Crabbe's merits and demerits. The poet is out of fashion, and not likely to come back into favour, but his devotees are fervent if few.

1905

F79 Bailey, J. The Commemoration of Crabbe. *The Times Literary Supplement*: 15 September 1905.

"Good sense and good verse" are the essence of Crabbe. His knowledge of human character distinguishes him especially, but this is purveyed by a sensibility which is of the world of the eighteenth century moral essayists, not of the Romantic poets. He probably missed his chance of fame in the years between 1783 and 1807, when he chose to remain silent. There would then have been no rival to him, but by the time he re-appeared in print he was old-fashioned.

(Repeated in *Poets and Poetry*. Oxford: 1911, and in *The Living Age* Vol. 247, 21 October 1905, pp. 179–183.

F80 Groves, J. Crabbe as a botanist. *Proceedings of the Suffolk Institute of Archaeology and Natural History*, vol. 12, part II: 1905.

Presents the evidence for taking Crabbe quite seriously as a botanist.

1906

F81 Boynton, H. W. The Life and Work of Crabbe. *Bookman* (New York), vol. 23 : March 1906. pp. 49–54.

Crabbe mistook his own greatness, thinking himself a moralist rather than an imaginative realist. Despite the unpopularity of the heroic couplet he "made the instrument his own". The tone of the article is vaguely jocular and patronizing.

1907

F82 Shorter, C. To the immortal memory of George Crabbe. In *Immortal Memories*. Hodder: 1907. pp. 97–127.

Originally an address given at the 1905 Aldeburgh celebration for Crabbe's birth. Reviews the history of the decline in Crabbe's reputation. Explores him as a poet bound to and influenced by his birthplace, and suggests the current depreciation of him is a mistake.

F83 [Anon.] A new study of Crabbe. *Nation*, vol. 1: 23 May 1907. pp. 82–83.

Ostensibly a review of Huchon. Affirms that while Crabbe is praised by the discerning few, he is and has always been ignored by most readers.

F84 Collins, J. C. The poetry of Crabbe. *The Fortnightly Review*, n.s. vol. 82: October 1907. pp. 575–591.

What distinguishes the work of Crabbe from poetry as normally understood is a difference of kind rather than of quality, for Crabbe's are "the utterances of strict truth". With all his faults of diffuseness and prolixity, and even with the gloom which he too frequently allows into his work, yet he is a master of pathos, sometimes of genuine tragedy.

1908

F85 Carlyle, A. J. & R. M. Introduction to the *Poetical Works*, Oxford University Press: 1908.

Crabbe is neglected, and a good deal of the neglect is justified by the intransigence of his material, the carelessness of his style, and his commonplace – sometimes offensive – subject matter.

1909

F86 Elton, O. The poetry of Crabbe. *Blackwood's Magazine*, vol. 185: January 1909. pp. 78–90.

Crabbe is a predecessor of the Romantic movement, not a prophet of it. Yet he is a refreshing change from "the Alastors of literature". He is "by far the greatest English novelist between Sterne and Scott", and if his popularity does ever return, it should be a permanent restoration.

1910

F87 Courthope, W. J. Chapter entitled "Anti-romanticism in English poetry: Crabbe": in *A history of English poetry*. Macmillan: 1910. vol. vi, pp. 357–380.

> "The time had . . . come for a poet, inspired with something of the old Chaucerian humour, to turn the light of Truth on the constitution of English society . . ." His poetical aim was to "extend the range of imaginative sympathy, by applying the traditional forms of poetry to objects scientifically observed in the domain of real life."

Courthope stresses the sympathy which underlies the observation.

1912

F88 Holme, W. J. The treatment of nature in Crabbe. In *Primitiae: essays by students of Liverpool University*. Constable: 1912. pp. 43–53.

Crabbe has little indebtedness to Wordsworth, even though his effect in "reviving the more humane and emotional elements in English poetry" is similar. Partly through the country upbringing he had, he strove to present the opposite of Goldsmith's pastoral sentimentality. This led him to concentrate on minute and particular objects in nature. Hence his great clarity, though "he lifts no veil, and the hidden mysteries behind the externals are never revealed".

1913

F89 Strang, W. George Crabbe. *The Quain Essay for 1913*. London; University College: 1913. pp. 123.

A concise survey of Crabbe's life and major works. The poet is defended against the kind of attack initiated by Hazlitt, through analogies drawn between himself and Chaucer.

1914

F90 [Anon.] The non-couplet poetry of Crabbe. *Spectator*, vol. 112: 14 March 1914. p. 426.

A reminder that the stanzaic poems like 'Sir Eustace Grey' and 'The Hall of Justice' are a valuable part of Crabbe's work, though most readers know him mainly through his couplet verse.

F91 Child, H. George Crabbe. Chapter VII of *The Cambridge History of English Literature*: 1932. vol. II, pp. 140–152.

"The desire to tell the truth as he saw it was the intellectual passion which governed Crabbe in all his mature poetry . . ." He revived a tradition of truthful fiction which had been current at the time of the eighteenth century essayists, but which had nearly died out when Crabbe started writing.

1915

F92 Glover, T. R. Crabbe. In *Poets and puritans*. Methuen: 1915. pp. 211–241.

"It is Aldeburgh . . . rather than the *Tales*, the story of the poor rather than the story of the middle class, which forms the main interest of his work." Crabbe's insistence on "prudence" is a little wearing: "he is undone by his gift; his strong sense of fact overpowers him". Makes useful comparisons between Crabbe and Burns.

1916

F93 Jackson, F. J. Foakes. George Crabbe. In *Social life in England 1750–1850*. Macmillan: 1916. pp. 42–80.

Claims that there has been a renewal of interest in Crabbe. "Delineation of character" is the poet's strength.

F94 Wylie, L. J. The England of George Crabbe. In *Social studies in English Literature*. New York, Houghton Mifflin: 1916.

Crabbe's first had experience of lower class life makes him "the spokesman of the workaday men and women of England in his time". His studies of their characters and fortunes "infinitely widen our knowledge of human life and our sympathy with it".

1917

F95 Thomas, E. George Crabbe. In *A Literary Pilgrim in England*. Methuen: 1917. pp. 212–223.

Emphazises the shaping effect of Aldeburgh itself on Crabbe's character, and asserts that although his subjectivity may be a logical defect it is certainly a poetical strength.

F96 Pound, E. The Rev. George Crabbe, LL.B. *The Future*, 1917.

A passionate defence of Crabbe's "words that conform precisely with fact, of free speech without evasions or circumlocutions" against the "pretty embroideries" which the Victorians wanted in their verse.

No copy of this journal was available for consultation on volume and page numbers.

(Reprinted in *Literary essays of Ezra Pound*, edited by T. S. Eliot. Faber and Faber: 1954. pp. 276–279.)

1919

F97 [Anon.] Poets of the village. *The Times Literary Supplement*, Thursday, July 10, 1919. pp. 369–370.

Outlines Crabbe's unsentimental attitude to village life: finds his style harsh and uncompromising, though it suggests this mellowed with old age. Claims he wrote for the mind and the heart but never for the ear.

1920

F98 A.M.O. Stories of the Crabbe family. *The Bookman's Journal*, 31 December 1920. pp. 166.

Ephemeral and anecdotal fragments about Mary Crabbe, the poet's last grandchild, who died in March 1920.

1921

F99 Whitby, C. A student of humanity. *Poetry Review*, vol. 12: 1921. pp. 251–259.

Crabbe's peculiar power lay in the study and delineation of character. His poetry is for those who seek in their literature "a serious criticism of life". His valuations of character were spiritual "regardless of the accidents of rank, wealth, or intellect". The sober beauty of his work is an emanation of his own courageous, tolerant, and acquiescent spirit.

1922

F100 Lacey May, G. Church life as pictured in Crabbe. *Theology*, vol. 4: May 1922. pp. 273–281.

Asserts that Crabbe is now coming into his own. His picture of the Church and its institutions, based on his wide social span, is a true one. He lacks reforming zeal, partly because he is more interested in people than institutions. As a priest he had probity and acumen in a drab period in the history of the English Church.

1923

F101 Massingham, H. J. In *Untrodden ways. Adventures on English coasts . . . and also among the work of Crabbe, Hudson, etc.* T. Fisher Unwin: 1923. Chapter 17.

Some knowledge of East Anglia and of Aldeburgh is essential to an understanding of Crabbe. He is . . . "the genius of the East wind, which if it is good for the soul is bad for the liver". Crabbe turned Flora into flora in English poetry through "his amazing betrothal of art and science". He also had a genuine gift for tragedy of a kind like that of Hardy and Maupassant.

F102 Campbell, A. J. George Crabbe; poet and botanist. *The Holborn Review*, n.s. vol. 14: April 1923. pp. 198–207.

Though he cannot claim a place among first-rank botanists – partly through his antipathy to order, and his technical inability to classify accurately – Crabbe had a very real "feel" for plants, and his botanical work had value.

F103 Olivero, F. Crabbe's realism. *Nuovo Antologia*, vol. 1: 1923. pp. 79–92.

Seeks to define the precise nature of "realism" in Crabbe. Even the subjective landscapes of *Tales* and the vision world of 'Sir Eustace Grey' are, as Crabbe himself suggested, part of his method of describing things as they really are.

1928

F104 [Anon.] When Crabbe came to town. *The Times*, July 5 1928.

A brief account of Crabbe's visit to Hampstead in 1828.

1930

F105 Boyden, R. Masefield and Crabbe; an affinity. *The Bookman*, vol. 79: December 1930. p. 165.

A crass little piece which fails to establish any meaningful affinity between the two poets.

1931

F106 Lucas, F. L. A poet of prose. *Life and Letters*, vol. 6: February 1931. pp. 79–105.

Though the tendency to bathos is ever present in Crabbe, and though his background was drab, he is still a poet of substantial worth. The flashes in his dingy-looking texture offer relief. Truthfulness is his most important quality, for he has "an uncanting sense of the world's real sorrows".

(Reprinted in 1933 as the introduction to the Crabbe anthology Lucas put out.)

F107 Looker, S. J. In praise of Crabbe. *Nineteenth century*, vol. 110: October 1931. pp. 489–502.

Crabbe's real strength lies in his psychological insight, in his profound knowledge of human character and his mastery and understanding of the tragi-comedy of life. Defends him against Saintsbury's charge of being unmusical, as well as against the general complaint that he is too gloomy. Expresses particular admiration for *Tales of the Hall*.

1932

F108 [Anon.] Introduction to *The Augustan Books of Poetry* edition, Benn: 1932.

Crabbe was a realist who set his face against dishonest sentimentality about misery. He suffers through his unqualified grimness, and his complacent technique, though in places he has great power.

F109 Deane, A. C. Revised introduction to the re-issue of the Methuen edition of 1903. Series now called "The Gateway Library".

An interesting re-assessment after a space of nearly thirty years. Deane now believes Crabbe has both historic and intrinsic interest, but modern readers are indifferent to him. Although he is a link-figure in the history of English verse, he has individuality and integrity. He managed "a union of eighteenth century manner with nineteenth century matter". He is full of longeurs, odd diction, and lumbering couplets, but cumulatively his merits outweigh these faults.

F110 Masefield, J. E. George Crabbe. In *Recent prose*. Heinemann: 1932. pp. 305–321.

A transcript of a speech given at Trowbridge on February 3, 1932. Although for a long time he had "either disliked or shrunk from" Crabbe's work, a recent re-reading had lead Masefield to be more just to the poet now.

F111 Deane, A. C. George Crabbe, classicist and realist. *The Times*, February 3 1932. p. 13.

Suggests that the surge of interest in Crabbe which occurred at the beginning of the century is now over. Crabbe's merit lay in his ability to span the gap between Augustans and Romantics; to put his old wine in new bottles.

F112 [Anon.] Leader on the Crabbe anniversary celebrations. *The Times Literary Supplement*: February 4, 1932. pp. 65–66.

A survey of Crabbe's life and work on the occasion of the anniversary of his death.

F113 Forster, E. M. Crabbe. *Spectator*, vol. 147: February 20, 1932. pp. 243–245.

Questions Crabbe's standing as a great poet, a satirist in Pope's tradition, a novelist who missed his vocation, or a character writer. Concludes that he is primarily none of these. Even his vaunted powers of dialogue are limited. But a savour and a personality certainly come across from his work.

F114 Waugh, A. George Crabbe. *Bookman*, vol. 81: February 1932. pp. 264–265.

Crabbe went out of fashion because he was a realist, and hence was concerned with outward manifestations of life and conduct at a time when most readers demanded a more subjective approach. And when compared with the modern realists, like Lawrence or Joyce, Crabbe is too moral and too overt.

F115 Payen-Payne, de V. The Crabbe centenary. *Bookman*, vol. 81: February 1932. p. 309.

A brief description of the celebrations at Trowbridge to celebrate the poet's death.

F116 Otley, M. George Crabbe. *The London Mercury*, vol. 26: June 1932. pp. 153–162.

Crabbe, with Cowper and Burns, is one of the "bridge-builders" between the eighteenth and nineteenth centuries. Seeks "to allocate to a semi-forgotten poet his peculiar place of importance . . ." and to suggest some of the reasons why "his vivid and artless lines" should make a special appeal.

F117 Forster, E. M. Introduction to "The world's classics" edition of *The Life of Crabbe*. 1932.

A sympathetic and sensitive response to Crabbe and to his son's biography of him.

F118 Webb, C. J. Crabbe to Scott. *The Times Literary Supplement*, September 29, 1932. p. 691.

Seeking information about one of the persons mentioned in the letter published by Bullough. (T.L.S. of September 22, 1932.)

1933

F119 Richards, F. George Crabbe. *The Holborn Review*, vol. 158: January 1933. pp. 38–47.

The Village challenged all the old assumptions partly because of the author's particular human sympathy, and his pathos. Crabbe is prolix, "rhetorical", and lacking in self-criticism, but modern denigrators should ask themselves why Byron considered him, with Coleridge, as "the first of these times in point of power and genius".

F120 Lucas, F. L. Introduction to the 'Poets in brief' edition, Cambridge University Press, 1933.

A repeat of the essay of 1931 from *Life and Letters* (q.v.)

1934

F121 Abrams, M. H. *The milk of paradise: the effects of opium visions on the work of De Quincey, Crabbe, Francis Thompson and Coleridge.* Cambridge Mass.: 1934.

An investigation of the effect of opium-taking on image patterns, particularly in Crabbe's stanzaic poems; and of the relationship between these patterns in Crabbe and other poets who took the drug.

F122 Deane, A. C. Pillars of the English Church: George Crabbe. *The Listener*, 21 February 1934. p. 322.

Underneath the venality and the acceptance of things which are characteristic of the eighteenth century Church, Crabbe was a priest and a poet of courage and originality.

1936

F123 Leavis, F. R. In *Revaluation*. Chatto & Windus: 1936. pp. 124–129.

It is the later work – *Tales* and *Tales of the Hall* – which should make Crabbe a living classic. "His strength is that of a moralist and of an eighteenth century poet who is positively in sympathy with the Augustan tradition, and it is one strength". Leavis is emphatic that Crabbe is not "Pope in worsted stockings" but the skilled practitioner of a special use of the couplet. "In the use of description, of nature and of the environment generally, for emotional purposes, he surpasses any Romantic".

1938

F124 D, R. Crabbe: a note. *The Townsman*, vol. 1, no. 2: 1938. pp. 22–24.

"Crabbe gains in effect by a continuous use of epithets which avoid the platitudinous by nothing short of a miracle". He excells as a short-story teller.

F125 Lang, V. Crabbe and Tess of the D'Urbervilles. *Modern Language Notes*, vol. 53: 1938. pp. 369–370.

Suggests that Hardy may have drawn an element in the plotting of the character of Alec from 'The Maid's story' in *Tales of the Hall*.

F126 Lang, V. Crabbe and the eighteenth century: a portion of some aspects of Crabbe's realism. *English Literary History*, vol. 5: March 1938. pp. 305–333.

Examines the Augustan characteristics of Crabbe's thought, and his verse. They are grouped under headings as 'pastoral', 'satire', 'Humanism', 'Neo-classical theory'. Concludes that Crabbe knew the rules governing the way he chose to write, and knew what he was seeking to achieve within the framework they provided.

1941

F127 Shepherd, T. B. Crabbe and Methodism. *The London Quarterly*, vol. 166: April 1941. pp. 166–174.

An investigation, by a Methodist, of Crabbe's justification for calling Methodism "this spiritual influenza". Argues that the poet's own defence is dubious, since it relies on Warburton's *Doctrine of Grace*, much of which was already refuted by the time Crabbe wrote *The Borough*. The poet may have felt a covert sympathy with non-conformist religion, and this may be evident in the stanzas at the end of 'Sir Eustace Grey', and in the prayer meeting described in Letter IV of *The Borough*.

F128 Forster, E. M. George Crabbe: the poet and the man. *The Listener*, May 29, 1941. pp. 769–770.

"Though he notes occasional heroism, his general verdict on the working class is unfavourable". He is enormously atmospheric: . . . "there steals, again and again into his verse the sea, the estuary, the flat Suffolk coast, and local meanness, and an odour of brine and dirt, tempered occasionally by the scent of flowers". For his tartness and acid humour he can be forgiven lack of warmth of human heart, vivid imagination, and grand style.

1943

F129 Tennyson, C. George Crabbe and Suffolk. *The Geographical Magazine*, July 1943. pp. 143–146.

Suggests that poet and county have both been neglected until recently, for reasons which suggest an inter-action between the man and his environment. Both tend to be unexciting and "flat" to the casual viewer not trained to see the minutiae. The article is illustrated with various photographs and a map.

1944

F130 Stonier, G. W. In the article 'Books in general' *The New Statesman*, vol. 27: January 1, 1944. p. 11.

"The qualities of his art . . . (are) . . . his social morality, love of truth, (and not only an ugly fact), sense of character, sly wit, and avid eye." He is "one of the most original writers England has produced".

F131 Mills, H. A subject of curious speculation. *Delta*, Summer 1944. pp. 16–20. No copy available for inspection.

1945

F132 Slater, M. *Peter Grimes, an opera* . . . words by Montagu Slater. Music by Benjamin Britten. Boosey & Hawkes: 1945.

The introduction offers an explanation of why Crabbe's story was changed for the opera. Slater sees Grimes as "visionary, ambitious, impetuous, frustrated." His desire is to better himself so he can marry Ellen Orford!

(See also under FORSTER, E. M. *Two cheers for democracy*. below, 1951).

F133 Pedley, M. S. George Crabbe. *The Central Literary Magazine*, November 1945. pp. 173–178.

Crabbe is "an embryo novelist who never developed." His strength is in character description.

F134 Heath-Stubbes, J. Crabbe and the Eighteenth Century. *Penguin New Writing*, vol. 25: 1945. pp. 129–145.

Although he outlived many of the Romantics, Crabbe wrote poetry which "is wholly a logical development of the central Augustan tradition". His character writing descends from Dryden and Pope, though his concern with psychological states links the Augustan and the Romantic elements in him.

1946

F135 Henderson, P. Introduction to *George Crabbe's poems*, Lawson & Dunn: 1946.

Crabbe pictured country life as it really was. He lacks "exultation" but is redeemed from gloom by his wry humour. Though *Tales of the Hall* is a falling-off in his talents, he has "the solid permanance of good workmanship".

1947

F136 Mercier, V. The poet as sociologist. *The Dublin Magazine*, vol. 22: 1947. pp. 19–27.

Sees Crabbe as a verse-sociologist, and hence regards *The Borough* as his finest poem, full of honesty and minute detail.

F137 Sale, A. Chaucer in Cancer. *English*, vol. 6: summer 1947. pp. 240–244.

Valuable and stimulating comparisons between Chaucer and Crabbe.

F138 Blunden, E. Introduction to 'The cresset library' edition of *The life of Crabbe*. 1947.

Covers most of the familiar areas of discussion. Sympathetic without ever breaking new ground.

1948

F139 Brown, W. C. In *The triumph of form: a study of the later masters of the heroic couplet*. University of North Carolina Press: 1948. pp. 161–187.

Crabbe produced a "masterful adaptation" of the heroic couplet to suit the requirements of narrative verse. His full poetic achievement in this field was in *Tales* and was continued into *Tales of the Hall*. In this volume his use of the heroic couplet for narrative purposes was the most successful and interesting of any poet since Dryden.

1949

F140 Batdorf, F. P. The background to Crabbe's *Village*. *Notes and Queries*, vol. 194: 29 October, 1949. pp. 477–478.

Argues that Crabbe's realism in the handling of rural life was part of a movement, not a new departure. Cites Cowper's *Hope* as evidence.

1950

F141 Spingarn, L. P. Crabbe as realist. *The University of Kansas City Review*, vol. 17: 1950. pp. 60–65.

"Crabbe clove the eighteenth century into two parts, retaining the style but dispensing with the artificiality of its viewpoint." His is "a deeper realism than that of mere reporter". His humour tends to rub the raw edge off his pictures of social conflict, yet he possesses "awareness" of a high quality.

F142 Woolf, V. Crabbe. In *The Captain's Deathbed*. Hogarth Press: 1950. pp. 31–34.

A lyrical-biographical fragment. "This gnarled and sea-salted man had a passion for the rejected and injured, the stunted, the hardy, and the self-grown . . ."

F143 Grigson, G. Introduction to 'The Crown Classics' series; Grey Walls Press: 1950.

Crabbe wrote out of conflict, and the distress present in many of his poems is autobiographical, even when imagination supervenes. He endured "the servitude of self-knowledge", but made admirable use of his own limitations. The original in him was pinched and twisted by his childhood in Aldeburgh.

F144 Sale, A. Introduction to *The Village*; University Tutorial Press: 1950.

It is the vigour of treatment, not the theme itself which is original in *The Village*, for Gay, Churchill and Langhorne had all dealt with anti-pastoral themes before Crabbe did. Though it has structural faults, *The Village* is more coherent than many of the poems in the same genre.

F145 Forster, E. M. George Crabbe and Peter Grimes. In *Two cheers for democracy*. Edward Arnold: 1951. pp. 178–192.

Originally a lecture on the relationship between poem and opera, given at the Aldeburgh Festival. Stresses the bleakness of the town and the unhappiness of Crabbe's childhood there. Yet he never tore up his emotional links with the place. Offers a sensitive explanation of the changes made in the poem for the opera.

F146 Graham, W. H. The poet of penury. *The Contemporary Review*, vol. 172: February 1951. pp. 97–103.

Factually very inaccurate, and without anything of substance to add to the critical debate.

1952

F147 Sale, A. The development of Crabbe's narrative art. *The Cambridge Journal*, vol. 5: May 1952. pp. 480–498.

Traces the changes and developments in Crabbe's narrative techniques from *The Parish Register* to *Tales*, and suggests that, as a narrative poet, Crabbe has a very high status.

1953

F148 Broman, W. E. Factors in Crabbe's eminence in the early nineteenth century. *Modern Philology*, vol. 51: August 1953. pp. 42–49.

In his day Crabbe was hailed as "new" because of his "truth", "actuality", etc. Readers were, at that time, looking for novelty, and they seized on Crabbe, particularly the aspect of him revealed in *The Village*. This poem, which is not really typical of him at all, has continued to represent him falsely and to cloud or conceal the type and scope of his more characteristic work.

F149 Cranbrook, The Earl of. George Crabbe and Great Glemham. *The Proceedings of the Suffolk Institute of Archaeology and Natural History*, vol. 25, part 1: 1953. pp. 116–117.

A note about the exact location in Great Glemham park of the house Crabbe lived in.

1954

F150 Duncan-Jones, E. E. Jane Austen and Crabbe. *The Review of English Studies*, n.s. vol. 5: April 1954. p. 174.

Suggests that Jane Austen may have taken the name of the heroine of Mansfield Park from Book II of *The Parish Register* – the episode of Sir Edward Archer and his bailiff's daughter.

F151 Mabbot, T. A deliberate parody of Pope by Crabbe. *Notes and Queries*, n.s. 1: December 1954. pp. 525–526.

Points to a parody of Pope's lines

> When Ajax strives some rock's vast weight to throw
> The line too labours, and the words move slow . . .

in the lines footnoted in *The Library*

> Soon as the chiefs, whom once they chose, lie low,
> Their praise too slackens, and their aid moves slow . . .

F152 Harvey, N. Crabbe of Aldeburgh 1754–1832. *The Journal of the Ministry of Agriculture*, vol. 61: December 1954. pp. 442–445.

"He left on record a peculiarly observant picture of country life in Suffolk in the last generation of an older simpler tougher England."
Treats the poet throughout as a versified social historian.

F153 Whitehead, F. Introduction to 'The Queen's Classics' selection. Chatto & Windus: 1955.

Manages to present Crabbe as a major poet, convincingly but without hyperbole or exaggeration. An excellent all-round introduction to the poet, also with sensible and informative notes.

F154 Cruttwell, P. The last Augustan. *The Hudson Review*, vol. 7: winter 1955. pp. 533–554.

Crabbe was a man of turbulent feelings and his poetry is, therefore, caught uneasily between the demands of neo-classical decorum – (reinforced by contemporary prudishness) and Crabbe's natural frankness – (reinforced by the new realism in literature). Emphasizes the poet's range by an interesting comparison of him with Dickens.

F155 Gregor, I. The last Augustan. *The Dublin Review*, vol. 179: 1955. pp. 37–50.

Crabbe's *Village* has many elements which are within Augustan norms. The poem "blends its colours" afresh, but it remains traditional elegaic pastoral. The "bizarre strength" of Crabbe's realism comes from his regional roots in East Anglia.

F156 Ker, W. P. In *On modern literature: lectures and addresses*; edited by T. P. Spencer & J. Sutherland. Clarendon Press: 1955. pp. 62–77.

Crabbe's subject matter and style are not disgusting or unpoetic: they are, rather, "admirable for narrative poetry". The poet is essentially good-humoured, a "chronicler of human life without any prejudice in favour of misery". Though the essay does not strive to be contentious or self-consciously original, it makes a persuasive case for seeing Crabbe with more moderation than has been used by those who customarily decry him as a gloomy pessimist.

1956

F157 Pollard, A. The theology of Crabbe and its effect on his work. *Church Quarterly Review*, vol. 157: 1956. pp. 309–316.

The claims that Crabbe "floated into the haven of the Anglican Ministry" for reasons of worldly security are examined and rejected. Evidence is used both from his attitude before he ever expected to be ordained, and from his thought and practice after he joined the Church.

F158 Brett, R. L. George Crabbe. *"Writers and their work"* series. Longman: 1956. pp. 43.

Surveys the common critical objections to Crabbe, and makes a strong but balanced defence of him against them.

F159 Thale, R. M. Crabbe's *Village* and topographical poetry. *The Journal of English and Germanic Philology*, vol. 55: 1956. pp. 618–623.

Structural anomalies in *The Village* are to be understood in terms of the genre of the topographical poem – a very popular eighteenth century form. The issue is bedevilled for us in that the realism and anti-pastoralism of *The Village* do not look like characteristic elements of a poem in this genre, which normally has far more of the Georgic element in it. Yet, even parts as diffuse as the praise of Lord Robert Manners, and the discursions into sanitary conditions, are meant to be held together "in the loose and often associative fashion of the topographical poem".

1957

F160 Batdorf, F. P. John Bonnycastle – friend of George Crabbe. *Notes and Queries*, n.s. 4: 1957. pp. 382–383.

Biographical details about one of Crabbe's friends from his penurious years in London, who eventually rose to be a distinguished mathematician.

1958

F161 Whitehead, F. George Crabbe. In *The pelican guide to English literature*, vol. 5: Blake to Byron. Penguin Books: 1958. pp. 85–93.

Crabbe is not merely an eighteenth century poet who happened to survive. "His tales are a highly original achievement in a wholly new art form . . . only possible to someone who had exposed himself . . . to the new currents of feeling."

1960

F162 Thomas, W. K. The flavour of Crabbe. *The Dalhousie Review*, vol. 40: winter 1960. pp. 489–504.

Discusses Crabbe's use of natural descriptions, his preference for types, and his dependence on moral norms. These identify him as an Augustan, yet they have kept his work from dating.

1962

F163 Chamberlain, R. L. George Crabbe and Darwin's amorous plants. *The Journal of English and Germanic Philology*, vol. 61: October 1962. pp. 833–852.

Investigates Crabbe's awareness of Erasmus Darwin's declining reputation as a way of estimating the degree to which Crabbe responded to a change in the temper of the age between 1873 and 1807, when he re-commenced as poet with his new volume, *Poems*.

1964

F164 Hodgart, P. & Redpath, T. In *Romantic perspectives: the work of Crabbe, Blake, Wordsworth, and Coleridge, as seen by their contemporaries and themselves*. Harrap & Co.: 1964.

The chapter on Crabbe, which reprints some of the more famous critical passages on his works is pp. 84 seq., but the introduction, which discusses the position and status of the critical reviews in the early nineteenth century, is valuable and rewarding too.

F165 Nowell-Smith, S. Landor echoes Crabbe. *The Times Literary Supplement*: 2 April, 1964. p. 273.

Suggests that a stanza in Landor's elegy on Rose Aylmer may have been influenced by some lines in *The Village*.

F166 Brady, M. B. Crabbe, "Clutterbuck & Co." *Brigham Young University Studies*, vol. 5: 1964. pp. 19–30.

Most critics undervalue Crabbe's ideas on poetic technique. He uses tone consciously to create pre-determined effects. Analyses 'The Elder Brother's Tale' from *Tales of the Hall* to demonstrate this thesis.

1965

F167 Edwards, O. Talking of books. *The Times*, Thursday January 14 1965. p.13.

A brief introduction to the poet, urging his merits upon new readers.

1966

F168 Hibbard, G. R. Crabbe and Shakespeare. In *Renaissance and modern essays for Vivian da Sola Pinto's seventieth birthday*. Edited by G. R. Hibbard Routledge: 1966. pp. 83–93.

Most of the Romantics made a mish-mash of Shakespeare because they tried to imitate him slavishly. They finished up with a pastiche, whereas Crabbe had apprehended Shakespeare's attitudes much more finely – particularly attitudes to forgiveness and sin. *Tales* reveals the extent of Crabbe's knowledge of Shakespeare, and how fruitfully he let it influence him.

F169 Thomas, W. K. Crabbe's view of the poor. *Revue de l'Université d'Ottowa*, Vol. 36: 1966. pp. 453–485.

Crabbe portrays the poor, not as he actually knew them to be, but through "filters" of sensibility which lighten the picture of virtuous labour, whilst emphasizing the grim facts of poverty when associated with vice. His stance may be influenced by Burke's pamphlet *Thoughts and details on scarcity*.

F170 Thomas, W. K. Crabbe's *Borough*: the process of montage. *University of Toronto Quarterly*, vol. 36: 1966. pp. 181–192.

An examination of the structure of *The Borough* and of repeated motifs which give structural firmness to the poem.

F171 Gallon, D. N. Silford Hall, or the happy day. *Modern Language Review*, vol. 61: July 1966. pp. 384–394.

'Silford Hall', the first of the *Posthumous Poems*, is full of "fruitful ambiguities". The poem is concerned with a knightly quest, half ironically and half seriously given to its youthful hero – (Crabbe himself as a young man.) Suggestions have been made that, unlike most of Crabbe's mature work, this poem is purely descriptive. The quest theme shows how far from the truth such a view really is.

F172 Swinnerton, F. In *A galaxy of fathers*. Hutchinson: 1966. pp. 48–58.

Mainly biographical. Contends that Crabbe "sacrificed nothing of truth to the charm of style; yet he produced his own charm by means of continuous accuracy and interestingness".

F173 Speirs, J. Crabbe as master of the verse tale. *The Oxford Review*, vol. 1: 1966. pp. 3–40.

Crabbe is "one of the great English provincials," yet, with Jane Austen, he is the natural successor to the urbanity of Pope and Johnson as a moral observer. This quality is encapsulated in his re-creation of the verse-tale where "his rational and moral intelligence . . . (exposes) . . . human nature and human life to conscious appraisal and judgement and concise, lucid, sharp-edged or pointed expression". The last works are a "gentle decline" of his tautness and compression.

1967

F174 Mills, H. Introduction to *Tales 1812*. Cambridge University Press: 1967.

Stresses the importance of the change which occurred in Crabbe between *The Village* and *Tales*. The poet's life was *not* uneventful, and the resultant "traumas" are manifest in his work. The notion of "Heart" is central to an understanding of him, and a good story is more important than overt moralizing. His reaction to language can be lazy or inert, but he can be masterful with words. The last work represents some falling-off for he allows sentiment to replace sharpness of vision.

F175 Newbold, G. Introduction to his *Crabbe selection*.

Crabbe produced a great body of truthful, incisive and honest verse. "His poetry never attempts to transcend ordinary experience. . . . He continued to abide by the Augustan positives – good sense, dignity, and endurance". His greatest achievement is in *Tales*. Crabbe is a patient searcher after truth, not a mechanical moralizer.

1968

F176 Hayter, A. *Opium and the romantic imagination*. Faber & Faber: 1968.

The chapter on Crabbe is pp. 165–190, though the general chapters on literature and opium are valuable too. Pursues the themes raised by Abrams (q.v., 1934), but much more fully and informatively.

F177 Aden, J. M. A Johnsonian echo in Crabbe's *The Village*. *The Johnsonian Newsletter*, vol. 28: March 1968. p. 16.

Perhaps Johnson's approval of *The Village* may have been conditioned by the echoes of himself he could have found in it.

F178 Wiltshire, J. The poetry of human nature. *The Cambridge Quarterly*, vol. 3: Spring 1968. pp. 185–194.

Takes the chance of a review of Mills's selection of Crabbe to write a long essay on the poet. Crabbe is difficult to come to terms with, since the first excitement of his novel approach to poetry has long since gone, and one must now ask how "deep" he is. He is "sternly moral" even in his comedy . . . "His real study is the soul itself" . . . and "he manages a clarifying of the everyday through the medium of the permanent".

F179 Thomas, W. K. George Crabbe – not quite the sternest. *Studies in romanticism*, vol. 7: 1968. pp. 166–175.

Questions Byron's claim that Crabbe was "Nature's sternest painter". Langhorne's *Country Justice* is more honest and much sterner in the way it emphasizes its facts about the effect of contemporary legislation upon the lot of the poor. Crabbe may have deliberately suppressed such details.

Though possibly over-stated this essay is a timely corrective to the tired old view that Crabbe is primarily a verse-sociologist, who simply recorded everything he saw.

1969

F180 Thomas, W. K. Crabbe's workhouse. *Huntington Library quarterly*, vol. 32: February 1969. pp. 149–161.

Crabbe's picture of workhouse conditions is highly selective. He creates atmosphere to arouse pity but not nausea, though, as contemporary documents show, the picture could have been made repulsive in the extreme. Crabbe chooses to describe emotionally rather than pictorially, and his object is rather religious than sociological.

F181 Diffey, C. T. Journey to experience: Crabbe's 'Silford Hall'. *The Durham University Journal*, vol. 30, no. 3 : 1969. pp. 129–134.

Takes further the suggestion by Gallon, (q.v. 1966), that the poem is about a knightly quest. Sees this quest as underlying a journey by the youthful hero from innocence to experience.

F182 Thomas, L. C. H. "Die Judenbuche" and English Literature. *Modern Language Review*, vol. 64: 1969. pp. 352–354.

Suggests that Annette von Droste-Hulshoff may have been influenced by Crabbe when writing "Die Judenbuche".

F183 Bareham, T. Crabbe's studies of derangement and hallucination. *Orbis Litterarum*, vol. 24, no. 3 : 1969. pp. 161–181.

Examines Crabbe's accounts of abberative and disturbed mental states, and the way in which they are usually presented through the 'romantic' trappings of ghosts, visions, etc. Emphasizes that these apparent dabblings in Gothic machinery usually have a declared and overt moral purpose.

1970

F184 Burden, D. Crabbe and the Augustan tradition. In *Essays and poems presented to Lord David Cecil*, edited W. W. Robson. Constable: 1970. pp. 77–92.

Crabbe's realism represented the best use of his experience. His attitudes to the basic phenomena of life were coloured by "clerical habituation". Although he worked within an established tradition he made something individual and recognizably his own from it. He staked a claim for poetry to have a wider province, but perhaps too late, since the novel had taken over the area in question.

F185 Hsia, C. T. Crabbe's poetry: its limitations. *The Tamkang Review*, vol. 1: 1970. pp. 61–77.

Crabbe is "an imitator" rather than "a maker". He uses his primary sensibility to register externals, and his moral sensibility to evaluate them. This method of working leaves weaknesses in his sense of structure and complex organization, though he can sometimes create poems where both are amalgamated.

1971

F186 Hsia, C. T. Pope, Crabbe, and the tradition. *The Tamkang Review*, vol. 2: 1971. pp. 51–97.

Traces the evolution of ideas on character, setting, and dialogue, through the poets from Pope to Crabbe, by means of descriptive and eclogue poetry. Crabbe's fusion of these elements into the verse-tale is skilful, and frequently creates a unique and original kind of poetry.

F187 Brewster, E. Two friends: George Crabbe and Sir Walter Scott. *Queen's Quarterly*, vol. 78: 1971. pp. 602–613.

Suggests natural affinities between the two poets, which explain an otherwise rather unlikely friendship.

1972

F188 Rendall, W. K. In *The American transcendental quarterly*, no. 14: Spring 1972. pp. 83–84.

Gives details of a letter from J. R. Lowell to Edward Fitzgerald concerning Crabbe. Lowell praises Crabbe's "pithy force", and his "honest doggedness of purpose". He sees a great deal of subtle calculation in Crabbe's practice of his art.

1973

F189 Hatch, R. B. George Crabbe, the Duke of Rutland, and the Tories. *The Review of English Studies*, vol. 24, no. 95: 1973, pp. 429–443.

Crabbe is normally presented as a 'liberal' chaplain serving in a 'conservative' establishment. But the Duke of Rutland had a Whiggish background, and was close to the Rockingham Whigs in opposition to Lord North. After Rockingham's death, Shelburne and Fox split their party, the former taking Rutland with him, while Burke went with Fox. Rutland remained liberal in his personal attitudes. It was not politics, but personal careers which might have created tension between Crabbe's two patrons, hence causing embarrassment to the poet.

F190 Brewster, E. George Crabbe and William Wordsworth. *University of Toronto Quarterly*, vol. 42, no. 2: winter 1973. pp. 142–156.

Jeffrey's reviews of the two poets may have served to put them out of sympathy with each other, since he chose to use Crabbe as an illustration of how wrong Wordsworth's line was. Yet there was probably a good deal of inter-influence between them. Crabbe may have purged his later work of poetic diction through the influence of the Preface to *Lyrical Ballads*, and for all he lacks Crabbe's "dry wit" Wordsworth may have learned from him.

F191 Lewis, C. Day. Essay in the *Poet to Poet* series. Penguin Books: 1973.

Crabbe's verse is not unlike the East Anglian countryside where "we have to look for the subtle variations of an apparently monotonous surface". He blended melodramatic plots with "quiet decorum of diction". His concentration, up to *Tales of the Hall*, upon low-life subjects, makes him unique among the English poets. His moral ideal is a kind of normality to which every civilized being should aspire.

1974

F192 Hatch, R. B. George Crabbe and the tenth muse. *Eighteenth Century Studies*, vol. 7: September 1974. pp. 274–294.

Crabbe's poetry "embodies alternate or antithetic visions of the world. . . ." *The Village* thus "combines Crabbe's perceptions of an empirically based world with his belief in man's ability to find values and goals." Hence the elegaic ending on Robert Manners attempts to bridge the gap between classical manner and village reality.

F193 Ostman, H. The silent years of George Crabbe. *Moderna Sprak*, vol. 68: 1974. pp. 233–244.

Suggests that although Crabbe published little or nothing between 1785 and 1807, he was hard at work altering his style to suit the changing tastes of readers during that period.

F194 Edwards, G. Review of Pollard's 'Critical Heritage' volume. *Essays in Criticism*, vol. 24: 1974. pp. 77–86.

Even those critics who recognize that Crabbe is neither "passive", nor "superficial", have found it difficult to give expression to the precise nature of his work.

1975

F195 Swingle, L. J. Late Crabbe in relation to the Augustans and Romantics: the temporal labyrynth of his *Tales in Verse*, 1812. *English Literary History*, vol. 42: 1975. pp. 580–594.

"Crabbe leans a good deal further away from an Augustan moral-didactic impulse in his 1812 *Tales* than most critics think he does." What most concerns him is "the phenomenon of change, the temporal condition of human life . . ." This "draws us into a lower-case view of the world . . . (and) . . . in this most basic respect, Crabbe stands on the modern side not only of the Augustans but also of the Romantics."

F196 Hatch, R. B. Crabbe and the Suffolk workhouses. *The Philological Quarterly*, vol. 54: Summer 1975. pp. 689–698.

Notes that the type of workhouse described in *The Borough* is very different from that of *The Village*. *The Borough* describes the relatively new East Anglian experimental workhouses, which were larger than the old villages poor houses, and whose machine-like impersonality Crabbe particularly deplored. Such institutions destroyed the self-hood of the inhabitants. Crabbe believed the poor must retain their sense of individual worth.

1976

F197 Wilson, P. B. Crabbe's narrative world. *The Durham University Journal*, vol. 68: June 1976. pp. 135–143.

Crabbe had persistent difficulties of structure because he tried to shape his narratives around an omniscient narrator. In 'The Parish Register' and *The Borough* he sought to surmount this with a kind of frame narrative or connecting device, in neither case quite successfully. In *Tales* he makes no such attempt, but accumulates the significance of each poem on a single point of character, moral process, dilemma or human experience.

Appendix

I WORKS OF CRABBE IN TRANSLATION.

THE BOROUGH

Letter XXII, (Peter Grimes) was translated into French in 1831 by P. Chasles in *Revue de Paris* vol. 26, pp. 197 seq. Reprinted in *Caracteres et paysages*: 1833.

THE NEWSPAPER

Translated into German as

Die Zeitung. Ein Lehrgedicht von Georg Crabbe. Nach dem Englischen von Dr Carl Abel. Berlin: 1856. pp. 30.

THE PARISH REGISTER

Translated into Dutch as

De Kerkregisters, naar het englisch van George Crabbe en de Predikants-dochter door K. Sijbrandi. Amsterdam: 1868. pp. 156.

Extracts were translated into Russian in 1875. (NCBEL).

TALES

Extracts were translated into Russian in 1902.

Tales XVII & XX were also translated into Russian [n.d.]

II CRITICAL ARTICLES IN LANGUAGES OTHER THAN ENGLISH.

This list is probably not exhaustive.

1825

Pichot, A. *Voyage historique et litteraire en Angleterre et en Ecosse*. Paris: 1825. Vol. 2, letter 63.

1855/56

Druzhinin, A. V. Krabb i ego proizvedenia. In *Sovremennik*. St Petersburg: 1855/56. Repeated in Druzhinin's *Collected Works*: 1865.

1899

Pesta, H. *Crabbe: eine Wurdigung seiner Werke*. Vienna: 1899.

1910

Wohlgemüth, J. *Der Stil in Crabbes Dichtungen*. Wurtzburg: 1910.

1921

Roth, G. Sainte-Beuve, Crabbe et le conte en vers. *The French Quarterly*, vol. 3: 1921. pp. 15–34.

1929

Bär, H. *Crabbe als Epiker; eine Studie zur Technik seiner Verserzählungen.* Leipzig: 1929.

1932

Hartmann, H. *Lord Byrons Stellung zu den Klassizisten seiner Zeit: Rogers . . . Crabbe, etc.* Bottrop: 1932.

1935

Heinlein, H. *Die sozialen Anschauungen Crabbes.* Kallmünz: 1935.

Kellner, K. *Crabbe und seiner Stellung zu den sozialen Ergebnissen der Industrie-Revolution.* Göttingen: 1935.

1945

Van Den Bergh, G. Der Pessimismus bei Hardy, Crabbe und Swift. Menziken: 1945.

1955

Levin, Y. D. Krest'yanskaya teme v anglyskoy poezii. . . . In *Iz istorii demokraticheskoy litaratury v Anglii xvii–xix vekov: sbornik statey.* Leningrad: 1955.

1965

Levin, Y. D. Kyukhel'beker & Crabbe. Oxford Slavonic papers, 12: 1964. pp. 99–113.

III OTHER WORKS WITH CONTRIBUTION BY CRABBE.

1859

The poetical works of Lord Byron. Collected and arranged with notes by Sir Walter Scott, Lord Jeffrey, Professor Wilson, Thomas Moore, William Gifford, Rev. George Crabbe. . . . London, John Murray: 1859.

Though Crabbe's name appears on the title page, the extent of his contribution to this volume is not clear.

IV THE CRABBE APOCRYPHA.

a) A poem called *The Skull* was attributed to Crabbe by a number of journals during the poet's lifetime. (For bibliographical description see p. 91–93).

At the end of the article on him in *The European Magazine*, September 1819, a list of Crabbe's publications is given. In this *The Skull* appears, after *The Village*, for the year 1783.

A poem of that title did appear in 1783, as is confirmed by *The Monthly Review* for December 1783, where a brief resumé of the plot is furnished. This is far from conclusive evidence that Crabbe wrote the poem. However, *The Monthly Review* for June 1808 has a critique of *Poems*, and this too attributes

The Skull to Crabbe. It congratulates him on having the discretion to leave this poem out of his new volume.

In *The Skull* a young man seduces a pretty girl and then abandons her. She gradually sinks to becoming a prostitute and, seeking custom at a public gathering, is struck by a coach. She is so seriously injured that her leg has to be amputated, despite which – (or because of which) – she dies. The surgeon preserves her skull because he admires its especially handsome teeth! In due course the seducer sees the skull and discovers to whom it belonged. The conclusion of the poem is taken up with his expressions of grief, and with some banal moralizing.

If Crabbe did write this as early as 1783 it completely upsets all the usual theses to the effect that his bent for narrative came slowly and un-consciously as he was working towards 'The Parish Register', and, more markedly, *The Borough*.

Stylistic evidence as to Crabbe's authorship is inconclusive, though on balance the poem is probably not his.

b) *The National Union Catalog* has the following among its entries for Crabbe:
A characteristic description of the Parochial Officers of a populous parish in the sixteenth century . . . Printed for the author, by J. Tilling, Grosvenor-Row, Chelsea. [n.d.]
In style this blank-verse poem is quite unlike anything Crabbe wrote, though the sardonic approach to many of the characters may owe something to him. The catalog compiler was probably mislead by the fact that most of the intro-ductory epigraphs to the sections of the poem are by Crabbe, and these are properly attributed to him in an otherwise anonymous publication.

Addendum

The following list has been compiled by Peter New of the Department of English, University of Exeter. In most cases it covers works where substantial discussions of Crabbe occur in works not principally about him, though one or two critical articles directly concerning Crabbe are included, having eluded the compiler of the main list.

1834 A. C. Cunningham: *A Biographical and Critical History of the British Literature of the Last Fifty Years*. pp. 25–32.

1845 J. R. Lowell: *Conversations on Some of the Old Poets*. Cambridge, Mass. p. 35.

1887 L(eslie) S(tephen) George Crabbe in D.N.B. Vol. 12, 1887. pp. 428–431.

1893 A. L. Humphries: *Piccadilly Bookmen: memoirs of the house of Hatchard*.

A. C. Swinburne: *Nineteenth Century* Vol. 15, pp. 583–598.

1896 G. Saintsbury: *A History of Nineteenth Century Literature 1780–1895*.

1908 Sir Spencer Walpole: *Essays Political and Biographical*, New York 1908, pp. 71–100.

1914 F. J. Foakes-Jackson: 'A Country Person'; *The Modern Churchman*, vol. 4, 1914. pp. 429–435.

1932 H. J. C. Grierson: 'Scott, Shelley and Crabbe' *The Times Supplement*. 1932.

1933 T. E. Welby: *Second Impressions*.

1940 Viola Meynell, (ed.) *Friends of a Lifetime: Letters to Sydney Carlyle Cockerell*.

1945 E. M. W. Tillyard: *Poetry Direct and Oblique*.

1948 E. Bernbaum: A Guide through the Romantic Movement.

1949 A. Sale: 'Chaucer and the Art of Narrative Verse'. *English*, vol. 7, 1949. pp. 216–220.

1952 M. R. Smith: 'Medecine and Poetry' *Notes & Queries*, 1952, pp. 423–425.

1955 F. P. Gant: 'George Crabbe – Nature's Sternest Painter and the Best'. *London Quarterly & Holborn Review*, vol. 180, pp. 282–284.

1957 D. Hubble: 'Opium Addiction and English Literature' *Medical History*, vol. 1, pp. 329–335.

1958 F. Berry: *Poet's Grammar: Person Time and Mood in Poetry*.

1960 M. Millgate: 'The Poetry of Crabbe' *Venture* vol. 1, pp. 314–324.

1963 A. Rodway: *Essays on Style and Language*, ed. R. Fowler.

1963 A. Rodway: *The Romantic Conflict*.

1963 J. W. Garbutt 'Music and Motive in "Peter Grimes"' *Music and Letters*, vol. 44, pp. 334–342.

1967 R. Williams: 'Literature and Rural Society' *The Listener* Nov. 15, 1967. pp. 630–632.

1968 J. D. Jump: Review of Mills selection (q.v.). *Notes & Queries* Vol. 213, pp. 348–349.

1970 R. B. Hatch: 'This Will Never Do'. *Review of English Studies*, Vol. 21, pp. 56–62.

A84a *The Village*, *The Library*, and extracts from 'The Parish Register' and *The Borough* appeared in *Chambers' Miscellany* vol. IX, 1846. The extracts are 'Phoebe Dawson', 'The Condemned Felon', and 'Trades'.

Index

Most items are indexed by main entry numbers. Page numbers, where given for appendices and addendum, are in *italics*. **Bold** type is used for editions of Crabbe's work published during his lifetime. Where an ambiguity exists over the proper designation of an edition, two citations are given: the first is the true bibliographical description, and the second is that actually appearing on the title page. Thus, Tales 2nd edition, 2nd issue, ('3rd edition') indicates that the volume is a re-issue though the title page conceals this fact.

Italic script is used

(i) for editions of Crabbe's work published after his death. Where more than one volume has the same title—'Poems', 'Selections',—these are further differentiated by citation of the *publisher* in brackets. This practice is adopted, for uniformity, since not all of these volumes cite an editor. Collections and selections are indexed strictly according to the rubric on their title page.

(ii) for titles of books and articles.

(iii) for page numbers as indicated above.

Quotation marks are used for contributions by Crabbe to periodicals and books, and for individual poems which first appeared in places other than complete volumes of his work.

Abel, C.P. *181*

Abrams, M.H. F121

Academy F66

Aden, J.M. F177

Ainger, A.C. E12, F77

'Air' A49

Aldeburgh Magazine, The F30

'Allegorical Fable, An' A48

American Transcendental Quarterly, The F188

Annual Bibliography of English Literature, The *124*

Annual Biography and Obituary for 1833, The A61, F2

Annual Register, The A55

Annual Review, The D21

Anti-Jacobin Review and Magazine, The D15

Art Journal, The F35

'Atheist Reclaimed, The' A49a

Athenaeum, The D64, F10, F52, F77

Atlantic Monthly F44, F71

Augustan Books of Poetry: George Crabbe, The A129, F108

Bailey, J. F79

Bär, H. *182*

Bareham, T. E25, F183

Batdorf, F.P. B7, B8, B10, B11, F140, F160

Beauties of the Rev. George Crabbe F14

'Bee, The' A48

Belfast, The Earl of F26

Bernbaum, E. *184*

Berry, F. *184*

Bibliographical Notes and Queries B6

Biographical and Critical History of the British Literature of the Last Fifty Years *184*

Blackburne, N. C7, E20

Blackwood's Magazine A178, D48, F7, F86

Blair, D. B2

Blunden, E. F138

Bobart, H.T. B1

Bodleian Library Record, The B16

Book Monthly A186

Bookman, The (London) F105, F114, F115

Bookman (New York) F81

Bookman's Journal, The F98

Borough, The 1st edition A15

Borough, The Facsimile of 1st edition A139
Borough, The 2nd edition A16
Borough, The 3rd edition A17
Borough, The 4th edition A18
Borough, The 5th edition A19
Borough, The 5th edition 2nd issue, A New Edition A20
Borough, The 5th edition 2nd issue (variant) A21
Borough, The 6th edition A40
Borough, The 6th edition (variant) A41
Borough, The 'A new edition' A42
Borough, The (Bradford and Inskeep) A66
Borough, The (Bradford and Inskeep) A176
Borough, The (Cook) A95
Borough, The (Daly) A80
Borough, The (Dent) A121, F74, F76
Borough, The (Perry) A171, (cf. A80)
Borough, The (Smith) A78, A79
Botanist's Guide Through England and Wales, The A60
Boyden, R. F105
Boynton, H.W. F81
Brady, M.B. F166
Bransby, J.H. F9
Brett, R.L. F158
Brewster, E. F187, F190
Brief Appreciation . . . of the Crabbe Collection . . . at Bath B4
Brigham Young University Studies F166
British Critic, The D20, D34, D46, D52, D67
British Magazine and Review, The D8
British Review, The D37
Broadley, A.M. E15
Broman, W.E. F148
Brown, W.C. F139
Burden, D. F184
Burney, C. D12

Cambridge History of English Literature, The F91
Cambridge Journal, The F147
Cambridge Quarterly, The F178

Campbell, A.J. F102
Candidate, The A2
Captain's Deathbed, The F142
Caracteres et Paysages 181
Carlyle, A.J. & R.M. F85
Carnavon Herald, The F9
Cartwright, E. D2, D6, D9
Casket, The A53
Catalogue of the exhibition at Aldeburgh, A B13
Celebrations of the 150th anniversary of the birth of Crabbe at Aldeburgh, The B5
Central Literary Magazine, The F133
Chamberlain, R.L. C5, E18, F163
'Character of Lord Robert Manners, The' A55
Characteristic Description of the Parochial Officers . . . , A 183
Chasles, P. 181
Child, H. F91
Christian Observer, The D35, D57
Church Quarterly Review, The F157
Clarke, F. C3, E14
Clodd, E. E10, F30
Collection of Poems Chiefly from the Manuscript, A A52
Collins, J.C. F84
Comparative Estimate of Modern English Poets, A F40
Contemporary Review, The F146
Conversations with Some of the Old Poets . . . 184
Cornhill Magazine, The F42, F69
Country Magazine, The D47
Courthope, W.J. F87
Crabbe, G. F2, F4
Crabbe, G. (the poet's son) E1
Crabbe (Critical Heritage) C6, E21
Crabbe (English Men of Letters) E12
Crabbe (Penguin) A140, F191
Crabbe Selection, A (Macmillan) A138, F175
Crabbe's Arabesque C9, E24
Crabbe's Tales (Routledge) A116, F59
Cranbrook, The Earl of F149
Critical Review, The D1, D4, D7, D11, D14, D28, D40

Crutwell, P. F154
Cullings from Crabbe F12
Cunningham, A.C. F19 *184*
'Cupid' A49

Dalhousie Review, The F162
Dana, R.H. F3
Deane, A.C. A119, F73, F109, F111, F122
Delta F131
Denman, T. D19, D24, D42
'Despair' A49
Devey, J. F40
Dictionary of National Biography, The 184
Diffey, C.T. F181
Discourse read in the Chapel at Belvoir Castle, A 1st edition A5
Discourse read in the Chapel at Belvoir Castle, A 2nd edition A5
Dowden, E. A183, B3
Druzhinin, A.V. *181*
Dublin Magazine, The F136
Dublin Review, The F155
Duncan, S.J. F13
Duncan-Jones, E.E. F150
Durham University Journal F181, F197

East Anglian Notes and Queries F37
Eclectic Review, The D23, D26, D41, D62, D69
Edinburgh Monthly Review, The D53
Edinburgh Review, The D18, D25, D39, D51, D71, F74
Edwards, G. F194
Edwards, O. F167
Eighteenth Century Studies F192
Elton, O. F86
Empson, W. D71
English F137, *184*
English Language Notes A199
English Literary History F126, F195
'Epitaph on William Springall Levett' A54
Essays (S.F. Williams) F32
Essays in Criticism F194
Essays and Poems for Lord David Cecil F184

Essays Political and Biographical 184
Essays on Style and Language 184
European Magazine, The F4
Evans, J.H. E16

'Farewell, dear Crabbe' F13
Fitzgerald, E. F37, F45
Forster, E.M. A189, F113, F117, F128, F145
Fortnightly Review, The F84
Frank, P. F25
Fraser's Magazine F11
Friends of a Lifetime 184
Future, The F96

Galaxy of Fathers, A F172
Gallon, D.N. F171
Gant, F.P. *184*
Gantz, C. B5
Garbutt, J.W. *185*
Gentleman's Magazine, The D3, D5, D10, D13, D27, D43, D59, D70, F64, F78
Geographical Magazine, The F129
George Crabbe (Twayne) C5, E18
George Crabbe (Vision Press) E25
George Crabbe: an anthology (Cambridge U.P.) A130, A131, F120
George Crabbe: a biography E10, F30
George Crabbe and His Times C3, E14
George Crabbe. Poems (C.U.P.) A122, C2
George Crabbe: Poems (Grey Walls Press) A133, F143
George Crabbe: Selections (Chatto) A135, F153
George Crabbe: Tales 1812, with other selected poems A137, F174
George Crabbe's Poems (Chidley) A84
George Crabbe's Poems (Lawson and Dunn) A132, F135
George Crabbe's Poetical Works (Daly) A82 (cf A156–A167)
George Crabbe's Poetry C8, E23
George Crabbe's Tales (Smith) A81
Gifford, W. D31
Giles, H. F23
Gilfillan, G. F22

Glover, T.R. F92
Graham, W.H. F146
Green Man, The D50
Gregor, I. F155
Gribble, F. F70
Grierson, H.J.C. 184
Grigson, G. A133, F143
Groves, J. F80
Guardian, The F72
Guide Through English Literature, A 184

Haddakin, L. E17
Hall, S.C. F35
Hartmann, H. 182
Harvey, N. F152
Hastings, J.D. A180
Hatch, R.B. C9, E24, F189, F192, F196
Hayter, A. F176
Hazlitt, W. F6
Heath-Stubbes, J. F134
Heinlein, H. 182
Henderson, P. F135
Hibbard, G.R. F168
Hillier, A.C. F63
History and Antiquities of the County of Leicester, The A58
History of English Poetry, A (Courthope) F87
History of Framlingham, The A54, A59
History of Nineteenth Century Literature 183
Hodgart, P. F164
Holborn Review, The F102, F119, 184
Holgate, C.W. F61
Holland, B. F65, F74
Holme, W.J. F88
Homes and Haunts of the Most Emminent British Poets F21
'Hope and Memory' A52
Howitt, W. F21
Hsia, C.T. F185, F186
Hubble, D. 184
Huchon, R. A185, B4, E13, F83
Hudson Review, The F154
Humphries, A.L. 184
Huntington Library Quarterly, The F180
Hutton, W.H. F69, F72

Illustrated London News, The A183, B3
Immortal Memories F82
Inebriety A1

Jackson, F.J. F93 184
Jackson, W. A181
Jain, B.B. E22
Jeffrey, F. D18, D25, D39, D51
Jerrold, W. E15
Johnsonian Newsletter, The F177
Journal of English and Germanic Philology, The F159, F163
Journal of The Ministry of Agriculture, The F152
Jump, J.D. 185

Kebbel, T.E. C1, E11
Kellner, K. 182
Ker, W.P. F156

La Belle Assemblée D29, D61
Lacey May, G. F100
Lady's Magazine (G. Robinson) A49b
Lady's Magazine (J. Wheble) A49a
Lamplough, E. A110, F50
Lang, V. F125, F126
Lawrence, F. F24
Lawson, J. F78
Leadbeater Papers, The A182
Leavis, F.R. F123
Lectures and Essays E23
Leisure Hour, The F36
Levin, Y.D. 182
Lewis, C.D. A140, F191
Library, The 1st edition A3
Library, The Facsimile of 1st edition A177
Library, The 2nd edition A4
Library, The (de la More Press) A128
Library, The (Routledge) A111
Life of George Crabbe (Kebbel) C1, E11
Life and Letters F106, F120
Life and New Poems (Carey, Lee and Blanchard) A70, E4
Life and Poetical Works (Murray, 1847) A86–A93, E6
Life of the Rev. George Crabbe (Chanticleer) E9

Life of the Rev. George Crabbe (Cresset Press) E8, F138
Life of the Rev. George Crabbe (Dearborn) E5
Life of the Rev. George Crabbe (Munroe and Co.) A69, E3
Life of the Rev. George Crabbe (Murray 1834) E1
Life of the Rev. George Crabbe (O.U.P.) E7, F117
Life of the Rev. George Crabbe (Spottiswoode) E2
Lines: 1822 A34
'Lines to the Dowager Duchess of Rutland' A53
Listener, The F122, F128, *185*
Literary Anecdotes of the Nineteenth Century A184
Literary Chronicle and Weekly Review, The D49
Literary Essays of Ezra Pound F96
Literary Gazette, The A51, D60
Literary History of the Nineteenth Century F46
Literary Pilgrim in England, A F95
Literature F68, F70
Lockhart, J.G. D62
London Magazine, The F6
London Mercury, The A187, F116
London Quarterly, The F127
London Review, The D73
Looker, S.J. F107
Lowell, J.R. *184*
Lucas, F.L. A130, F106, F120
Lucas, J. A139

Mabbott, T. F151
Macmillan's Magazine F55
Masefield, J.E. F110
Massingham, H.J. F101
Medical History 184
'Memoir' A61
Mental Hygeine A188
Mercier, V. F136
Methodist Quarterly, The F18
Meynell, V. *184*
Miles, A.H. F60
Milk of Paradise, The F121

Millgate, M. *184*
Mills, H. A137, F131, F174
Miscellany, A A111
Modern Churchman, The 184
Modern Language Notes F125
Modern Language Review F171, F182
Modern Philology F148
Moderna Sprak F193
Montgomery, J. D23, D26
Monthly Magazine, The D55
Monthly Mirror ,The D30
Monthly Review, The A185, D2, D6, D9, D12, D19, D24, D42, D58, D68, *182*
More, P.E. F71
Morley, H. F59
Music and Letters 185

Nation F83
National Review, The F29
'Natural History of the Vale of Belvoir, The' A58
Nature's Sternest Painter C4, E19
New Annual Register, The D32
New British Lady's Magazine, The D54
New Cambridge Bibliography of English Literature [124]
New England Magazine, The D72
New Monthly Magazine, The A61, D56, F2
New, P. C8, E23
New Poems by George Crabbe A136, A197
New Review, The D44
New Statesman, The F130
New York Review, The D74
Newbold, G. A137, F175
Newspaper, The A6
Nineteenth Century F107 *184*
North American Review, The D66, F3, F15, F39
Notes and Queries A192, A195, A198, B1, B2, B12, F31, F41, F43, F49, F51, F54, F56, F57, F62, F140, F151, F160
Nowell-Smith, S. F165
Nuovo Antologia F103

Old fashioned wit and humour A181

Oliphant, Mrs M. F46
Olivero, F. F103
'On Melancholy' A48
On Modern Literature F156
'On the Wonders of Creation' A49
Opium and the Romantic Imagination F176
Orbis Litterarum F183
Ostman, H. F193
Ottley, M. F116
Oxford Review, The (1808) D17
Oxford Review, The (1966) F173

Pamphleteer, The F1
Papers of the Bibliographical Society of America B7, B8, B9
Parish Register, The (Chambers) A101, F33
Patmore, C. F47
Payen-Payne, de V. F115
Peabody, O.W.B. D66
Pedley, M.S. F133
Pelican Guide to English Literature, The F161
Penguin New Writing F134
People's Journal, The F25
Pesta, H. *181*
Peter Grimes, an Opera F132
Philological Quarterly, The F196
Picadilly Bookmen 184
Pichot, A. *181*
Pocket Magazine of Classic and Polite Literature, The F5
'Poem for the Anniversary of the Literary Fund, 1809, A' A50
Poems 1st edition A7
Poems 2nd edition A8
Poems 3rd edition A9
Poems 4th edition A10
Poems 5th edition A11
Poems 6th edition A12
Poems 7th edition A13
Poems 7th edition 2nd issue A14
Poems 8th edition A36
Poems 8th edition (variant) A37
Poems 9th edition A38
Poems A New Edition A39
Poems (Arnold) A117, A118, F65

Poems (Cassell) A109
Poems (Inskeep and Bradford, New York) A64
Poems (Inskeep and Bradford, Philadelphia) A65
Poems by George Crabbe (Cassell) A175
Poems of George Crabbe, The (Sheldon) E16
Poet's Grammar [*184*]
'Poetical Essay on Hope' A48
Poetical Register, The D16, D33
Poetical Works: 1829 A46, F8
Poetical Works: 2nd impression A47
Poetical Works (Allman) A73a, A73b, A74
Poetical Works (Blackwood) A103
Poetical Works (Daly) A75, A76, F16
Poetical Works (Gall and Inglis) A96, A97, A98 See also F27
Poetical Works (T. Holmes) A99
Poetical Works (Lippincott) A168, (cf A96)
Poetical Works (Oxford) A125, A126, A127, F85
Poetical Works (Perry) A169, A170, (cf A75)
Poetical Works (Routledge) A100, F28
Poetical Works (Walter Scott) A110, F50
Poetical Works of Chaucer and Crabbe (Blackwood) A104
Poetical Works of Crabbe, Heber and Pollok A141–A154, F17
Poetical Works with Life by A.C. Cunningham (Daly) A82, F19 See also A156–A167
Poetry of Crabbe, The E17
Poetry Direct and Oblique 184
Poetry of George Crabbe, The (Salzburg) E22
Poetry Review F99
Poets and Poetry of the Century A112–A115, F60
Poets and Poetry of the Nineteenth Century F26
Poets and Puritans F92
Pollard, A. A136, A196, A197, C6, E21, F157

Pollard, G. B16
Posthumous Sermons A180
Principle in Art F47
Proceedings of the Suffolk Institute of Archaeology B15, F2, F80, F149
Prospectus for Works: 1834 94
Pound, E. F96
Prichard, M.F.L. B12
Primitiae F88
Prower, M. F64

Quain Essay, The F89
Quarterly Review, The D31, D63, F67
Queen's Quarterly F187

Rae, W.F. F48
Readings in Crabbe, Tales of The Hall A106–A108, F45
Recent Prose F110
Redpath, T. F164
Rendall, W.K. F188
Renaissance and Modern Essays F168
Restless Ocean, The C7, E20
Revaluation F123
Review of English Studies, The A193, A196, A200, F150, F189
Revue de l'Université d'Ottowa F169
Richards, F. F119
Rodway, A. *184*
Romance of an Elderly Poet, The E15
Romantic Conflict, The 184
Romantic Perspectives F164
Roscoe, W.C. F29
Roth, G. *181*
Rural Poetry of the English Language, The A172

Sacred Casket, The A179
St James's Gazette, The F47
St James's Magazine, The F38
Saintsbury, G. F55 *184*
Sale, A. A134, F137, F144, F147
Saturday Review, The F34, F53, F76
Scotish (sic) *Review, The* D36
Scourge D38
Second Gallery of Literary Portraits, A F22

Second Impressions 184
Selections from Poems (Clarendon) A123, A124
Selections from the Poems of George Crabbe (Methuen) A119, A120, F73, F109
Sermon: The Variation of Public Opinion . . . A62
Sharpe's London Journal F24
Sheldon, F. F39
Shepherd, T.B. F127
Shorter, C. F82
Sigworth, O.F. C4, E19
Sijbrandi, K. *181*
Skull, The 1st edition A71,
Skull, The 2nd edition A72
Slater, M. F132
Smith, M.R. *184*
Social Life in England 1750–1850 F93
Social Studies in English Literature F94
'Solitude' A49
'Song' A49
Souvenir of the Crabbe Celebrations at Aldeburgh B5
Sparrow, J. B6
Spectator, The A189, F75, F90, F113
Speirs, J. F173
Spingarn, L.P. F141
Spirit of the Age, The F6
Statham, H. F67
Stephen, Sir L. F42 *184*
Stonier, C.W. F130
Strang, W. F89
Studies in Bibliography B10, B11
Studies in Letters and Life F44
Studies in Romanticism F179
Summer Scenes . . . A102
Swinburne, A.C. *184*
Swingle, L.J. F195
Swinnerton, F. F172

Tait's Edinburgh Magazine D65, F22
Tales 1st edition A22
Tales 2nd edition A23
Tales 2nd edition 2nd issue ('3rd edition') A24
Tales 3rd edition ('4th edition') A25

Tales 3rd edition 2nd issue ('5th edition') A26

Tales 4th edition ('6th edition') A27

Tales 4th edition 2nd issue ('7th edition') A28

Tales 4th edition 4th issue ('A New Edition') A29

Tales 5th edition ('A New Edition') A30

Tales (Eastburn, New York) A67

Tales (Cook) A94

Tales (Smith) A81

Tales and Miscellaneous Poems (Bohn) A85

Tales and Miscellaneous Poems (Chidley) A83

Tales of The Hall 1st edition A31

Tales of The Hall 2nd edition A32

Tales of The Hall 3rd edition A33

Tales of The Hall (Wells and Lilley, Boston) A68

Tales of The Hall, The (Burgess and Stringer) A155

Talfourd, Sir T.N. F1

Tamkang Review, The F185, F186

Taylor, T. F12

Temple Bar, F48, F58, F63

Tenbury Letters, The A194

Tennyson, C. F129

Thale, R.M. F159

Theology F100

Thomas, E. F95

Thomas, L.C.H. F182

Thomas, W.K. F162, F169, F170, F179, F180, F182

Thoughts on The Poets F20

Tillyard, E.M.W. *184*

Times, The F104, F111, F167

Times Literary Supplement, The A190, A191, A194, B14, F79, F97, F112, F118, F165, *184*

'To Emma' A49

'To Mira' A48

Townsman, The F124

Triumph of Form, The F139

Tuckerman, H. F20

Two Cheers for Democracy F145

'Tyrsis and Damon' A49

Un Poete Realiste Anglais: George Crabbe E13

Universal Magazine, The D22, D45

University of Kansas City Review, The F141

University of Toronto Quarterly, The F170, F190

Untrodden Ways F101

Van den Bergh, G. p *182*

Venture p [*184*]

'Verses: 1817' A51

Village, The A5

Village, The 4th edition A63

Village, The (Blackie) A105

Village, The (Clark and Maynard) A173a, A173b

Village, The (Maynard Merrill and Co) A174

Village, The (University Tutorial Press) A134, F144

Village, The Parish Register and Other Poems, The (Chambers) A77

Walpole, Sir S. p [*184*]

Ward, A.W. A122, C2

Waugh, A. F114

Webb, C.J. F118

Welby, T.E. p [*184*]

Whitby, C. F99

Whitehead, F. A135, F153, F161

Williams, R. p. [*185*]

Williams, S.F. F32

Wilson, J. D48, F7

Wilson, P.B. F197

Wiltshire Archaeological and Natural History Magazine F61

Wiltshire, J. F178

Wohlgemüth, J. p [*181*]

Woodbury, G.E. F44

Woolf, V. F142

Works: 1816. 4 volumes A35

Works: 1820. 7 volumes A43

Works: 1823. 5 volumes A44

Works: 1823. 8 volumes A45

Works: 1834. 8 volumes A48

Writers and their Work F158

Wylie, L.J. F94